THE
BOUNDARIES
OF
HUMANITY

THE BOUNDARIES OF HUMANITY

HUMANS, ANIMALS, MACHINES

EDITED BY
JAMES J. SHEEHAN
AND MORTON SOSNA

UNIVERSITY OF CALIFORNIA PRESS

Berkeley   Los Angeles   Oxford

University of California Press
Berkeley and Los Angeles, California
University of California Press
Oxford, England
Copyright © 1991 by
The Regents of the University of California

Library of Congress Cataloging-in-Publication Data

The boundaries of humanity : humans, animals, machines / edited by
James J. Sheehan, Morton Sosna.
p.   cm.
Includes bibliographical references and index.
ISBN 0-520-07153-0 (hard). — ISBN 0-520-07207-3 (pbk.)
1. Sociobiology.   2. Artificial intelligence.   3. Culture.
4. Human-animal relationships.   5. Human-computer interaction.
I. Sheehan, James J.   II. Sosna, Morton.
GN365.9.B67   1990   90-22378
304.5—dc20   CIP

Printed in the United States of America

1   2   3   4   5   6   7   8   9

For Bliss Carnochan and Ian Watt, directors
extraordinaires, and the staff and friends of
the Stanford Humanities Center

CONTENTS

ACKNOWLEDGMENTS

The editors would like to acknowledge some of those who made possible the 1987 Stanford University conference, "Humans, Animals, Machines: Boundaries and Projections," on which this volume is based. We are particularly grateful to Stanford's president, Donald Kennedy, and its provost, James Rosse, for their support of the conference in connection with the university's centennial. We also wish to thank Ellis and Katherine Alden for their generous support.

Special thanks are owed the staff of the Stanford Humanities Center and its director, Bliss Carnóchan, who generously assisted and otherwise encouraged our endeavors in every way possible. We are also indebted to James Gibbons, Dean of Stanford's School of Engineering, who committed both his time and the Engineering School's resources to our efforts; Michael Ryan, Director of Library Collections, Stanford University Libraries, who, along with his staff, not only made the libraries' facilities available but arranged a handsome book exhibit, "Beasts, Machines, and Other Humans: Some Images of Mankind"; and John Chowning, Center for Computer Research in Music and Acoustics, who organized a computer music concert. Other Stanford University members of the conference planning committee to whom we are very grateful include James Adams, Program in Values, Technology, Science, and Society; William Durham, Department of Anthropology; and Thomas Heller, School of Law. Several members of the planning committee, John Dupré, Stuart Hampshire, and Terry Winograd, contributed to this volume.

Not all who participated in the conference could be included in the book. We wish, nonetheless, to thank Nicholas Barker of the British Library, Davydd Greenwood of Cornell University, Bruce Mazlish of the Massachusetts Institute of Technology, Langdon Winner of the Rensselaer Polytechnic Institute, and from Stanford, Joan Bresnan and Carl Degler, for their important contributions. Their views and observations greatly enriched the intellectual quality of the conference and helped focus our editorial concerns.

Finally, we wish to thank Elizabeth Knoll and others at the University of California Press for their steadfast support.

J. J. S.
M. S.

General Introduction

Morton Sosna

The essays in this volume grew out of a conference held at Stanford University in April 1987 under the auspices of the Stanford Humanities Center. The subject was "Humans, Animals, Machines: Boundaries and Projections."

The conference organizers had two goals. First, we wanted to address those recent developments in biological and computer research—namely, sociobiology and artificial intelligence—that are not normally seen as falling in the domain of the humanities but that have reopened important issues about human nature and identity. By asking what it means to be human, these relatively new areas of research raise the question that is at the heart of the humanistic tradition, one with a long history. We believed such a question could best be addressed in an interdisciplinary forum bringing together humanities scholars with researchers from sociobiology and artificial intelligence, who, despite their overlapping concerns, largely remain isolated from one another. Second, we wanted to link related but usually separate discourses about humans and animals, on the one hand, and humans and machines, on the other. We wished to explore some of the parallels and differences in these respective debates and see if they can help us understand why, in some cases, highly specialized and even esoteric research programs in sociobiology or artificial intelligence can become overriding visions that carry large intellectual, social, and political implications. We recognized both that this is a daunting task and that some limits had to be placed on the material to be covered.

We have divided this volume into several sections. It opens with a general statement by philosopher Bernard Williams on the range of problems encountered in attempting to define humanity in relation either to animals or machines. This is followed by sections on humans and

1

animals and on humans and machines. These are separately introduced by James J. Sheehan, who provides historical background and commentary to the essays in each section while exploring connections between some of the issues raised by sociobiology and artificial intelligence. Sheehan further develops these connections in a concluding afterword. Together, Sheehan's pieces underscore the extent to which sociobiology and artificial intelligence have reopened issues at the core of the Western intellectual tradition.

In assembling the contributors, we chose to emphasize the philosophical, historical, and psychological aspects of the problem as opposed to its literary, artistic, theological, and public policy dimensions. We sought sophisticated statements of the sociobiological and pro-artificial intelligence viewpoints and were fortunate to obtain overviews from two of the most active and influential researchers in these areas, Melvin Konner and Allen Newell. Konner probes the ways genetic research and studies of animal behavior have narrowed the gap between biological and cultural processes, and he raises questions about the interactions between genetic predispositions and complex social environments. Newell outlines some of his and others' work on artificial intelligence, arguing that the increasingly sophisticated quest for a "unified theory of mind" will, if successful, profoundly alter human knowledge and identity. Although neither Konner nor Newell claims to represent the diversity of opinion in the fields of sociobiology or artificial intelligence (as other essays in the volume make clear, considerable differences of opinion exist within these fields), each holds an identifiably "mainstream" position. The reader who wishes to know more about the specifics of sociobiology or artificial intelligence might wish to start with their essays.

Since the question of what it means to be human is above all philosophical, however, the volume begins with the reflections of Bernard Williams. In "Making Sense of Humanity," Williams criticizes some of the claims made in the names of sociobiology and artificial intelligence without denying their usefulness as research programs that have contributed to human understanding. He focuses on the problem of reductionism, that is, reducing a series of complex events to a single cause or to a very small number of simple causes. For Williams, both the appeal and shortcomings of sociobiology and artificial intelligence lie in their powerfully reductive theories that provide natural and mechanistic explanations for what William James once called "the blooming, buzzing confusion of it all." In making the case for human uniqueness, Williams contends that, unlike the behavior of animals or machines, only human behavior is characterized by consciousness of past time, either historical or mythical, and by the capability of distinguishing the real from the representational, or, as he deftly puts it, distinguishing a rabbit from a picture of a rabbit. And unlike animal ethologies, human ethology must take culture into account. According to Williams, neither "smart" genes nor "smart" machines affect such attributes of humanity as imagination, a sense of the past, or a search for transcendent meaning. These, he insists, can only be understood culturally.

The section, Humans and Animals, focuses more directly on the relationship between biology and human culture. Arnold I. Davidson takes up some of the philosophical problems in a specific historical context, the century or so prior to the scientific revolution of the seventeenth century, when human identity stood firmly between the divine and natural orders. Davidson's "The Horror of Monsters" is a useful reminder that in earlier times, definitions of humanity were formed more by reference to angels than to animals, let alone machines. Since science as it emerged from medieval traditions was often indistinguishable from theology, the task of defining the human readily mixed the two discourses. Among other things, Davidson shows how the notion of monsters tested the long-standing belief in Western culture in the absolute distinction between humans and other animal forms in ways that prefigured some contemporary debates about sociobiology and artificial intelligence. His essay traces repeated attempts to reduce the human to a single a priori concept, to uncover linkages between moral and natural orders (or disorders), and to create allegories that legitimate a given culture's most cherished beliefs. Our own culture may find our predecessors' fascination with animal monsters amusingly misguided, but we continue to take more seriously—and are appropriately fascinated by—representations of monsters, from Dr. Frankenstein's to Robocop, that combine human intention with mechanical capacity.

In "The Animal Connection," Harriet Ritvo, a specialist in nineteenth-century British culture, brings Davidson's discussion of marginal beasts as projections of human anxiety closer to the present. By examining the ideas of animal breeders in Victorian England, she shows that much of their thought owed more to pervasive class, racial, and gender attitudes than to biology. Unlike the theologically inspired interpreters of generation analyzed by Davidson, the upper- and middle-class breeders described by Ritvo did not hesitate to tinker with the natural order by "mixing seeds." What one age conceived as monstrous became to them a routine matter of improving the species and introducing new breeds. Still, projections from these breeders' understandings of human society so permeated their views of biological processes that they commonly violated an essential element of Victorian culture: faith in the absolute dichotomy between human beings and animals. For Victorians, this was no small matter. Shocked by Darwin's theories but as yet innocent of Freud's, many saw the open violation of the boundary between humans and beasts as a sure recipe for disaster. In Robert Louis Stevenson's *The Strange Case of Dr. Jekyll and Mr. Hyde,* for example, when the kindly Dr. Henry Jekyll realizes that his experiment in assuming the identity of the apelike and murderous Edward Hyde has gone terribly awry, he is horrified at both his own enjoyment of Hyde's depravity and at his inability to suppress the beast within himself, save by suicide.[1] But Victorian animal breeders who claimed they could distinguish "depraved" from "normal" sexual activities on the part of female dogs were, according to Ritvo, openly (if unselfconsciously) acknowledging this very "animal connection." Ritvo also observes that the greatest slippage—that is, the displacement of human moral judgments onto cows, dogs, sheep, goats, and cats—occurred precisely in those areas where contemporary understanding of the actual physiology of reproduction was weakest.

Human "slippage" under the guise of science, especially at the frontiers of knowledge, is Evelyn Fox Keller's main concern in "Language and Ideology in Evolutionary Theory: Reading Cultural Norms into Natural Law." Keller argues that the concept of competitive individualism on which so much evolutionary theory depends is not drawn from nature. Rather, like the rampant anthropomorphism described by Ritvo, it, too, is a projection of human social, political, and psychological values. Focusing on assumptions within the fields of population genetics and mathematical ecology, Keller questions whether individualism necessarily means competition, pointing out many instances in nature—not the least being sexual reproduction—where interacting organisms can more properly be said to be cooperating rather than competing. Yet, so deeply is the notion of competition embedded in these fields that Keller wonders whether such linguistic usage is symptomatic of a larger cultural problem, ideology passing as science, which makes evolutionary theory as much a prescriptive as a descriptive enterprise. For Keller, language and the way we use it, not to mention our reasons for using it as we do, limit our discussion of what nature is. Not opposed to a concept of human nature, as such, Keller objects to the ideologically charged terms on which such a concept often rests.

The problem of linguistic slippage permeates discussion of both sociobiology and artificial intelligence. As a general rule, the greater the claims made by either of these disciplines, the greater is the potential for slippage. Like philosophical reductionism, linguistic slippage can simultaneously energize otherwise arcane scientific research projects, providing them with readily graspable concepts, while undermining them through oversimplification and distortion. In any case, sociobiology and artificial intelligence raise traditional questions about the relationship between language and science, between the observer and the observed, and between the subjects and the objects of knowledge. To one degree or another, all the essays in this volume confront this problem.

Is sociobiology merely the latest attempt to transfer strictly human preoccupations to a biological, and hence scientific, realm? Not according to Melvin Konner. In "Human Nature and Culture: Biology and the Residue of Uniqueness," Konner, an anthropologist and physician, makes the case for the sociobiological perspective. Drawing on recent genetic and primate research, he argues that categories like "the mental" or "the psychological," previously thought to be distinctively human cultural traits, are in fact shared by other species. As Konner sees it, this is all that sociobiology claims. Moreover, he acknowledges significant criticisms that undermined the credibility of earlier social Darwinists: their refusal to distinguish between an organism's survival and its reproduction, their inability to account for altruism in human and animal populations, or their misunderstanding of the exceedingly complex and still not fully understood relation between an organism and its environment. If left at that, apart from further reducing the already much narrowed gap separating humans from other animals, there would not be much fuss. But Konner also suggests that this inherited biological "residue," as he puts it, constitutes an essential "human nature." He then raises the question, If human nature does exist, what are the social implications? His answers range from the power of genes to determine our cognitive and emotional capacities to the assertion that, in human societies, conflict is inherent rather than some "transient aberration." If there is human uniqueness, according to Konner, it consists in our possessing the "intelligence of an advanced machine in the mortal brain and body of an animal."

Given the diminished role of culture in such an analysis, sociobiology has aroused strong criticism. In his general reflections on the theme of biology and culture, philosopher John Dupré characterizes it as a flawed project that combines reductionism with conservative ideology. Davidson, Ritvo, and Keller, he notes, provide interesting case studies of how general theories can go wrong. Dupré finds Konner's view of science inadequate, both in its faith in objectivity and in its epistemological certainty. Although not a cultural relativist in the classic sense, Dupré, much like Williams, would have us pay more attention to human cultures in all their variability as a better way of understanding human behavior than biological determinism grounded in evolutionary theory.

Among the strongest appeals of any explanatory theory is its appeal to mechanism. This is as true for Newton's physics, Adam Smith's theory of wealth, or Marx's theory of class conflict as for evolution or sociobiology. Know a little and, through mechanism (as if by magic), one can predict a lot. This brings us to humanity's other alter ego, the machine. As with the boundary between humans and animals, the one between humans and machines not only has a history but has been equally influential in shaping human identity. In some ways, our relationship to machines has been more pressing and problematic. No one denies that human beings are animals or that animals, in some very important respects, resemble human beings. The question has always been what kind of animal, or how different from others, are we. But what does it mean if we are machines or, perhaps more disturbingly, if some machines are "like us"?

Roger Hahn begins the section, Humans and Machines, with several historical observations, which provide a useful context for considering current debates about the computer revolution and artificial intelligence. In "The Meaning of the Mechanistic Age," Hahn distinguishes between machines and the concept of mechanism as it came to be understood in seventeenth-century Europe. Machines, he notes, have been with us since antiquity (if not before), but prior to the Scientific Revolution, their creators rarely strove to make their workings visible. Indeed, as a way of demonstrating their own cleverness, they often deliberately hid or disguised the inner workings of their contrivances, much like magicians who keep their tricks secret. Early machines, in other words, did not offer themselves as blueprints for how the world worked. Nor did they principally operate as a means of harnessing and controlling natural forces for distinctively human purposes; more likely, they served as amusing or decorative curios. However, in the wake of the new astronomy, the new physics, and other discoveries emphasizing the universe as a well-ordered mechanism, the machine, according to Hahn, became something quite different: a device that openly displayed its inner workings for others to understand. By calling attention to their mechanisms, often through detailed visual representations, machines came to symbolize a new age of scientific knowledge and material progress attainable through mechanical improvements. "The visual representation of the machine forever stripped them of secret recesses and hidden forces," writes Hahn. "The tone of the new science was to displace the occult by the visible, the mysterious by the palpable." To see was to know, and to know was to change the world, presumably for the better.

At best, machines have only partially fulfilled this hope, and we are long past the day when diagrams of gears and pulleys could alone guarantee their tangibility and utility. Yet the concept of mechanism—what it means and what it can do—continues to generate controversy. Biological and evolutionary theories, despite their mechanistic determinism, could still leave us with minds, psyches, or souls. But with the advent of computers and artificial intelligence, even these attributes of humanity are in danger of giving way for good. The essays by Allen Newell, Terry

Winograd, and Sherry Turkle consider the implications of the computer revolution.

In "Metaphors for Mind, Theories of Mind: Should the Humanities Mind?" Newell reminds us that the computer is a machine with a difference, "clearly not a rolling mill or a tick-tock clock." The computer threatens not only how we think about being human and the foundation of the humanities as traditionally conceived but all intellectual disciplines. Noting that a computational metaphor for "mind" is very common, Newell expresses dissatisfaction with such metaphorical thinking, indeed with *all* metaphorical thinking when it applies to science. For Newell, the better the metaphor, the worse the science. A scientific "theory of mind," however, if achieved (and Newell believes we are well on our way toward achieving one), would be quite another matter. He insists that, unlike the artificial rhetorical device of metaphor, theories formally organize knowledge in revealing and useful ways. In urging cognitive scientists to provide a unified theory of mind that can be represented as palpably as the workings of a clock, Newell exemplifies the epistemological spirit of the mechanistic age described by Hahn. He also believes that "good science" can and should avoid the kind of linguistic slippage that has characterized the debate about biology and culture.

As to what such a theory of mind (if correct) will mean for the humanities, Newell speculates that it will break down the dichotomy between humans and machines. Biological and technological processes will instead be viewed as analogous systems responding to given constraints and having, quite possibly, similar underlying features. At most, there will remain a narrower distinction between natural technologies, such as DNA, and artificial ones, such as computers, with both conceived as operating according to the same fundamental principles. Even elements frequently thought to be incommensurably human, such as "personality" or "insight," might be shown to be part of the same overall cognitive structure. And technology itself might finally come to be viewed as an essential part of our humanity, not an alien presence.

Newell's analysis treats artificial intelligence (AI) as an exciting research project, ambitious and potentially significant, yet still limited in its claims and applications. But critics have questioned whether AI has remained, or can or ought to remain, unmetaphorical. Is not, they ask, the concept of artificial intelligence itself a profoundly determining metaphor? As the editor of a special *Daedalus* issue on AI recently put it, "Had the term *artificial intelligence* never been created, with an implication that a machine might be able to replicate the intelligence of a human brain, there would have been less incentive to create a research enterprise of truly mythic proportions."[2] Among other difficulties, a science without metaphor may be a science without patronage.

Terry Winograd, himself a computer scientist, is less sanguine about AI. In "Thinking Machines: Can There Be? Are We?" Winograd characterizes AI research as inextricably tied to its technological—and hence metaphorical—uses. Why seek a theoretical model of mind, he asks, unless we also desire to create "intelligent tools" that can serve human purposes? Winograd is troubled by the slippage back and forth between these parts of the AI enterprise, which he feels comprises its integrity and leads to exaggerated expectations and overdetermined statements, such as Marvin Minsky's notorious assertion that the mind is nothing more than a "meat machine." The human mind, Winograd argues, is infinitely more complicated than mathematical logic would allow. Reviewing AI efforts of the past thirty years, Winograd finds that a basic philosophy of "patchwork rationalism" has guided the research. He compares the intelligence likely to emerge from such a program to rigid bureaucratic thinking where applying the appropriate rule can, all too frequently, lead to Kafkaesque results. "Seekers after the glitter of intelligence," he writes, "are misguided in trying to cast it in the base metal of computing." The notion of a thinking machine is at best fool's gold—a projection of ourselves onto the machine, which is then projected back as "us." Winograd urges researchers to regard computers as "language machines" rather than "thinking machines" and to consider the work of philosophers of language who have shown that, to work, human language ultimately depends on tacit understandings not susceptible to mechanistically determinable mathematical logic.

In "Romantic Reactions: Paradoxical Responses to the Computer Presence," social scientist Sherry Turkle provides a third perspective on AI. Where Hahn emphasizes the palpability of machines and their mechanisms as leading to "the age of reason," Turkle's empirical approach underscores a paradoxical reaction in the other direction. "Computers," she reminds us, "present a scintillating surface and exciting complex behavior but no window, as do things that have gears, pulleys, and levers, in their internal structure." Noting that romanticism was, at least in part, a reaction to the rationalism of the Enlightenment, Turkle raises the possibility that the very opacity of computer technology, along with the kind of disillusionment expressed by Winograd, might be leading us to romanticize the computer. This could, she suggests, lead to a more romantic rather than a more rationalistic view of people, because if we continue to define ourselves in the mirror of the machine, we will do so in contrast to computers as rule-processors and by analogy to computers as "opaque." These questions of defining the self in relation and *in reaction* to computers takes on new importance given current directions in AI research that focus on "emergent" rather than rule-driven intelligence.

By emphasizing the computer as a projection of our psychological selves—complex, divided, and unpredictable as we are—Turkle speaks to Winograd's concern that computers cannot be made to think like humans by reversing the question. For her, the issue is not only whether computers will ever think like people but, as she puts it, "the extent to which people have always thought like computers." Turkle does not regard humans' inclination to define themselves in relation to machines or animals as pathological; rather, she views it as a normal expression of our own psychological uncertainties and of the machine's ambivalent nature, a marginal object poised between mind and not-mind. At the same time, in contrast to Newell, Turkle suggests that computers are as much metaphorical as they are mechanistic and that there are significant implications for non-rule-based theories of artificial intelligence in researchers' growing reliance on metaphors drawn from biology and psychology.

The section concludes with some reflections on the humans/animals/machines trichotomy by philosopher Stuart Hampshire. Philosophy, he confesses, often seems like "a prolonged conspiracy to avoid the rather obvious fact that humans have bodies and are biological beings," a view that allows sociobiology more legitimacy than Williams and Dupré would perhaps be willing to give it. But, as opposed to Turkle's notion of "romantic" machines, Hampshire goes on to make the point that, precisely because humans possess biologically rooted mental imperfections and unpredictabilities, the more machines manage to imitate the workings of the often muddled human mind, the *less* human they become. Muddled humans, he notes, at times still perform inspired actions; muddled machines, however, are simply defective. Hampshire's thoughts, in any event, are delightfully human.

The essays in *The Boundaries of Humanity* consider the question, whether humanity can be said to have a nature and, if so, whether this nature (or natures) can be objectively described or symbolically reproduced. They also suggest that sociobiology and artificial intelligence, in all their technical sophistication, put many old questions in a new light.

NOTES

1. Robert Louis Stevenson, *The Strange Case of Dr. Jekyll and Mr. Hyde* (Oxford and New York: Oxford University Press, 1987), 65–67. On the dichotomizing tendency within Victorian culture, see Walter E. Houghton, *The Victorian Frame of Mind, 1830–1870* (New Haven and London: Yale University Press, 1957), 162, and Daniel Joseph Singal, *The War Within: From Victorian to Modernist Thought in the South, 1919–1945* (Chapel Hill: University of North Carolina Press), 5, 26–29.

2. Stephen R. Graubard, "Preface to the Issue, 'Artificial Intelligence,'" *Daedalus* 117 (Winter 1988): v.

PROLOGUE

Making Sense of Humanity

Prologue:
Making Sense of Humanity

Bernard Williams

Are we animals? Are we machines? Those two questions are often asked, but they are not satisfactory. For one thing, they do not, from all the relevant points of view, present alternatives: those who think that we are machines think that other animals are machines, too. In addition, the questions are too easily answered. We are, straightforwardly, animals, but we are not, straightforwardly, machines. We are a distinctive kind of animal but not any distinctive kind of machine. We are a kind of animal in the same way that any other species is a kind of animal—we are, for instance, a kind of primate.

ETHOLOGY AND CULTURE

Since we are a kind of animal, there are answers in our case to the question that can be asked about any animal, "How does it live?" Some of these answers are more or less the same for all human beings wherever and whenever they live, and of those universal answers, some are distinctively true of human beings and do not apply to other animals. There are other answers to the question, how human beings live, that vary strikingly from place to place and, still more significantly, from time to time. Some other species, too, display behavior that varies regionally—the calls of certain birds are an example—but the degree of such variation in human beings is of a quite different order of magnitude. Moreover, and more fundamentally, these variations essentially depend on the use of language and, associated with that, the nongenetic transmission of information between generations, features that are, of course, themselves among the most important universal characteristics distinctive of human beings. This variation in the ways that human beings live is cultural

13

variation, and it is an ethological fact that human beings live under culture (a fact represented in the ancient doctrine that their nature is to live by convention).

With human beings, if you specify the ethological in detail, you are inevitably led to the cultural. For example, human beings typically live in dwellings. So, in a sense, do termites, but in the case of human beings, the description opens into a series of cultural specifications. Some human beings live in a dwelling made by themselves, some in one made by other human beings. Some who make dwellings are constrained to make them, others are rewarded for doing so; in either case, they act in groups with a division of labor, and so on. If one is to describe any of these activities adequately and so explain what these animals are up to, one has to ascribe to them the complex intentions involved in sharing a culture.

There are other dimensions of culture and further types of complex intention. Some of the dwellings systematically vary in form, being four-bedroom Victorians, for instance, or in the Palladian style, and those descriptions have to be used in explaining the variations. Such styles and traditions involve kinds of intentions that are not merely complex but self-referential: the intentions refer to the tradition, and at the same time, it is the existence of such intentions that constitutes the tradition. Traditions of this kind display another feature that they share with many other cultural phenomena: they imply a consciousness of past time, historical or mythical. This consciousness itself has become more reflexive and complex in the course of human development, above all, with the introduction of literacy. All human beings live under culture; many live with an idea of their collective past; some live with the idea of such an idea.

All of this is ethology, or an extension of ethology; if one is going to understand a species that lives under culture, one has to understand its cultures. But it is not all biology. So how much is biology? And what does that question mean? I shall suggest a line of thought about similarities and differences.

The story so far implies that some differences in the behavior of human groups are explained in terms of their different cultures and not in biological terms. This may encourage the idea that culture explains differences and biology explains similarities. But this is not necessarily so. Indeed, in more than one respect, the question is not well posed. First, there is the absolutely general point that a genetic influence will express itself in a particular way only granted a certain sort of environment. A striking example of such an interaction is provided by turtles' eggs, which if they are exposed to a temperature below 30 degrees Celsius at a certain point in development yield a female turtle but if to a higher temperature, a male one. Moreover, the possible interactions are complex, and many cases cannot be characterized merely by adding together different influences or, again, just in terms of triggering.[1] Changes in the environment may depend on the activities of the animals themselves. In the case of human beings, the environment and changes in it may well require cultural description.

Granted these complexities, it may not be clear what is meant by ascribing some similarity or difference between different groups of human beings to a biological rather than a cultural influence. But insofar as it makes sense to say anything of this sort, it can be appropriate to ascribe a *difference* in human behavior to a biological factor. Thus, the notable differences in the fertility rates of human societies at different times (a phenomenon that defies simple explanation) may be connected to a differential perception of risk.[2] This would provide a strong analogy to differences in the reproductive behavior in groups of other species, and in this sense, it would suggest a biological explanation. But many features of the situation would demand cultural description, such as the reproductive behaviors so affected, the ways in which risks are appreciated, and, of course, what events counted as dangerous (e.g., war).

In the opposite direction, it has been a pervasive error of sociobiology to suppose that if some practice of human culture is analogous to a pattern of behavior in other species, then it is all the more likely to be explained biologically if it is (more or less) universal among human beings. If this follows at all, it does so in a very weak sense. Suppose (what is untrue) that the subordinate role of women were a cultural universal. This might nevertheless depend on other cultural universals and their conditions, for example, the absence up to now of certain kinds of technology; it could turn out to be biologically determined at most to this extent, that if roles related to gender were to be assigned in those cultural contexts, biology favored this assignation.

We cannot be in a position to give a biological explanation of any phenomenon that has a cultural dimension, however widespread the phenomenon is, unless we are also in a position to interpret it culturally. This is simply an application, to the very special case of human beings, of the general truth that one cannot explain animal behavior biologically (in particular, genetically) unless one understands it ethologically.

COGNITIVE SCIENCE AND FOLK PSYCHOLOGY

The claim that we are animals is straightforwardly true. The claim that we are machines, however, needs a determinate interpretation if it is to mean anything. What some people mean by it (despite the existence of machines capable of random behavior) is merely that we, like other large things, can be deterministically characterized, to some acceptable approximation, in terms of physics. This seems to me probably true and certainly uninteresting for the present discussion. Any more interesting version must claim that we are *each* a machine; and I take the contemporary content of this to be that we are each best understood in terms of an information-processing device. This, in turn, represents a belief in a research program, that of psychology as cognitive science. However, the claim that human beings are in this sense machines involves more than the claim that human beings are such that cognitive science is a good program for psychology. It must also imply that psychology provides an adequate program for understanding human beings; this is a point I shall come back to.

To some extent, the claim that human beings can be understood in terms of psychology as cognitive science must surely be an empirical one, to be tested in the success of the research program. For an empirical claim, however, it has attracted a surprising amount of a priori criticism, designed to show that the undertaking is mistaken in principle. Less extreme, obviously, than either the comprehensive research program or the comprehensive refutation of it is the modest suggestion that this kind of model will be valuable for understanding human beings in some respects but not others. The suggestion is initially attractive but at the same time very indeterminate, and, of course, it may turn out that, like some other compromises, it is attractive only because it is indeterminate. I should like to raise the question of how the compromise might be made more determinate.

Those who want to produce a comprehensive refutation of the program sometimes make the objection that only a living thing can have a psychology. This can mean two different things. One is that psychological processes, of whatever kind, could be realized only in a biological system, that a mind could only be secreted by a brain.[3] This, if true, would certainly put the research program out of business, since, whatever other refinements it receives, its central idea must be that psychological processes could in principle be realized by any system with an adequate information-theoretical capacity. However, I see no reason why in this form the objection should be true: that mind is essentially biochemical seems a no more appealing belief than that it is essentially immaterial.

A more interesting version of the objection that only a living thing can have a psychology takes the form of saying that a human psychology, at least, can be possessed only by a creature that *has a life,* where this implies, among other things, that its experience has a meaning for it and that features of its environment display salience, relevance, and so on, particularly in the light of what it sees as valuable. This seems to me much more likely to be true, and it has a discouraging consequence for the research program in its more ambitious forms, because the experience described in these terms is so strongly holistic. An example is provided by complex emotions such as shame, contempt, or admiration, where an agent's appreciation of the situation, and his or her self-reflection, are closely related to one another and also draw on an indefinitely wide range of other experiences, memories, social expectations, and so on. There is no reason to suppose that one could understand, still less reproduce, these experiences in terms of any system that did not already embody the complex interconnections of an equally complex existence.[4]

Another example is worth mentioning particularly because it has so often appeared in the rhetoric of arguments about such questions. This is creativity. An information-processing device might be a creative problem solver, and it might come up with what it itself could "recognize" as fruitful solutions to problems in mathematics or chess (wagers on this being impossible were always ill-advised). But it could not display a similar creativity in some less formalized intellectual domain or in the arts. This is not (repeat, *not*) because such creativity is magical or a resplendent counterexample to the laws of nature.[5] It is simply that what we call creativity is a characteristic that yields not merely something new or unlikely but something new that strikes us as meaningful and interesting; and what makes it meaningful and interesting to us can lie in an indeterminately wide range of associations and connections built up in our existence, most of them unconscious. The associations are associations *for us*: the creative idea must strike a bell that we can hear. In the sense that a device can be programmed to be a problem solver, there may be, in these connections, no antecedent problem. (Diaghilev, asking Cocteau for a new ballet, memorably said, "*Étonne-moi, Jean.*") None of this is to deny that there may be a description in physical terms of what goes on when a human being comes up with something new and interesting. The difficulty for the research program is that there is no reason to expect that in these connections, at least, there will be an explanatory psychological account at the level that it wants, lying between the physical account, on the one hand, and a fully interpretive account, which itself uses notions such as meaning, on the other.

The activities and experiences that I have mentioned as providing a difficulty for the research program are all specifically human. Although it may sometimes have been argued that some such holistic features must belong to any mentality at all, the most convincing account of the problem connects them with special features of human consciousness and culture. The question on these issues that I should like to leave for consideration is the following: If we grant this much, what follows for activities and, particularly, abilities that human beings do prima facie share with other creatures? If we grant what has just been suggested, there will not be an adequate cognitive-scientific account of what it is to feel embarrassment, or of recognizing a scene as embarrassing, or (perhaps) of seeing that a picture is a Watteau. But there could be, and perhaps is, such an account of seeing that something is a cylinder or of recognizing something as a rabbit. Other animals have abilities that can be described in these terms, but are they just the same abilities in human beings and in other animals? (Consider, for instance, the relations, in the human case, between being able to recognize a rabbit and being able to recognize a rabbit in many different styles of picture.) What does seem clear, at the very least, is that a cognitive-scientific program for rabbit recognition, and a human being skilled in recognizing rabbits, would not be disposed to make quite the same mistakes. What we shall need here, if this kind of research program is to help us in understanding human beings, is an effective notion of a *fragment* of human capacities. There is no reason to think that there cannot be such a notion, but we need more thoughts about how it may work.

The cognitive science research program and the hopes that may be reasonably entertained for it are a very different matter from the ambitions that some people entertain on the basis of a metaphysics of the cognitive science program, in particular, that the concepts of such a science will eventually replace, in serious and literal discourse, those of "folk psychology." The main difficulty in assessing this idea is that the boundaries of "folk psychology" are vague. Sometimes it is taken to include such conceptions as Cartesian dualism or the idea that the mental must be immediately known. These conceptions are indeed unsound, but if you attend to what "the folk" regularly say and do rather than to what they may rehearse when asked theoretical questions, it is far from clear that they have these conceptions in their psychology. If they do, it does not need cognitive science to remove them, but, if anything, reflection, that is to say, philosophy.

In any case, the interesting claims do not concern such doctrines but rather the basic materials of folk psychology, notions such as belief, desire, intention, decision, and action. These really are used by the folk in understanding their own and other people's psychology. These, too, the metaphysicians of cognitive science expect to be replaced, in educated thought, by other, scientific, conceptions.[6] In part, this stance may depend on confusing two different questions, whether a given concept belongs to a particular science and whether it can coexist with that science, as opposed to being eliminated by it. "Golf ball" is not a concept of dynamics, but this is quite consistent with the truth that among the things to which dynamics applies are golf balls.[7] It may be said here that the situation with concepts such as *belief, desire,* and *intention* is different, because they, unlike the concept of a golf ball, have explanatory ambitions, and folk psychology, correspondingly, is in the same line of business as the theory, call it cognitive science, that will produce more developed explanations. But this is to presuppose that cognitive science does not need such concepts to characterize what it has to explain. No science can eliminate what has to exist if there is to be anything for it to explain: Newton's theory of gravitation could not show that there are no falling bodies or Marr's theory of vision, that there is no such thing as vision.

The metaphysicians perhaps assume that there is a neutral item that cognitive science and folk psychology are alike in the business of explaining, and that is behavior. But to suppose that there could be an adequate sense of "behavior" that did not already involve concepts of folk psychology—the idea of an intention, in particular—is to fall back into a basic error of behaviorism. Cognitive science rightly prides itself on having left the errors of behaviorism behind; but that should mean not merely that it has given up black box theorizing but, connectedly, that it recognizes that the kinds of phenomena to be explained cannot be brought together by purely nonpsychological criteria, as, for instance, classes of displacements of limbs.[8]

HUMANITY AND THE HUMAN SCIENCES

The claim that we are machines was the claim, I said earlier, that we are each a machine, and this, as I paraphrased it, entailed the idea that psychology is adequate for the understanding of human beings. What I have particularly in mind here relates to the much-discussed idea that for most purposes, at least, of explaining what human beings do, we can adopt the posture of what is called methodological solipsism and think of these creatures, in principle, as each existing with its own mental setup, either alone or in relation to a physical environment not itself characterized in terms of any human science. This approach has been criticized in any case for reasons in the theory of meaning.[9] My concern here, however, is not with those issues but with the point that to make sense of the individual's psychology, it may well be necessary to describe the environment in terms that are the concern of other human sciences. It may be helpful, in this connection, to see how the false conception of methodological solipsism differs from another idea, which is correct. The correct idea is inoffensive to the point of triviality; I label it "formal individualism,"[10] and it states that there are ultimately no actions that are not the actions of individual agents. One may add to this the truth that the actions of an individual are explained in the first place by the psychology of that individual: in folk psychological terms, this means, for instance, that to the extent those actions are intentional, they are explained in the first place by the individual's intentions.

The simple truths of formal individualism are enough to rule some things out. They imply, for instance, that if some structural force brings about results in society, it must do so in ways that issue in actions produced by the intentions of individuals, though those intentions, of course, will not adequately express or represent those forces. It also follows (unsurprisingly, I hope) that if Germany declared war, then some individuals did things that, in the particular circumstances, constituted this happening. But none of this requires that such things as Germany's declaring war are *logically reducible* to individual actions. (Germany embarked on war in 1914 and again in 1939, but the types of individual action that occurred were different. For one thing, Germany had different constitutions in these years.) Nor is it implied that the concepts that occur in individuals' intentions and in the descriptions of their actions can necessarily be reduced to individualist terms; in the course of Germany's declaring war on some occasion, someone no doubt acted *in the capacity of chancellor,* and there is no credible unpacking of that conception in purely individualist terms. Again, it is a matter not only of the content of agents' intentions but of their causes. Some of the intentions that agents have may well require explanation in irreducibly social terms. Thus, some intentions of the person who is German Chancellor will have to be explained in terms of his being German Chancellor.[11]

What is true is that each action is explained, in the first place, by an individual's psychology; what is not true is that the individual's psychology is entirely explained by psychology. There are human sciences other than psychology, and there is not the slightest reason to suppose that one can understand humanity without them.

How the human sciences are related to one another—indeed, what exactly the human sciences are—is a much-discussed question that I shall not try to take up. I hope that if we are able to take a correct approach to the whole issue, this will make it less alarming than some obviously find it to accept that the human sciences should essentially deploy notions of intention and meaning and that they should flow into and out of studies such as history, philosophy, literary criticism, and the history of art which are labeled "the humanities" and perhaps are not called "sciences" at all. If it is an ethological truth that human beings live under culture, and if that fact makes it intelligible that they should live with ideas of the past and with increasingly complex conceptions of the ideas that they themselves have, then it is no insult to the scientific spirit that a study of them should require an insight into those cultures, into their products, and into their real and imagined histories.

Some resistance to identifying the human sciences in such terms—

"humanistic" terms, as we might say—comes, no doubt, simply from vulgar scientism and a refusal to accept the truth, at once powerful and limiting, that there is no physics but physics. But there are other reasons as well, to be found closer to the human sciences themselves. I have suggested so far that biology, here as elsewhere, requires ethology and that the ethology of the human involves the study of human cultures. Looking in a different direction, I have suggested that psychology as cognitive science, whatever place of its own it may turn out to have, should not have universalist and autonomous aspirations. But there is a different kind of challenge to the humane study of humanity, which comes from cultural studies themselves. I cannot in this context do much more than mention it, but it should be mentioned, since it raises real questions, sometimes takes the form of extravagantly deconstructive ambitions, and often elicits unhelpfully conservative defenses.

This challenge is directed to the role of the humanities now. It is based not on any scientific considerations, or on any general characteristics of human life, but on certain features of the modern—or perhaps, in one sense of that multipurpose expression, postmodern—world.

The claim is that this world is liberated from, or at least floating free from, the past, and that in this world, history is *kitsch*. Above all, it is a world in which particular cultural formations are of declining importance and are becoming objects of an interest that is merely nostalgic or concerned with the picturesque—that is to say, a commercial interest.

If applied to our need for historical understanding, such a view is surely self-defeating, because the ideas of modernity and postmodernity are themselves historical categories; they embody an interpretation of the past. This would be true even if the conception of a general modernity completely transcending local and cultural variation were correct. But it remains to be seen whether that conception is even correct; there is no reason at the moment, as I understand the situation, to suppose that patterns of development are independent of history and culture; South Korea and Victorian England are by no means the same place. But however that may be, these are indisputably matters for historical and cultural understanding.

What is more problematic is our relation in the modern world to the literature and art of the past. Our historical interest in it—our interest in it as, for instance, evidence of the past—raises no special question, but the study of the humanities has always gone beyond this, in encouraging and informing an interest in certain works, picked out both by their quality and their relation to a particular tradition, as cultural objects for us, as formative of our experience. There is obviously a great deal to be said about this and about such phenomena as the interest shown by all developing countries in the canon of European painting and music.

Some of what needs to be said is obviously negative, and it is a real question whether certain famous artworks can survive—a few of them physically, all of them aesthetically—their international marketing. But the conversion of works of art into commodities is one thing, and their internationalization is another, even if the two things have up to now coincided, and we simply do not yet know, as it seems to me, what depth of experience of how much of the art of the past will be available to the human race if its cultural divergences are in fact diminished. However, it is worth recalling the number of cultural transitions that have already been effected by the works of the past in arriving even where they now are in our consciousness. What was there in classical antiquity itself, or in the complex history of its transmission and its influence, that might have led us to expect that as objects of serious study seven plays of Sophocles should now be alive and well and living in California?

"Humanity" is, of course, a name not merely for a species but for a quality, and it may be that the deepest contemporary reasons for distrusting a humanistic account of the human sciences are associated with a distrust of that quality, with despair for its prospects, or, quite often, with a hatred of it. Some legatees of the universalistic tendencies of the Enlightenment lack an interest in any specific cultural formation or other typically human expression and at the limit urge us to rise above the local preoccupations of "speciesism." Others, within the areas of human culture, have emphasized the role of structural forces to a point at which human beings disappear from the scene. There are other well-known tendencies with similar effects. But the more that cultural diversity within the human race declines, and the more the world as a whole is shaped by structures characteristic of modernity, the more we need not to forget but to remind ourselves what a human life is, has been, can be. This requires a proper understanding of the human sciences, and that requires us to take seriously humanity, in both senses of the term. It also helps us to do so.

NOTES

1. See Patrick Bateson, "Biological Approaches to the Study of Behavioural Development," *International Journal of Behavioural Development* 10 (1987), to which I owe the example of the turtle eggs.

2. See Richard M. Smith, "Transfer Incomes, Risk and Security: The Roles of the Family and the Collectivity in Recent Theories of Fertility Change," in David Coleman and Roger Schofield, eds., *The State of Population Theory: Forward from Malthus* (Oxford: Blackwell, 1986).

3. John Searle has suggested this in *Minds, Brains and Science* (Cambridge: Harvard University Press, 1985).

4. This argument has been forcefully developed by Charles Taylor in articles collected in his *Human Agency and Language* (Cambridge and New York: Cambridge University Press, 1985).

5. Advocates of this kind of research often claim that the only alternative to their program lies in superstition and mystification; Marvin Minsky's book *The Society of Mind* (New York: Simon and Schuster, 1986) provides some (relatively mild) examples of this rhetoric.

6. The most extreme of these believers are Paul Churchland and Patricia Churchland, who once said that folk psychology "is a stagnant or degenerating research program, and has been for millennia." An extended statement may be found in Patricia Churchland, *Neurophilosophy* (Cambridge: MIT Press, 1986). A more moderate line is taken by Stephen Stich in his book *From Folk Psychology to Cognitive Science* (Cambridge: MIT Press, 1983).

7. A related point is central to Donald Davidson's treatment of causality; see *Essays on Actions and Events* (Oxford: Clarendon Press, 1980).

8. A detailed and very effective argument is provided by Jennifer Hornsby's "Physicalist Thinking and Concepts of Behaviour," in Philip Pettit and John McDowell, eds., *Subject, Thought and Context* (Oxford: Clarendon Press, 1986).

9. Recent discussion has been shaped by Hilary Putnam's important article, "The Meaning of 'Meaning,' " reprinted in his *Mind, Language and Reality* (Cambridge: Cambridge University Press, 1975). The issues are set out in the introduction to Pettit and McDowell, *Subject, Thought and Context*.

10. The doctrine is weaker than several that could be expressed in those words. I have given some account of it in "Formal and Substantial Individualism," *Proceedings of the Aristotelian Society* 85 (1984/85).

11. Arguments on these points are well deployed in David Hillel-Ruben, *The Metaphysics of the Social World* (London: Routledge & Kegan Paul, 1985).

PART ONE

Humans and Animals

ONE

Introduction

James J. Sheehan

In 1810, William Blake painted a picture that came to be known as *Adam Naming the Beasts*. Blake's portrait of the first man reminds us of a Byzantine icon of Christ: calm, massive, and immobile, Adam dominates the scene. One of his arms is raised in an ancient gesture signifying speech, while around the other a serpent meekly coils. In the background, animals move in an orderly, peaceful file. Of course, we know the harmony depicted here will not last. Soon Adam and his progeny will lose their serene place in nature; no longer will they be comfortable in their sovereignty over animals or secure in the unquestioned power of their speech. Our knowledge of what is coming gives Blake's picture its special, melancholy power.[1]

Since the Fall, man's place in nature has always been problematic. The problems begin with Genesis itself, where the story of creation is told twice. In the second chapter, the source of Blake's picture, God creates Adam and then all other living things, which are presented to man "to see what he would call them: and whatsoever Adam called every living creature, that was the name thereof." The first chapter, however, has a somewhat different version of these events. Here man is the last rather than the first creature to be made; while still superior to the rest by his special relationship to God, man nevertheless appears as part of a larger natural order. A similar ambiguity can be found in Chapter Nine, which begins with a divine promise to Noah that all beings will fear him but then goes on to describe a covenant between God and Noah and "every living creature of all flesh." From the very start of the Judeo-Christian tradition, therefore, humanity is at once set apart from, and joined with, the realm of other living things.[2]

In Greek cosmology, humanity's relationship to animals was yet more uncertain. Like the Hebrews, the Greeks seemed eager to establish human hegemony over nature. Animal sacrifice, which was so central to Greek religion, ritually affirmed the distinctions between humans and beasts, just as it sought to establish connections between the human and divine. Aristotle, the first great biologist to speculate about human nature, developed an elaborate hierarchy of living beings, in which all creatures— beginning with human females—were defined on a sliding scale that began with adult males. But the line between humanity and its biological neighbors was more permeable for Greeks than for Hebrews. Gods frequently took on animal form, which allowed them to move about the world in disguise. As punishment, humans could be turned into beasts. Moreover, a figure like Heracles, who was human but with supernatural connections, expressed his association with animals by wearing skins on his body and a lion's head above his own. And if animal sacrifice set humans and animals apart, there were other rituals that seemed to blur the distinction between them. Dionysus's Maenads, for instance, lived wild and free, consumed raw flesh, and knew no sexual restraint. By becoming like beasts, the Maenads achieved a "divine delirium" and thus direct contact with the gods.[3]

Christians saw nothing godlike in acting like a beast. To them, the devil often appeared in animal form, a diabolic beast or, as Arnold Davidson points out, in some terrible mix of species. Bestiality, sexual transgression across the species barrier, was officially regarded as the worst sin against nature; it remained a capital crime in England until the second half of the nineteenth century. Humanity's proper relationship to animals was that of master; beasts existed to serve human needs. "Since beasts lack reason," Saint Augustine taught, "we need not concern ourselves with their sufferings," an opinion echoed by an Anglican bishop in the seventeenth century who declared, "We may put them [animals] to any kind of death that the necessity either of our food or physic will require." Even those who took a softer view of humanity's relationship with animals believed that our hegemony over the world reflected our special ties to the creator. "Man not only rules the animals by force," the Renaissance philosopher, Ficino, wrote, "he also governs, keeps and teaches them. Universal providence belongs to God, who is the universal cause. Hence man who generally provides for all things, both living and lifeless, is a kind of God."[4]

Although set apart from the rest of creation by their privileged relationship with God, many Christians felt a special kinship to animals. As Keith Thomas shows in his splendid study, *Man and the Natural World,* so close were the ties of people to the animals among whom they lived that often "domestic beasts were subsidiary members of the human community." No less important than these pressing sympathies of everyday interdependence were the weight of cultural habit and the persistent power of half-forgotten beliefs. Until well into the eighteenth century, many Europeans viewed the world anthropomorphically, imposing on animals human traits and emotions, holding them responsible for their "crimes," admiring them for their alleged expressions of pious sentiment. Although condemned by the orthodox and ridiculed by secular intellectuals, belief in the spirituality of animals persisted. As late as the 1770s, an English clergyman could write, "I firmly believe that beasts have souls; souls truly and properly so-called."[5]

By the end of the eighteenth century, such convictions were surely exceptional among educated men and women. The expansion of scientific knowledge since the Renaissance had helped to produce a view of the world in which there seemed to be little room for animal souls. The great classification schemes of the late seventeenth and eighteenth centuries encouraged rational, secular, and scientific conceptions of the natural order. As a result, the anthropomorphic attitudes that had invested animals—and even plants—with human characteristics gradually receded; nature was now seen as something apart from human affairs, a realm to be studied and mastered with the instruments of science. Here is Thomas's concise summary of this process:

> In place of a natural world redolent with human analogy and symbolic meaning, and sensitive to man's behavior, they [the natural scientists] constructed a detached natural scene to be viewed and studied by the observer from the outside, as if by peering through a window, in the secure knowledge that the objects of contemplation inhabited a separate realm, offering no omens or signs, without human meaning or significance.[6]

Within this new world, humans' claims to hegemony were based on their own rational faculties rather than divine dispensation. Reason became the justification as well as the means of humanity's mastery. Because they lack reason, Descartes argued, animals were like machines, without souls, intelligence, or feeling. Animals do not act independently, "it is nature that acts in them according to the arrangement of their organs, just as we see how a clock, composed merely of wheels and springs, can reckon the hours." Rousseau agreed. Every animal, he wrote in *A Discourse on Inequality,* was "only an ingenious machine to which nature has given sense in order to keep itself in motion and protect itself." Humans are not in thrall to their instincts and senses; unlike beasts, when nature commands, humans need not obey. Free will, intellect, and above all, the command of language gives people the ability to choose, create, and communicate.[7]

Not every eighteenth-century thinker was sure that humanity's unquestioned uniqueness had survived the secularization of the natural order. Lord Bolingbroke, for example, still regarded man as "the principal inhabitant of this planet" but cautioned against making too much of humanity's special status.

> Man is connected by his nature, and therefore, by the design of the Author of all Nature, with the whole tribe of animals, and so closely with some of them, that the distance between his intellectual faculties and theirs, which constitutes as really, though not so sensibly as figure, the difference of species, appears, in many instances, small, and would probably appear still less, if we had the means of knowing their motives, as we have of observing their actions.

When Alexander Pope put these ideas into verse, he added that the sin of pride that brought Adam's fall came not from his approaching too close to God but rather from drawing too far away from other living things:

> Pride then was not, nor arts that pride to aid;
> Man walk'd with beast, joint tenants of the shade;

And it was Pope who best expressed the lingering anxiety that must attend humanity's position between gods and beasts:

> Plac'd in this isthmus of a middle state,
> A being darkly wise and rudely great,
> With too much knowledge for the sceptic side,
> With too much weakness for the stoic pride,
> He hangs between; in doubt to act or rest;
> In doubt to deem himself a god or beast;
> In doubt his Mind or Body to prefer;
> Born but to die, and reas'ning but to err. . . .
> Chaos of Thought and Passion all confus'd,
> Still by himself abus'd, or disabus'd;
> Created half to rise, and half to fall,
> Great lord of all things, yet a prey to all;
> Sole judge of Truth, in endless error hurl'd;
> The glory, jest, and riddle of the world.[8]

In the second half of the eighteenth century, what Pope had once called the "vast chain of being" began to be seen as dynamic rather than static, organic rather than mechanistic. The natural order now seemed to be the product of a cosmic evolution that, as Kant wrote in 1755, "is never finished or complete." This meant that everything in the universe—from species of plants and animals to the structure of distant galaxies and the earth's surface—was produced by and subject to powerful forces of change. By the early nineteenth century, scientists had begun to examine this evolutionary process in a systematic fashion. In 1809, Jean Baptiste de Lamarck published *Philosophie zoologique,* which set forth a complex theory to explain the transformation of species over time. Charles Lyell, whose *Principles of Geology* began to appear in 1830, doubted biological evolution but offered a compelling account of the earth's changing character through the long corridors of geologic time. Thus was the stage set for the arrival of Darwin's *Origin of Species,* by far the most famous and influential of all renditions of "temporalized chains of being." With this book, Darwin provides the basis for our view of the natural order and thus links eighteenth-century cosmology and twentieth-century evolutionary biology.[9]

Even before Darwin formulated his theory of natural selection, he seems to have sensed that his scientific observations would have powerful implications for the relationship between humans and animals. In a notebook entry of 1837, Darwin first sketched what would become a central theme in his life's work:

> If we choose to let conjecture run wild, then animals, our fellow brethren in pain, diseases, death, suffering and famine—our slaves in the most laborious works, our companions in our amusements—they may partake [of] our origins in one common ancestor—we may be all netted together.

When he published *Origin of Species* twenty-two years later, he approached the matter delicately and indirectly: "it does not seem incredible" that animals and plants developed from lower forms, "and if we admit this, we must likewise admit that all the organic beings which have ever lived on this earth may be descended from some one primordial form." In any event, he promised that in future research inspired by the theory of natural selection, "much light will be thrown on the origin of man and his history."[10]

The meaning of Darwinism for human history quickly moved to the center of the controversies that followed the publication of *Origin.* In 1863, T. H. Huxley, for example, produced *Man's Place in Nature.* Darwin himself turned to the evolution of humanity in *The Descent of Man,* where he set out to demonstrate that "there is no fundamental difference between man and the higher mammals in their mental faculties." Each of those characteristics once thought to be uniquely human turn out to be shared by higher animals, albeit in lesser degrees: animals cannot speak, but they do communicate; they are intellectually inferior to humans, but they "possess some power of reasoning"; they cannot work as we do, but they can even use tools in a rudimentary way. Darwin's discussion of animal self-consciousness is worth quoting at length, not simply because it conveys the flavor of his argument but also because it illustrates the ease with which he slipped from talking about differences between humans and animals to describing differences between "races" of men.

> It may be freely admitted that no animal is self-conscious, if by this term it is implied that he reflects on such points, as whence he comes or whither he will go, or what is life and death, and so forth. But how can we feel sure that an old dog with excellent memory and some power of imagination, as shewn by his dreams, never reflects on his past pleasures and pains in the chase? And this would be a form of self-consciousness. On the other hand, as Büchner has remarked, how little can the hard-worked wife of a degraded Australian savage, who uses very few abstract words, and cannot count above four, exert her self-consciousness, or reflect on the nature of her own existence.

Darwin carried on his examination of humans and animals in *The Expression of the Emotions in Man and Animals*. Here he seeks to demonstrate that basic emotions have common origins and a biological base by pointing out the similarity of emotional expressions among human societies and between humans and animals. Like reason, language, and consciousness, emotions such as love, fear, and shame are not the sole and undisputed property of humanity.[11]

The research program suggested in this work on human and animal emotions was not immediately taken up by Darwin's many disciples. There were, to be sure, many who sought to apply Darwinism to human society, but they usually did so without a systematic examination of the resemblances between human and animal behavior. To social scientists influenced by Darwin, what mattered was less that people were animals than that they were still—in Harriet Ritvo's phrase—"the top animals," separated from the rest by what Darwin himself had called man's "noble qualities" and "godlike intellect." Most of the natural scientists who followed Darwin turned in the opposite direction, away from humans toward other species with longer evolutionary histories and more accessible biological structures. As a result, empirical work on the connection between human and animal behavior, so central to Darwin's work on emotions, did not become an important part of his legacy until the second half of the twentieth century.[12]

The direct heirs of Darwin's research on human and animal emotion were scientists who studied behavioral biology, the discipline that would come to be called ethology. Although important research on ethology had been conducted during the 1920s and 1930s, the subject did not become prominent until the 1960s; in 1973, three leading ethologists shared the Nobel Prize. The new interest in ethology encouraged the publication of a variety of works of quite uneven quality, but all shared the conviction that studying the similarity of behavior existing across animal species could yield important insights into the character of human individuals and groups. For example, Konrad Lorenz, a pioneer in the field and one of the Nobel laureates, maintained that, in both man and animals, aggressive behavior was instinctual. "Like the triumph ceremony of the greylag goose, militant enthusiasm in man is a true autonomous instinct: It has its own releasing mechanisms, and like the sexual urge or any other strong instinct, it engenders a specific feeling of intense satisfaction." Such deeply rooted instincts, ethologists warned, will inevitably pose problems for, and set limits on, humans' ability to control themselves and their societies.[13]

By the 1970s, popular and scientific interest in ethology had become enmeshed with a larger and more ambitious set of ideas and research enterprises conventionally called sociobiology. Edward O. Wilson, perhaps sociobiology's most vigorous exponent, describes it as the "scientific study of the biological basis of all forms of social behavior in all kinds of organisms, including man." Wilson began to define his view of the field in the concluding chapter of *The Insect Societies* (1971), which called for the application of his work on the population biology and zoology of insects to vertebrate animals. Four years later, he concluded *Sociobiology: The New Synthesis* with a chapter entitled "Man: From Sociobiology to Sociology." This was followed in 1978 with the more popularly written *On Human Nature*, which examined what Wilson regarded as "four of the elemental categories of behavior, aggression, sex, altruism, and religion," from a sociobiological perspective. Wilson brought an ethologist's broad knowledge of animal behavior to these subjects but added his own growing concern for the genetic basis of instincts and adaptations. This genetic dimension has become increasingly important in Wilson's most recent work.[14]

Sociobiology in general and Wilson in particular have been the subject of intense attacks from a variety of directions. In the course of these controversies, the term has tended to become a catchall for a variety of different developments in behavioral biology. Like many other controversial movements, sociobiology often seems more solid and coherent to its opponents, who can easily define what they oppose, than to its advocates, who have some trouble agreeing on what they have in common. It is worth noting, for example, that Melvin Konner, while sympathetic to Wilson in many ways, explicitly denies that his own work, *The Tangled Wing* (1982), is sociobiology. But what Konner and the sociobiologists do share is the belief that most studies of human beings have been too "anthropocentric." If, as Wilson and others claim, "homo sapiens is a conventional animal species," then there is much to be learned by viewing the human experience as part of a broader biological continuum. Doing so will help us to understand what Darwin, in the dark passage at the end of *The Descent of Man,* referred to as "the indelible stamp of his lowly origin" which man still carries in his body and what Konner, in a contemporary version of the same argument, calls the "biological constraints on the human spirit."[15]

We will return to some of the questions raised by sociobiology in the conclusion to this volume. For the moment, it is enough to point out that the conflicts surrounding it—illustrated by the works of Konner and Dupré in the following section—are new versions of ancient controversies. These controversies, while informed by our expanding knowledge of the natural world and expressed in the idiom of our scientific culture, have at their core our persistent need to define what it means to be human, a need that leads us, just as it led the authors of Genesis, to confront our kinship with and differences from animals.

NOTES

1. For an analysis of this painting, see Robert Essick, *William Blake and the Language of Adam* (Oxford: Clarendon Press, 1989).

2. These issues are treated in John Passmore, *Man's Responsibility for Nature: Ecological Problems and Western Traditions* (London: Charles Scribner's Sons, 1974).

3. On the role of animals in Greek religion, see Walter Burkert, *Structure and History in Greek Mythology and Ritual* (Berkeley, Los Angeles, London: University of California Press, 1979) and J. P. Vernant, "Between the Beasts and the Gods," in *Myth and Society in Ancient Greece* (Hassocks, Sussex: 1980). There is a fine analysis of Aristotle in G. E. R. Lloyd, *Science, Folklore, and Ideology: Studies in the Life Sciences in Ancient Greece* (Cambridge: Cambridge University Press, 1983).

4. Keith Thomas, *Man and the Natural World: A History of the Modern Sensibility* (New York: Pantheon Books, 1983), 21; Clarence Glacken, *Traces on the Rhodian Shore: Nature and Culture from Ancient Times to the End of the Eighteenth Century* (Berkeley and Los Angeles: University of California Press, 1967), 463.

5. Thomas, *Man and the Natural World,* 98, 140.

6. Ibid., 89. As Harriet Ritvo's contribution to this volume makes clear, in the nineteenth century this tendency to anthropomorphize nature was translated into a more appropriate vocabulary.

7. Mary Midgley, *Beast and Man: The Roots of Human Nature* (Ithaca: Cornell University Press, 1978), 210; J.-J. Rousseau, *A Discourse on Inequality* (New York: Penguin Books, 1984), 87.

8. A. O. Lovejoy, *The Great Chain of Being* (Cambridge: Harvard University Press, 1936), 195–196, 199.

9. See Lovejoy, *Great Chain of Being,* Chap. Nine, and D. G. Charlton, *New Images of the Natural in France: A Study in European Cultural History, 1750–1800* (Cambridge: Cambridge University Press, 1984), esp. 77 ff.

10. Donald Worster, *Nature's Economy: A History of Ecological Ideas* (Cambridge: Cambridge University Press, 1977), 180; Philip Appleman, ed., *Darwin: A Norton Critical Edition* (New York: Norton, 1979), 128, 130.

11. There is a useful collection of Darwin's writing on this subject edited by Alexander Alland, *Human Nature: Darwin's View* (New York: Columbia University Press, 1985). The quotation is from p. 153.

12. Appleman, *Darwin*, 208.

13. There is a sympathetic discussion of ethology in Melvin Konner, *The Tangled Wing: Biological Constraint on the Human Spirit* (New York: Holt, Rinehart, and Winston, 1982), 143 ff. The Lorenz quotation is from Arthur L. Caplan, ed., *The Sociobiology Debate: Readings on Ethical and Scientific Issues* (New York: Harper and Row, 1978), 72.

14. Edward O. Wilson, *On Human Nature* (New York: Bantam Books, 1979), 230. The Caplan collection just cited provides a good introduction to the discipline and its critics.

15. Konner, *Tangled Wing*, 16; Appleman, *Darwin*, 208.

TWO

The Horror of Monsters*

Arnold I. Davidson

As late as 1941, Lucien Febvre, the great French historian, could complain that there was no history of love, pity, cruelty, or joy. He called for "a vast collective investigation to be opened on the fundamental sentiments of man and the forms they take."[1] Although Febvre did not explicitly invoke horror among the sentiments to be investigated, a history of horror can, as I hope to show, function as an irreducible resource in uncovering our forms of subjectivity.[2] Moreover, when horror is coupled to monsters, we have the opportunity to study systems of thought that are concerned with the relation between the orders of morality and of nature. I will concentrate here on those monsters that seem to call into question, to problematize, the boundary between humans and other animals. In some historical periods, it was precisely this boundary that, under certain specific conditions that I shall describe, operated as one major locus of the experience of horror. Our horror at certain kinds of monsters reflects back to us a horror at, or of, humanity, so that our horror of monsters can provide both a history of human will and subjectivity and a history of scientific classifications.

The history of horror, like the history of other emotions, raises extraordinarily difficult philosophical issues. When Febvre's call was answered, mainly by his French colleagues who practiced the so-called history of mentalities, historians quickly recognized that a host of historiographical and methodological problems would have to be faced. No one has faced these problems more directly, and with more profound results, than Jean Delumeau in his monumental two-volume history of fear.[3] But these are issues to which we must continually return. What will be required to write the history of an emotion, a form of sensibility, or type of affectivity? Any such history would require an investigation of gestures, images, attitudes, beliefs, language, values, and concepts. Furthermore, the problem quickly arose as to how one should understand the relationship between elite and popular culture, how, for example, the concepts and language of an elite would come to be appropriated and transformed by a collective mentality.[4] This problem is especially acute for the horror of monsters, since so many of the concepts I discuss which are necessary to our understanding of monsters come from high culture—scientific, philosophical, and theological texts. To what extent is the experience of horror, when expressed in a collective mentality, given form by these concepts? Without even attempting to answer these questions here, I want to insist that a history of horror, at both the level of elite concepts and collective mentality, must emphasize the fundamental role of description. We must describe, in much more detail than is usually done, the concepts, attitudes, and values required by and manifested in the reaction of horror. And it is not enough to describe these components piecemeal; we must attempt to retrieve their coherence, to situate them in the structures of which they are a part.[5] At the level of concepts, this demand requires that we reconstruct the rules that govern the relationships between concepts; thus, we will be able to discern the highly structured, rule-governed conceptual spaces that are overlooked if concepts are examined only one at a time.[6] At the level of mentality, we are required to place each attitude, belief, and emotion in the context of the specific collective consciousness of which it forms part.[7] At both levels, we will have to go beyond what is said or expressed in order to recover the conceptual spaces and mental equipment without which the historical texts will lose their real significance.

In 1523, Martin Luther and Phillip Melancthon published a pamphlet entitled *Deuttung der czwo grewlichen Figuren, Bapstesels czu Rom und Munchkalbs czu Freyerbeg ijnn Meysszen funden.*[8] It was enormously influential and was translated into French, with Calvin's endorsement, in 1557, and into English in 1579 under the title *Of two wonderful popish monsters.* The pamphlet consisted of a detailed interpretation of two monsters: a pope-ass, discussed mainly by Melancthon, supposedly left on the banks of the Tiber River in 1496, and a monk-calf, interpreted by Luther, that was born on December 8, 1522, in Freiburg (figs. 2.1, 2.2). Both of these monsters were interpreted within the context of a polemic against the Roman church. They were prodigies, signs of God's wrath against the Church which prophesied its imminent ruin. There were two dimensions to the Lutheran exegesis of these monsters.[9] On the one hand, there is a prophetic or eschatological dimension, only diffidently mentioned in this pamphlet, in which monsters and prodigies, as a general phenomenon, were taken to be signs of fundamental changes about to

Fig. 2.1. The Pope-Ass.

affect the world. Often these signs were interpreted as nothing less than
an announcement that the end of the world was at hand, and support for
this prophetic interpretation was adduced by citing the Book of Daniel, a
biblical text invoked by both Melancthon and Luther. The other dimension, which, following Jean Céard, we can call allegorical, is the one with
which this pamphlet is most preoccupied. The allegorical exegesis of
these monsters is intended to show that each monster has a very specific

Fig. 2.2. The Monk-Calf.

interpretation that can be grasped because, in one way or another, it is
represented before our eyes in the constitution of the monster itself;
each monster is a divine hieroglyphic, exhibiting a particular feature of
God's wrath. So, for instance, the pope-ass, according to Melancthon, is
the image of the Church of Rome; and just as it is awful that a human
body should have the head of an ass, so it is likewise horrible that the
Bishop of Rome should be the head of the Church. Similarly, the overly

large ears of the calf-monk exhibit God's denouncement of the practice of hearing confessions, so important to the monks, while the hanging tongue shows that their doctrine is nothing but frivolous prattle.

A useful study could be made of the adjectives that appear in this text; in lieu of such a study, let me just note that "horrible" and "abominable" occur frequently in both Luther's and Melancthon's discussions, often modifying "monster." The mood of these adjectives is accurately conveyed in the translator's introduction to the 1579 English translation of the text. It begins:

> Among all the things that are to be seen under the heavens (good Christian reader) there is nothing can stir up the mind of man, and which can engender more fear unto the creatures than the horrible monsters, which are brought forth daily contrary to the works of Nature. The which the most times do note and demonstrate unto us the ire and wrath of God against us for our sins and wickedness, that we have and do daily commit against him.[10]

John Brooke goes on to tell us that his motive for translating this pamphlet is the better "to move the hearts of every good Christian to fear and tremble at the sight of such prodigious monsters,"[11] and he warns his readers not to interpret these two monsters as if they were but fables. He closes his preface with the hope that, after reading this pamphlet, we shall "repent in time from the bottom of our hearts of our sins, and desire him [God] to be merciful unto us, and ever to keep and defend us from such horrible monsters."[12] He concludes with a few more specific remarks about the pope-ass and calf-monk addressed, and we shall not overlook the form of the address, "unto all which fear the Lord."

In order to better understand the preoccupation and fascination with monsters during the sixteenth century, a fascination fastened onto by Luther and Melancthon, whose text is fully representative of an entire genre, we must place these discussions within a wider context. As Jean Delumeau has argued in the second volume of his history of fear, it is within "the framework of a global pessimistic judgment on a time of extreme wickedness that one must place the copious literature dedicated to monsters and prodigies between the end of the fifteenth century and the beginning of the seventeenth."[13] Sinfulness was so great that the sins of men extended to nature itself which, with God's permission and for the instruction of sinners, seemed to have been seized by a strange madness; the resulting monsters were to be understood as illustrations of these sins. Heresy and monsters were frequently linked during this period, both by reformers and Catholics alike. Prodigies were not only specific punishments for particular sins but they also announced greater punishments to come—war, famine, and perhaps even the end of the world. This proliferation of monsters presaged a dark future explained by God's wrath at the increase of wickedness on earth.[14] Français Belleforest summarized the shared sensibility: "The present time is more monstrous than natural."[15]

To make as clear as possible the relationship between horror and monsters, I am going to focus primarily on one text, Ambroise Paré's *Des monstres et prodiges*, originally published in 1573 and frequently reprinted after that.[16] Since I am going to set the conceptual context for my discussion of Paré in a rather unconventional way, I want to state explicitly that a full comprehension of this treatise requires that it be placed in relation to other learned and popular treatises on monsters that both preceded and followed it. We are fortunate in this respect to have Céard's thorough treatment of Paré in his brilliant *La Nature et les prodiges* and in the notes to his critical edition of *Des monstres et prodiges*;[17] moreover, in the best English-language treatment of monsters, Katharine Park and Lorraine Daston have provided a three-stage periodization—monsters as divine prodigies, as natural wonders, and as medical examples for comparative anatomy and embryology—that is indispensable in helping us to understand shifts in the conceptualization and treatment of monsters from the Middle Ages to the eighteenth century.[18] Rather than summarizing the work of these scholars, I am going to turn to a different kind of text to prepare my discussion of Paré, namely, Thomas Aquinas's *Summa Theologica*.

Aquinas's *Summa* is not only the greatest work of genius produced by medieval moral theology but also a profound synthesis of previous work, coherently connecting doctrines, ideas, and arguments whose relationships had never been made very clear; moreover, the *Summa* also made conceptually determinate notions that had had a deep and wide-ranging significance in the Middle Ages but that had not really been approached with sufficient analytical precision. I am going to use one portion of the *Summa* as representative of medieval attitudes, attitudes that have lasted, in one form or another, for many subsequent centuries. I shall not address the question of the *Summa*'s originality in this area; suffice it to say that I believe that this is one place in which Aquinas gave a conceptually powerful formulation to a set of ideas that had been essential, even if not very precise, to most of medieval moral theology.

Part II of Part II, Questions 153 and 154, of the *Summa Theologica* deal with lust and the parts of lust, respectively. Aquinas begins, in Article 2 of Question 154, by considering the question of whether the venereal act can be without sin. He argues as follows: if the dictate of reason makes use of certain things in a fitting manner and order for the end to which they are adapted, and if this end is truly good, then the use of these things in such a fitting manner and order will not be a sin. Now the preservation of the bodily nature of an individual is a true good, and the use of food is directed to the preservation of life in the individual. Similarly, the preservation of the nature of the human species is a very great good, and the use of the venereal act is directed to the preservation of the whole human race. Therefore, Aquinas concludes,

> wherefore just as the use of food can be without sin, if it be taken in due manner and order, as required for the welfare of the body, so also the use of venereal acts can be without sin, provided they be performed in due manner and order, in keeping with the end of human procreation.[19]

He proceeds in the first article of Question 154 to differentiate six species of lust—simple fornication, adultery, incest, seduction, rape, and the vice contrary to nature—all of which are discussed in the remaining articles.

My concern is with the vices contrary to nature, which are discussed in Articles 11 and 12. In Article 11, he argues that this type of vice is a distinct species of lust, since it involves a special kind of deformity; vices contrary to nature are not only contrary to right reason, as are all the lustful vices, but are also "contrary to the natural order of the venereal act as becoming to the human race," which order has as its end the generation of children.[20] Aquinas distinguishes four categories of vice contrary to nature—bestiality, sodomy, which he interprets as male/male or female/female copulation, the sin of self-abuse, and not observing the natural manner of copulation. It is difficult to determine exactly what falls under this last category, but it is clear from II-II, Question 154, Article 12, Reply to Objection 4, that male/female anal and oral copulation are two of the most grievous ways of not observing the right manner of copulation.

In Article 12, Aquinas rank-orders, from worst to least worst, all of the lustful vices. He claims, first, that all four categories of vice contrary to nature are worse than any of the other vices of lust. So that bestiality, sodomy, not observing the natural manner of copulation, and self-abuse are worse, because of their special deformity, than adultery, rape of a virgin, incest, and so on.[21] Vices contrary to nature are worse in kind and not merely in degree than other lustful vices. Aquinas then goes on to rank-order the vices contrary to nature. The least bad of these vices is self-abuse, since the "gravity of a sin depends more on the abuse of a thing than on the omission of the right use."[22] Next worse is the sin of not observing the right manner of copulation, and this sin is more grievous if the abuse concerns the right vessel than if it affects the manner of copulation in respect of other circumstances. Third worse is sodomy, since use of the right sex is not observed. Finally, the most grievous of all the vices contrary to nature, and so the most grievous of any lustful vice, is bestiality, since the use of the due species is not observed; moreover, in this instance, Aquinas explicitly cites a biblical text as support.[23] One final remark of Aquinas's must be mentioned before I turn to Paré. About the vices contrary to nature, from masturbation to bestiality, Aquinas writes,

> just as the ordering of right reason proceeds from men, so the order of nature is from God Himself: wherefore in sins contrary to nature, whereby the very order of nature is violated, an injury is done to God, the Author of nature.[24]

To act contrary to nature is nothing less than to act directly contrary to the will of God.

One may understandably be wondering how this discussion of Aquinas is relevant to the treatment of monsters, so let me turn immediately to Paré's *Des monstres et prodiges.* The preface to his book begins as follows:

> Monsters are things that appear outside the course of Nature (and are usually signs of some forthcoming misfortune), such as a child who is born with one arm, another who will have two heads, and additional members over and above the ordinary.
>
> Prodigies are things which happen that are completely against Nature, as when a woman will give birth to a serpent, or to a dog, or some other thing that is totally against Nature, as we shall show hereafter through several examples of said monsters and prodigies.[25]

Ceárd has argued that Paré was somewhat indifferent to the problem of precisely how one should distinguish monsters from prodigies. Monsters and prodigies did not constitute absolutely separate classes and during the successive editions of his book, Ceárd things Paré became more and more convinced that the term "monster" was sufficient to designate all of these phenomena.[26] But however imprecise and unarticulated this distinction might appear, the idea that there was a separate class of phenomena, prodigies, that were completely against nature affected the language, attitude, and conceptualization with which Paré approached his examples.

In the first chapter of *Des monstres et prodiges,* Paré distinguishes thirteen causes of monsters, which causes, although not completely exhaustive, are all the ones he is able to adduce with assurance. Ten of these causes are straightforwardly natural causes; two, the glory of God and the wrath of God, are straightforwardly supernatural causes; and one, demons and devils, has a long and complicated classificatory history.[27] Briefly, to classify the products of demons and devils as a result of supernatural causes was to threaten to place the devil on a par with God, granting him the same powers to overturn the natural order that God

possessed. The possibility of such a theologically untenable position led
to detailed discussions concerning the status of demonic causation; and
as we can see from chapters 26 to 34, Paré fit squarely into these discussions, concerned both to grant the reality of the devil and yet to limit his
powers. Of the two straightforwardly supernatural causes, Paré's treatment of the first, the glory of God, is exhausted by one example, the
restoration of a blind man's sight by Jesus Christ, an example literally
copied from Pierre Boaistuau's *Histoires Prodigieuses,* first published in
1560.[28]

The other supernatural cause, the wrath of God, is far more interesting for my purposes; most of the examples produced by Paré to illustrate
this category are of the same kind, and they are closely linked to the
natural cause of the mixture or mingling of seed. I want to discuss these
examples in detail in order to support some claims about the history of
horror. But I should make one more preliminary remark. Paré, like
virtually every writer during this period, had no intellectual difficulty in
referring to both supernatural and natural causes; he felt no incompati-
bility in discussing these two types of cause together. Yet although God
was always in the background of *Des monstres et prodiges,* by far the most
space is devoted to natural causes, with God's explicit appearances being
relatively few. This contrasts, for instance, with Jacob Rueff's *De conceptu
et generatione hominis,* a book known to Paré, published in 1554 and for a
long time the classic work on the problems of generation. Rueff also
discussed supernatural and natural causes together, but in Book V of *De
conceptu,* when he discusses monstrous births, Rueff considers them all as
divine punishment, and their physical causes, however active, are almost
ignored in favor of the evidence of the judgments of God. In Rueff's
text, whatever the physical or natural causes of the production of monsters, monsters are first of all punishments inflicted by God on sinners.[29]
So Paré's book already demonstrates a shift of emphasis that makes his
treatment of supernatural causes all the more interesting.

Paré's chapter on the wrath of God opens with these words:

> There are other creatures which astonish us doubly because they do not
> proceed from the above mentioned causes, but from a fusing together of
> strange species, which render the creature not only monstrous but prodi-
> gious, that is to say, which is completely abhorrent and against Nature. . . .
>
> It is certain that most often these monstrous and prodigious creatures
> proceed from the judgment of God, who permits fathers and mothers to
> produce such abominations from the disorder that they make in copula-
> tion, like brutish beasts. . . . Similarly, Moses forbids such coupling in Leviti-
> cus (Chapter 16) (fig. 2.3).[30]

The creatures discussed in this chapter are produced by the natural
cause of the fusing together of strange species, but, more important,

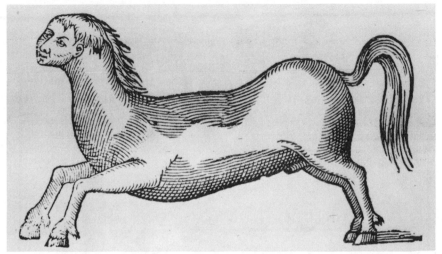

Fig. 2.3. A colt with a man's head.

their, so to speak, first cause is God's wrath at the copulation between human beings and other species, a practice that is explicitly forbidden in Leviticus. The result is not only a monster but a prodigy, a creature that is contrary to nature and that is described as completely abhorrent.

If we turn to the chapter that treats the natural cause of the mixture or mingling of seed, we find Paré endorsing the principle that nature always strives to create its likeness; since nature always preserves its kind and species, when two animals of different species copulate, the result will be a creature that combines the form of both of the species.[31] The kind of naturalistic explanation exhibited in this chapter is, however, framed by crucial opening and closing paragraphs, which I quote at length. The chapter begins with this statement:

> There are monsters that are born with a form that is half-animal and half-human . . . which are produced by sodomists and atheists who join together, and break out of their bounds contrary to nature, with animals, and from this are born several monsters that are hideous and very scandalous to look at or speak about. Yet the disgrace lies in the deed and not in words; and it is, when it is done, a very unfortunate and abominable thing, and a great horror for a man or woman to mix with and copulate with brute animals; and as a result some are born half-men and half-animals (figs. 2.4, 2.5).[32]

The chapter closes with this:

> Now I shall refrain from writing here about several other monsters engendered from such grist, together with their portraits, which are so hideous and abominable, not only to see, but also to hear tell of, that, due to their

Fig. 2.4. A monstrous lamb.

great loathsomeness I have neither wanted to relate them nor have them portrayed. For (as Boaistuau says, after having related several sacred and profane stories, which are all filled with grievous punishments for lechers) what can atheists and sodomists expect, who (as I said above) couple against God and Nature with brute animals?[33]

What I want to isolate is the conjunction of God's wrath at human disobedience of his laws (a supernatural cause) with the production of a creature contrary to nature, a prodigy, the reaction to which is horror; and, finally, I want to emphasize that the prime example for Paré of such human disobedience is bestiality. These features are in effect Paré's analogue to Aquinas's discussion in the *Summa Theologica*. For Thomas, there is a distinct category of lust, worse in kind than other species of lust, namely, lust contrary to nature (remember that prodigies, being completely against nature, are worse in kind than monsters, being only outside the course of nature), the most grievous example of which is bestiality; moreover, when such sins are committed, an injury is done to God. Paré physicalizes this framework of concepts by exhibiting the consequence of such an injury to God; the resulting bestial creature is a sym-

Fig. 2.5. A child, half dog.

bolic representation of God's wrath, and the reaction of horror we have
to such hideous creatures is intended to remind us of, and to impress
upon us, the horror of the sin itself. Thus, the special viciousness of sins
contrary to nature extends to the creatures produced by these sins. Paré
reserves his most charged language—horror, horrible, hideous, loathsome, abominable—for these creatures and the sins they represent.

The link between moral disorder and the disorder of nature was a constant theme during this period. It was widely believed that evil committed on earth could leave its mark on the structure of the human body.[34] And the way in which the physical form of the body gave rise to moral and theological questions went far beyond the case of prodigies. The issue of monstrous births as a whole raised practical problems for priests, since they had to decide whether any particular monstrous child was human, and so whether it should be baptized or not. There were, of course, disagreements about how to make these determinations, but the form of the body served as a guide to theological resolution. The kind of reasoning employed is well represented by Guido of Mont Rocher's *Manipulus Curatorum Officia Sacerdotus* of 1480:

> But what if there is a single monster which has two bodies joined together: ought it to be baptized as one person or as two? I say that since baptism is made according to the soul and not according to the body, howsoever there be two bodies, if there is only one soul, then it ought to be baptized as one person. But if there are two souls, it ought to be baptized as two persons. But how is it to be known if there be one or two? I say that if there be two bodies, there are two souls. But if there is one body, there is one soul. And for this reason it may be supposed that if there be two chests and two heads there are two souls. If, however, there be one chest and one head, however much the other members be doubled, there is only one soul.[35]

I mention this example to indicate that Paré's use of the body as a moral and theological cipher is only a special instance, and not an entirely distinctive one, of a much more general mentalité.

What is most remarkable about Paré's book is that when he confines himself to purely natural causes, he employs the concept of monster exclusively (phenomena outside the course of nature) and not the concept of prodigy. Furthermore, the experience of horror is absent from his descriptions. Horror is appropriate only if occasioned by a normative cause, the violation of some norm, as when the human will acts contrary to the divine will. The chapter that immediately follows Paré's discussion of the wrath of God concerns monsters caused by too great a quantity of seed. Compare its opening language with the language of the previous chapter already quoted.

> On the generation of monsters, Hippocrates says that if there is too great an abundance of matter, multiple births will occur, or else a monstrous child having superfluous and useless parts, such as two heads, four arms, four legs, six digits on the hands and feet, or other things. And on the contrary, if the seed is lacking in quantity, some member will be lacking, [such] as feet or head, or [having] some other part missing (figs. 2.6, 2.7).[36]

Even Paré's discussion of hermaphrodites in chapter 6 bears no trace of horror, and we see that their formation is due entirely to natural causes,

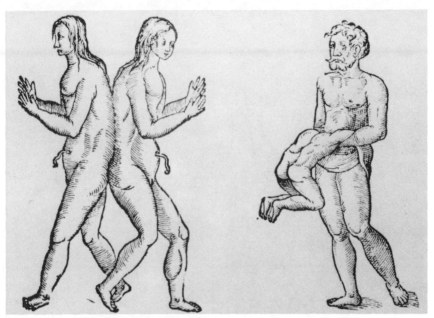

Fig. 2.6. Examples of too great a quantity of seed.

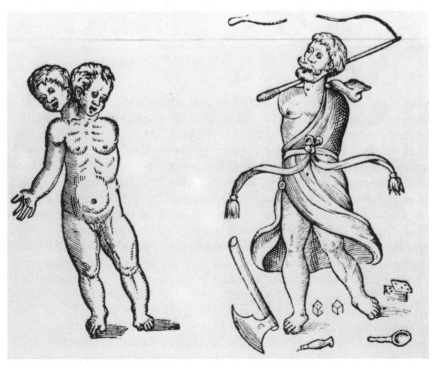

Fig. 2.7. Examples of lack in the quantity of seed.

Fig. 2.8.   Hermaphrodites.

with no admixture of willful violation of a norm (fig. 2.8). Hermaphrodites are monsters, not prodigies, naturally explicable and normatively neutral.

If we read Paré's treatise chapter by chapter, we find that horror is a normative reaction, a reaction engendered by a violation of a specific kind of norm. When causal knowledge, that is, knowledge of the natural causes, is produced to explain a monster, the effect of such explanation is to displace horror, to alter our experiences of the phenomenon with which we are confronted. Horror is linked to Paré's discussion of supernatural causes because the issue in these discussions is always the normative relation between the divine and human wills. A horrible prodigy is produced when the human will acts contrary to nature, contrary to the divine will, and so when this contrariness (as Aquinas makes conceptually articulate and as is reflected in Paré) involves the thwarting of a very particular kind of norm. I see no reason to doubt the accuracy of Paré's descriptions, of where and when he experienced horror, especially because this kind of description is confirmed in so many other treatises.[37] It strikes me as no odder that Paré and his contemporaries would experience horror only when confronted by a prodigy, by some especially vicious normative violation, than that the Israelites of the Old Testament would come to experience horror at the seemingly heterogeneous group of phenomena called "abominations." And the inverse relationship between horror and causal explanation is the other side of the similar relationship between wonder and causal explanation. A sense of wonder was the appropriate reaction to the production of a miracle, just as horror was the appropriate reaction to the production of a prodigy. Lorraine Daston has argued, in examining the decline of miracles and the sensibility of wonder, that "it was axiomatic in the psychology of miracles that causal knowledge drove out wonder, and in the seventeenth century the converse was also emphasized: wonder drove out causal knowledge."[38] The psychology of miracles and the psychology of prodigies were phenomenologically and analytically akin to each other.

In his chapter on the mixing and mingling of seed and the hideous monsters that result from bestiality (fig. 2.9), Paré describes a man-pig, a creature born in Brussels in 1564, having a man's face, arms, and hands, and so representing humanity above the shoulders, and having the hind legs and hindquarters of a swine and the genitals of a sow (fig. 2.10). This man-pig was one of a litter of six pigs and, according to Paré, "it nursed like the others and lived two days: then it was killed along with the sow on account of the horror the people had of it."[39] As one would expect from what I have argued, horror was in fact the reaction triggered by this man-pig, and it was so consuming as to push the people to kill both the sow and her monstrous offspring.

In 1699, Edward Tyson, a fellow of the Royal Society and Royal College of Physicians, communicated a report, published in the *Philosophical Transactions of the Royal Society,* entitled "A Relation of two Monstrous Pigs, with the Resemblance of Human Faces, and two young Turkeys joined by the Breast." Tyson announces his intention at the start:

> By the description of the following monsters I design to prove that the distortion of the parts of a fetus may occasion it to represent the figure of different animals, without any real coition betwixt the two species.[40]

He proceeds to describe, in much detail, a so-called man-pig, discovered at Staffordshire in 1699. His article contains no evidence of horror, disgust, dread, or any related emotion. As he continues, it becomes clear that his description of the seemingly human face of the pig is meant to show that it is the result of some depression of the pig's face, caused by a compression of the womb or by the pressure of the other pigs in the same part of the womb. No reference to bestiality is necessary to understand the production of this creature, and no horror is, or should be, occasioned by it. Tyson mentions the case of a man-pig reported by Paré,

Fig. 2.9.   A monster, half man and half swine.

Fig. 2.10.   A pig, having the head, feet, and hands of a man, and the rest of a pig.

the very case I have quoted, and is content to point out some differences between Paré's case and his, for example, that his man-pig did not possess human hands. Tyson is cautious about whether recourse to bestiality is ever required to explain such monsters, but the main thrust of his article is to show that causal explanations of the kind he has produced have a much greater explanatory relevance than has often been recognized. His attitude stands at a great distance from Paré's, and it is exemplified by his remark, made when discussing other reported cases of monstrous pigs, "I believe either fiction, or want of observation has made more monsters than nature ever produced"[41]—sometimes almost employing the concept of monster as if monsters were thought to be creatures contrary to nature, whereas the whole point of his communication has been to show that they result from abnormal deformations due to natural causes.

The displacement of horror as a result of causal explanation, as though knowing the cause of a monster calms the horror we might feel, can also be seen in the case of John Merrick, the so-called Elephant Man, and such displacement operates in one and the same individual, namely, Merrick's physician, Frederick Treves (figs. 2.11, 2.12). In the medical reports submitted to the Pathological Society of London, words such as "deformity," "abnormality," "remarkable," "extraordinary," and "grossly" describe Merrick's condition. The reports do not convey an experience of horror but rather an impression of how extreme Merrick's deformities are, and, because of that extremity, they indicate the immense medical interest of his condition. However, when we read Treves's memoir and he describes his and others' first encounters with the Elephant Man, the mood is completely different. Here we find words and phrases such as "repellent," "fright," "aversion," "a frightful creature that could only have been possible in a nightmare," "the most disgusting specimen of humanity that I have ever seen," "the loathing insinuation of a man being changed into an animal," and "everyone he met confronted him with a look of horror and disgust."[42] (See fig. 2.13.) It is as though we can describe Treves's emotional history by saying that when he attends to the complicated causal etiology of Merrick's condition, he can transform his own reaction from one of horror and disgust to pity and, eventually, sympathy. We often assume that the appellation "Elephant Man" derives from the fact that Merrick was covered with papillomatous growths, a derivation of this name reported in one of the medical communications. And certainly this appearance could have accounted for that title. But it is easy to forget that this is not the official reason that Merrick himself gave for his being called the Elephant Man. He reported that shortly before his birth, his mother was knocked down by a circus elephant and that this accident, with its horrifying consequences, was the source of the label, "Elephant Man." It is perfectly evident that this story conceals, and not very well, the fantasy of bestiality, and it is exactly this fantasy that is embedded in Treves's memoir when he speaks of "the loathing insinuation of a man being changed into an animal."

Although the adjective "abominable" occurs frequently in discussions of monsters and prodigies, I will not insist here on the obvious differences between this use of the term and the concept of abomination in the

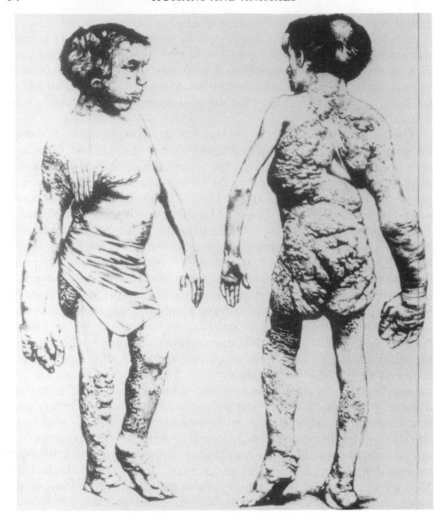

Fig. 2.11. John Merrick, 1884–85.

Old Testament. The use of "abominable" to describe prodigies remains inextricably linked to horror, as I have argued; but the doctrine of natural law, absent from the Old Testament, decisively alters one feature of the biblical conception. A study of the relevant biblical passages would show that it is primarily one uniquely specified people who, because of their special relation to God, feel horror at abominations. But in the texts I have discussed, it is rather as though the horror of sins contrary to nature, and of the products that result from them, is experienced by all human beings qua rational beings. For the use of natural reason alone is sufficient to grasp the viciousness of sins contrary to nature, and bestial-

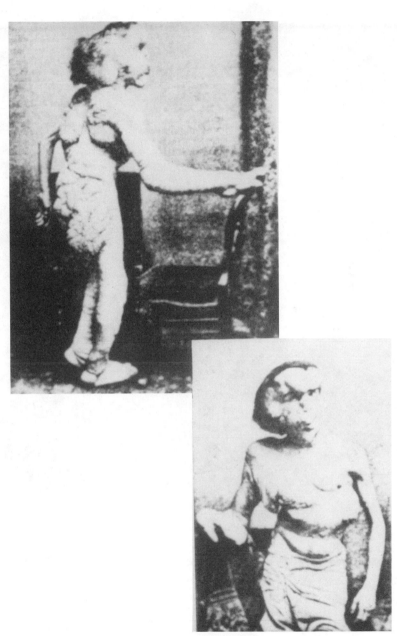

Fig. 2.12.   John Merrick.

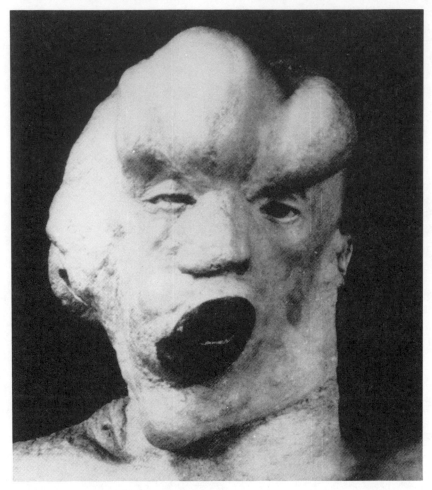

Fig. 2.13.   Postmortem cast of the head and neck of John Merrick.

ity, for example, is a violation of natural law, which requires no special act of divine revelation to be known but is nothing else than the rational creature's participation in God's eternal law.[43] So every human being ought to experience horror at that which he knows, as a rational being, to be contrary to nature. In this context, the doctrine of natural law helped to conceal the recognition that horror is a cultural and historical product and not demanded by reason alone, a fact that is more easily recognized in the pertinent biblical texts. Since horror came to be enmeshed in the framework of natural law and natural reason, prodigies, and the wrath of God, could be described in a way that was intended to represent the

experience of every human being, not simply the experience of a culturally specific group. Objects of horror could now directly appear to be
naturally horrifying.

As I have already shown, bestiality, the worst of the sins contrary to
nature, exhibited its viciousness in the very structure of the human body
itself, in the creatures produced by the willful violation of God's natural
law. But this configuration, whereby a certain kind of undermining of
norms was exhibited in the effects of physical pathology, was not restricted only to this one form of lust contrary to nature. Eighteenth- and
early nineteenth-century treatises on onanism reproduce this same pattern of concepts; self-abuse, another one of Aquinas's sins contrary to
nature, ravages the physical structure of the body, producing, among its
effects, acute stomach pains; habitual vomiting that resists all remedies
during the time this vicious habit is continued; a dry cough; a hoarse,
weak voice; a great loss of strength; paleness; sometimes a light but
continuous yellowness; pimples, particularly on the forehead, temples,
and near the nose; considerable emaciation; an astonishing sensibility to
changes in the weather; an enfeeblement of sight sometimes leading to
blindness; a considerable diminution of all mental faculties often culminating in insanity; and even death (fig. 2.14).[44] Indeed, this relationship
between the viciousness of the sin and the pathology of the body even
gave rise to a genre of autopsy report, in which the autopsy of a mastur-
bator would reveal that the effects of this loathsome habit had pene-
trated within the body itself, affecting the internal organs no less than
the external appearance.[45] In Tissot's *L'Onanisme, Dissertation sur les maladies produites par la masturbation*, we find the same kind of terminology
and sensibility that accompanies Renaissance descriptions of prodigies.
Tissot opens his discussion of cases, with which he has had firsthand
experience, with the following preamble:

> My first case presents a scene which is dreadful. I was myself frightened
> the first time I saw the unfortunate patient who is its subject. I then felt,
> more than I ever had before, the necessity of showing young people all the
> horrors of the abyss into which they voluntarily plunge themselves.[46]

And he invokes the idea of masturbation as contrary to nature in strategi-
cally central passages.[47]

It is often said that Tissot's treatise is the first scientific study of masturbation, and his book is engulfed by medical terminology and punctu-
ated by attempts to give physiological explanations of the pathological
effects provoked by masturbation. But it is just as evident that his book
remains firmly placed within a tradition of moral theology, which begins
with a conception of masturbation as an especially vicious kind of lust. It
produces mental and physical disease and disorder, but even in the scien-

Fig. 2.14.   Death by masturbation.

tific treatments inaugurated by Tissot, it remains a vicious habit, not itself a disease but a moral crime against God and nature. Tissot begins his book with the claim, which he says that physicians of all ages unanimously believe, that the loss of one ounce of seminal fluid enfeebles one more than the loss of forty ounces of blood.[48] He immediately recognizes that he must then explain why the loss of a great quantity of seminal fluid by masturbation, by means contrary to nature, produces diseases so much more terrible than the loss of an equal quantity of seminal fluid by natural intercourse. When he offers an explanation, in Article II, Section 8 of his book, he attempts to frame it in terms of purely physical causes, the mechanical laws of the body and of its union with the mind. But try as he might, he cannot help but conclude this section by reintroducing the claim that masturbators "find themselves guilty of a crime for which divine justice cannot suspend punishment."[49]

Theorists of sodomy also exploited this same kind of connection between normative taint and physical deformation. The normative origin of attitudes toward sodomy is contained not only in the very word, with its reference to the episode of Sodom and Gomorrah in Genesis, but also in the emergence of other words to refer to the same practices. For instance, buggery derives from the French *bougrerie,* a word that refers to a Manichaean sect that arose at Constantinople in the ninth century, and which recognized a sort of pontiff who resided in Bulgaria. Thus, to be a *bougre* meant that one was a participant in heresy, and there is no reason to believe that this heretical sect had any special proclivity toward sodomy. However, eventually, the accusation of *bougrerie* came to be identified with an accusation of sodomy, and the link to heresy became submerged.[50] Moreover, in French, the phrase "change of religion" could be used to describe pederasty; to become a pederast was to change religion (*changer de religion*).[51] Both sex and religion have their orthodoxies, their heresies, their apostasies—their normative paths and deviations.

Even when the theological underpinnings of the concept of sodomy receded into the background, its normative content and origin was always close at hand. Ambroise Tardieu, whose enormously influential *Étude médico-légale sur les attentats aux moeurs* was first published in 1857, devotes about one-third of this book to a discussion of pederasty and sodomy. Tardieu restricts the term "pederasty" to the love of young boys, whereas the more general term "sodomy" is reserved for "acts contrary to nature, considered in themselves, and without reference to the sex of the individuals between whom the culpable relations are established."[52] Most of the cases of sodomy Tardieu describes concern either male/male anal intercourse or male/female anal intercourse. The fact that he repeatedly characterizes these acts as contrary to nature indicates the normative tradition into which his work fits. Although Tardieu acknowledges that madness may accompany pederasty and sodomy, he wishes to make certain that these acts escape "neither the responsibility of conscience, the just severity of law, nor, above all, the contempt of decent people."[53] He is aware that the "shame and disgust"[54] that these acts inspire have often constrained the reports of observers, and his book is intended to remedy this lack, and in extraordinary detail.

Much of Tardieu's discussion of pederasty and sodomy is concerned with the physical signs that permit one to recognize that these activities have transpired, with the material traces left by these vices in the structure of the organs. Tardieu believed that an exhaustive discussion of these signs is necessary if legal medicine was going to be able to determine with assurance whether such acts contrary to nature and public morality had taken place. He describes the deformations of the anus that result from the habit of passive sodomy, a topic that had already received much discussion in the French and German medicolegal literature. But he goes on to describe the signs of active pederasty, signs left on the viril member itself, which he claims have been completely ignored in previous treatises. Changes in the dimension and form of the penis are the most reliable indications of active sodomy and pederasty. The active sodomist has a penis that is either very thin or very voluminous. The excessively voluminous penis is analogized to "the snout of certain animals,"[55] while

Tardieu describes the much more common, excessively thin penis of active sodomists in the following remarkable way:

> In the case where it is small and thin, it grows considerably thinner from the base to the tip, which is very tapered, like the finger of a glove, and recalls completely the *canum more*.[56]

To confirm his general observations, he reports the physical conformation of the penises of many active sodomists:

> Having made him completely undress, we can verify that the viril member, very long and voluminous, presents at its tip a characteristic elongation and tapering that gives to the gland the almost pointed form of the penis of a dog.[57]

Another of Tardieu's active sodomists has a penis that "simulates exactly the form of the penis of a pure-bred dog."[58] As if to confirm that sodomy is contrary to nature and God, the relevant parts of the human body are transformed by this activity so that they come to resemble the bodily parts of a dog. What could be more horrifying than the moral and physical transformation of the human into a beast, a man-dog produced no longer by bestiality but by the disgusting practice of sodomy. Long after the classical discussions of prodigies, the category of the contrary to nature continued to mark out one fundamental domain of horror.

By the late nineteenth century, the experiences provoked by so-called freak shows already contrasted with the horror of the contrary to nature. Rather than exhibiting the physical consequences of normative deviation, the freaks exhibited in sideshows and circuses were intended to amuse, entertain, and divert their audiences. In general,

> the urban workers who came to stare at freaks were by and large an unsophisticated audience in search of cheap and simple entertainment. . . . In the early 1870s William Cameron Coup had introduced a two-ring concept while working with Barnum and by 1885 most shows revolved around a multiple ring system. The result was a drift toward glamour and spectacle as the basic product of the big shows. The tendency was well developed by the early nineties and brought specific changes to the exhibits. Contrasts of scale—fat ladies and living skeletons, giants and dwarfs—and exhibits involving internal contrasts—bearded ladies, hermaphroditic men and ladies toying with snakes—began to displace the more repulsive exhibits. As the shows were freighted with fewer mutilated horrors they became less emotionally loaded and less complex as experiences.[59]

It should be noted that part of the purpose of the multiple-ring circus would have been defeated by the displaying of horrors. For if having more than one ring was intended to get the spectators to look from exhibit to exhibit, to gaze periodically and repeatedly at each of the

Fig. 2.15. Fred Wilson, the Lobster Boy.

rings, to experience the circus in all of its diversity, then the exhibition of a horrifying object would have tended to thwart this experience. The experience of horror disposes us to fix on its object, unable to avert our gaze, fascinated as well as repulsed, blocking out virtually everything but the object before our eyes. Thus, horror is incompatible with the glamour, spectacle, and variety that is inherent in the multiple-ring circus.

Fig. 2.16.   Avery Childs, the Frog Boy.

The modern circus has to be set up so that no single exhibit so predomi-
nated that the many rings were, in effect, reduced to one.

Even if we put aside the fact that the categories of freaks and prodigies were by no means composed of the same specimens, we can see how
different this experience of freaks was by examining photographs of
them. Charles Eisenmann was a Bowery photographer who took many
portraits of freaks during the late nineteenth century. Some of these
photographs represent characters that are half-human and half-animal
and so, at least in this respect, can be thought of as successors to the
medieval and Renaissance prodigies produced by bestiality. But these
photographs exhibit no indication of horror. Avery Childs, the Frog Boy,
is evocative and amusingly photographed but no more horrifying than a
contortionist, his slippers emphasizing that he is more human than frog
(fig. 2.15). Indeed, these photographs insist on the humanity of their
subjects, precisely the opposite of Paré's discussions, which highlight the

Fig. 2.17. Jo Jo, the Russian Dog Face Boy.

bestiality of prodigies. Fred Wilson, the Lobster Boy, suffers from a serious congenital deformity, but dressed in his Sunday best, with his hair neatly combed, one is drawn as much to his human face as to his supposed lobster claws (fig. 2.16). And even Jo Jo, the Russian Dog Face Boy, one of Barnum's most famous attractions, wears a fringed velour suit and sports that great symbol of Western civilization, the watch chain (fig. 2.17). Furthermore, his right hand bears a ring, and his left hand is neatly placed on his knee. And he poses with a gun, as if to suggest that he is not an animal to be hunted but can himself participate in the all too human activity of the hunt. Horror at the prodigious, amusement by the freak—the history of monsters encodes a complicated and changing history of emotion, one that helps to reveal to us the structures and limits of the human community.

NOTES

*Among the many people who have offered comments and suggestions on earlier versions of this chapter, I am especially grateful to Daniel Brudney, Nancy Cartwright, Justine Cassell, Stanley Cavell, Lorraine Daston, Peter Galison, Jan Goldstein, Joel Snyder, David Wellbery, and the editors of this volume.

1. Lucien Febvre, "Sensibility and History: How to Reconstitute the Emotional Life of the Past," in *A New Kind of History* (London: Routledge and Kegan Paul, 1973), 24.

2. This chapter is a fragment of a much longer manuscript entitled "The History of Horror: Abominations, Monsters, and the Unnatural." That manuscript is a comparative historical analysis of the three concepts mentioned in the title, linking each of them to the reaction of horror and thus taking a first step toward writing a history of horror. I then use this comparative history to consider both the phenomenology of horror and its moral analysis, interlacing historical and philosophical concerns throughout.

3. Jean Delumeau, *La Peur en Occident: Une citié assiegié* (Paris: Fayard, 1978), and *Le Péché et la peur: La culpabilisation en Occident* (Paris: Fayard, 1983).

4. For useful discussion, see, among many others, Jacques Le Goff, "Mentalities: A History of Ambiguities," in Jacques Le Goff and Pierre Nora, eds., *Constructing the Past* (Cambridge: Cambridge University Press, 1985); Robert Mandrou, "L'histoire des mentalités," in the article "Histoire," *Encyclopedia Universalis* (Paris: Encyclopedia Universalis France, 1968); Jean Delumeau, "Déchristianization ou nouveau modèle de christianisme," *Archives de Science sociales des Religion* 40 (Juillet–Décembre 1975); and Carlo Ginzburg, *The Cheese and the Worms* (New York: Penguin Books, 1980), "Preface to the Italian Edition."

5. This is emphasized by Alphonse Dupront in his seminal essay, "Problémes et méthodes d'une histoire de la psychologie collective," *Annales* (Janvier–Fevrier 1961).

6. I have tried to do this for the history of sexuality in "How to Do the History of Psychoanalysis: A Reading of Freud's *Three Essays on the Theory of*

Sexuality," *Critical Inquiry* (Winter 1986); "Sex and the Emergence of Sexuality," *Critical Inquiry* (Autumn 1987); and "Closing Up the Corpses: Diseases of Sexuality and the Emergence of the Psychiatric Style of Reasoning," forthcoming in George Boolos, ed., *Mind, Method, and Meaning: Essays in Honor of Hilary Putnam* (Cambridge: Cambridge University Press).

7. See Dupront, "Problémes et méthodes," 9.

8. Martin Luther, *Werke* (Weimar: H. Böhlau, 1930–1985), XI:370–385.

9. In my interpretation of this pamphlet, I follow Jean Céard, *La Nature et les prodiges* (Geneva: Librarie Droz, 1977), 79–84.

10. Martin Luther and Phillip Melancthon, *Of Two Wonderful Popish Monsters,* trans. John Brooke. (Imprinted at London: Colophon, 1579.) I have modernized spelling and punctuation. The quotation comes from the first page of Brooke's preface, which is unpaginated in the 1579 edition of the pamphlet.

11. Ibid.

12. Ibid. The quotation comes from the second page of Brooke's preface.

13. Jean Delumeau, *Le Péché et la peur,* 153.

14. I am following Delumeau's account here. Ibid., 152–158. But chap. 4 as a whole should be read in this context.

15. Quoted in Delumeau, *La Péché et la peur,* 155.

16. Ambroise Paré, *Des monstres et prodiges* (Edition Critique et commentée par Jean Céard) (Geneva: Librarie Droz, 1971). There is an English translation under the title *On Monsters and Marvels* (Chicago: University of Chicago Press, 1982). I have tried to follow the English translation in my quotations, but I have altered it whenever I felt it was necessary to preserve Paré's meaning. For some inexplicable reason, the English renders *prodiges* as "marvels" rather than "prodigies," a translation that cannot help but result in obfuscation.

17. Jean Céard, *La Nature et les prodiges.*

18. Katharine Park and Lorraine J. Daston, "Unnatural Conceptions: The Study of Monsters in Sixteenth- and Seventeenth-Century France and England," *Past and Present* 92 (August 1981). For some premedieval treatments of monsters, see Bruce MacBain, *Prodigy and Expiation: A Study in Religion and Politics in Republican Rome* (Collection Latomus: Brussels, 1982); Raymond Bloch, *Les prodiges dans l'antiquité classique* (Paris: Presses Universitaire de France, 1963); and E. Leichty, "Teratological Omens," in *La Divination en Mésopotamie ancienne et dans les régions voisines* (Paris: Presses Universitaire de France, 1966).

19. Thomas Aquinas, *The Summa Theologica* (literally translated by the Fathers of the English Dominican Province) (New York: Benziger Brothers), Second Part of the Second Part, Question 53 Second Article. I have generally followed this translation, although in paraphrasing Aquinas, I have also consulted the Latin and facing-page English translation of the *Summa* by the Blackfriars (New York: McGraw–Hill, 1964–1980). I have appropriated terminology from each of the translations when I thought it appropriate.

20. Ibid., 157–158.

21. Ibid., II-II, Q. 154, Art. 12, Reply.

22. Ibid., 161.

23. Ibid., II-II, Q. 154, Art. 12, Rep. Obj. 4.

24. Ibid., 160. A useful discussion of this part of Aquinas can be found in John Boswell, *Christianity, Social Tolerance, and Homosexuality* (Chicago: University of Chicago Press, 1980). See esp. chap. 11.

25. Ambroise Paré, *On Monsters and Marvels*, 3. In 1579, Paré added a third category to that of monsters and marvels, namely, the maimed (*les mutilez*). I shall not discuss this category, since, as Céard notes, after the preface, Paré no longer uses the concept of the maimed. See Ambroise Paré, *Des monstres et prodiges*, 151.

26. Jean Céard, *La Nature et les prodiges*, 304–305.

27. On this topic, see Stuart Clark, "The Scientific Status of Demonology," in Brian Vickers, ed., *Occult and Scientific Mentalities in the Renaissance* (Cambridge: Cambridge University Press, 1984).

28. Paré, *On Monsters*, 152.

29. Céard, *La Nature et les prodiges*, 293–295.

30. Paré, *On Monsters*, 5. In this chapter, Paré also considers the monsters that are produced when a man copulates with a woman during her period; he analogizes such activity to bestiality, since "it is a filthy and brutish thing to have dealings with a woman while she is purging herself." Without discussing this important topic here, I simply note that the same chapter of Leviticus which prohibits bestiality also prohibits intercourse with a woman during her period (the relevant chapter is Leviticus 18, not 16 as Paré states).

31. Paré, *Des monstres*, chap. IX. This chapter appears as chap. XX in the English translation.

32. Paré, *On Monsters*, 67.

33. Ibid., 73.

34. See Delumeau, *La Péché et la peur*, 156.

35. Quoted in John Block Friedman, *The Monstrous Races in Medieval Art and Thought* (Cambridge: Harvard University Press, 1981), 182. Friedman's book is a useful introduction to the topic of monstrous races, a topic I shall not discuss here.

36. Paré, *On Monsters*, 8.

37. For an English example, see John Sadler's *The Sicke Woman's Private Looking-Glasse*, relevant portions of which are excerpted in Paré, *On Monsters*, 174–176.

38. Lorraine Daston, "The Decline of Miracles." Unpub. ms., 12.

39. Paré, *On Monsters*, 69. The practice of killing both the human being and the beast involved in bestial copulation has a long history that goes back to the law of Leviticus 20: 15–16. I have been able to find a few exceptions where the beast was spared. The most interesting of these exceptions is reported as follows:

> E. P. Evans states that at Vanvres in 1570 one Jacques Verrons was hung for copulating with a she-ass. The animal was acquitted on the grounds that she was a victim of violence and had not participated of her own free will. The prior of the local convent and several citizens of the town signed a certificate saying that they had known said she-ass for four years, and that she had always shown herself to be virtuous both at home and abroad and had never given occasion of scandal to anyone. This document was produced at the trial and is said to have exerted a decisive influence upon the judgment of the court.

Quoted in Harry Hoffner, "Incest, Sodomy and Bestiality in the Ancient Near East," Harry Hoffner, ed., *Orient and Occident*, Band 22 of *Alter Orient und Altes*

Testament (Germany: Verlag Butzon & Bercker Kevelaer, 1973), 83, fn. 13. This exceptional case should not misdirect one to think that trials for bestiality required the ascription of moral responsibility to animals. For discussion, see J. J. Finkelstein, *The Ox that Gored,* esp. 69–72.

40. Edward Tyson, "A Relation of two Monstrous Pigs, with the Resemblance of Human Faces, and two young Turkeys joined by the Breast," *Philosophical Transactions of the Royal Society* XXI (1669): 431. I have modernized spelling and punctuation.

41. Ibid., 434.

42. Both Treves's memoir and the relevant medical reports are reprinted in Ashley Montagu, *The Elephant Man* (New York: E. P. Dutton, 1979).

43. See Aquinas's discussion in *Summa Theologica,* I-II, Q. 91, Art. 2, and Q. 94.

44. I have taken my list from Art. I, Sect. 4, of S. Tissot, *L'Onanisme, Dissertation sur les maladies produites par la masturbation,* 5th ed. (Lausanne: Marc Chapuis, 1780). Tissot's list is entirely representative of other eighteenth-century discussions. An English translation of Tissot's book appeared in 1832: *Treatise on the Diseases Produced by Onanism* (New York: Collins and Hennay, 1832). I have often found it necessary to modify the English translation. For discussions of the masturbation literature, see T. Tarczylo, "L'*Onanisme* de Tissot," *Dix-huitième Siècle* 12 (1980), and *Sexe et liberté au siècle des Lumières* (Paris: Presses de la Renaissance, 1983); J. Stengers and A. Van Neck, *Histoire d'une grande peur: La masturbation* (Brussels: Editions de l'Universite de Bruxelles, 1984).

45. A representative example is Alfred Hitchcock, "Insanity and Death from Masturbation," *Boston Medical and Surgical Journal* 26 (1842).

46. Tissot, *L'Onanisme,* 33.

47. See, e.g., the last paragraph of the introduction to *L'Onanisme.*

48. Ibid., 3.

49. Ibid., 121.

50. Pierre Guiraud, *Dictionnaire historique, stylistique, rhétorique, étymologique, de la littérature érotique* (Paris: Payot, 1978), 76.

51. Ibid., 215.

52. Ambroise Tardieu, *Étude médico-légale sur les attentats aux moeurs,* Septième éd. (Paris: J. B. Ballière, 1878), 198. The category of sodomy has proven notoriously flexible and has been used to encompass a variety of activities. However, despite the flexibility, I believe that this category has more conceptual unity than has sometimes been attributed to it. I discuss this issue in the manuscript of which this chapter is an excerpt.

53. Ibid., 255.

54. Ibid., 195.

55. Ibid., 237.

56. Ibid., 236.

57. Ibid., 258.

58. Ibid., 260.

59. Michael Mitchell, *Monsters of the Guilded Age: The Photographs of Charles Eisenmann* (Toronto: Gauge Publishing Limited, 1979), 28, 30. I am indebted to Ian Hacking for providing me with this book.

THREE

The Animal Connection*

Harriet Ritvo

The dichotomy between humans and animals—or man and beast, as it used to be called—is so old and automatic that we scarcely notice it. It was enshrined near the beginning of our tradition, in the second chapter of Genesis, when God presented the animals to Adam one by one, in the vain hope that one of them would prove a fit helpmeet for him. In the end, of course, none of them would do, and God had to provide Adam with a creature more like himself.[1] At least since then, the notion that animals are radically other, on the far side of an unbridgeable chasm constructed by their lack of either reason or soul, has been a constant feature of Western theology and philosophy.[2] It has completely overshadowed the most readily available alternative, which would define human beings as one animal kind among many others.

And the advent of modern science has not made much difference. Most scientific research about animals has been founded on the assumption that they constitute a distinct class to which human beings do not belong. Thus, eighteenth- and nineteenth-century zoologists were confident that "the prerogative of reason," which animals lacked, distinguished humanity "as . . . intended for higher duties, and a more exalted destiny."[3] This confidence insulated them from the implications of such disquieting recognitions as the following, taken from an early Victorian zoological popularizer: "When we turn our attention to Mammalia . . . we find some startling us by forms and actions so much resembling our own, as to excite unpleasant comparisons."[4] Nor did Charles Darwin's formulations necessarily change things. The gap between humans and animals remained axiomatic even, or perhaps especially, in fields like comparative psychology, which focused on the kinds of intellectual and emotional qualities that were also assumed to distinguish us as a species.

George Romanes, a pioneer in such research and the friend and pro-
tégé of Darwin, tried to quantify this discontinuity in a book entitled
Mental Evolution in Animals, published in 1883. It included a graphic scale
of emotional and intellectual development, presented as a ladder with
fifty steps. Civilized human adults, capable of "reflection and self-
conscious thought," were at the top. Then there was a large hiatus. The
highest animals were anthropoid apes and dogs, which Romanes considered capable of "indefinite morality" as well as shame, remorse, deceitful-
ness, and a sense of the ludicrous. They occupied step 28, along with
human infants of fifteen months. Close behind them, on step 25, were
birds, which could recognize pictures, understand words, and feel terror; and they were followed on step 24 by bees and ants, which could
communicate ideas and feel sympathy.[5] The details of this schemati-
zation sound quaint now, but its underlying taxonomy, which defines
humans and animals as separate and equivalent categories on the basis of
their intellectual, spiritual, and emotional capacities, continued to determine the course of research on animal behavior for the succeeding century. As Donald Griffin, a contemporary critic of this taxonomy, has
pointed out, "Throughout our educational system students are taught
that it is unscientific to ask what an animal thinks or feels . . . [and] field
naturalists are reluctant to report or analyze observations of animal behavior that suggest conscious awareness . . . lest they be judged uncriti-
cal, or even ostracized from the scientific community."[6]

Although the dichotomy between humans and animals is an intellectual construction that begs a very important question, we are not apt to
see it in that light unless it is challenged. And serious challenges have
proved difficult to mount. Those who have based their thinking on the
uniqueness of our species (i.e., its uniqueness in a different sense than
that in which every species is unique) have often resisted even the attempt to make the dichotomy controversial. The scientific consensus
cited by Griffin exemplifies entrenched institutional reluctance to acknowledge that an alternative taxonomy might be possible. An analogous refusal by philosopher Robert Nozick structured his review, which
appeared several years ago in the *New York Times Book Review,* of Tom
Regan's *The Case for Animal Rights.* Instead of grappling seriously with
Regan's carefully worked out and elaborately researched argument,
Nozick simply dismissed it by asserting that animals are not human and
therefore cannot possibly have any rights. That is, he claimed that Regan
had made a crippling category mistake by failing to recognize the insu-
perable barrier that separated humans from all other creatures and that
it was therefore not necessary to think seriously about anything else that
he said.[7] Such views are not confined to scholars and scientists; so, despite its evasiveness, Nozick's stratagem is unlikely to have bothered

many of his readers. Recent research suggests that most ordinary Americans explicitly endorse the dichotomy that Nozick postulates, whatever else they may think or feel about animals, for example, whether or not they like them, or whether they wish to protect them or to exploit them.[8]

But this repeatedly avowed taxonomy is not the whole story, either about the relationship of human beings to other species or about the way that people have perceived and interpreted that relationship. There are other indexes of belief and understanding than explicit declarations. In the case of other animals, and especially the mammalian species that human beings resemble most closely, the explicit denial of continuity may paradoxically have freed people to articulate, in a veiled and unselfconscious way, their competing sense of similarity and connection. A lot of evidence suggests that when people are not trying to deny that humans and animals belong to the same moral and intellectual continuum, they automatically assume that they do. Discourses that seem to refer exclusively to animals are frequently shaped by cultural constructions clearly derived from human society, even in the scientific and technological fields where it might seem that such constructions would be counterproductive, out of place, and easy to identify and discard. The consequences of this unacknowledged connection have often been enormous, even in the behavioral sciences most strongly committed to reinforcing the dichotomy between humans and animals. Thus, it is no accident that the baboon studies published by S. L. Washburn and Irven DeVore in the 1950s and 1960s stressed the importance of male dominance hierarchies. Analogously, the research undertaken by the increasing number of female primatologists in the past two decades has emphasized the extent to which female primates aggressively manage their own reproductive careers, radically revising earlier characterizations of them as sexually passive and even "coy."[9]

Thus animal-related discourse has often functioned as an extended, if unacknowledged metonymy, offering participants a concealed forum for the expression of opinions and worries imported from the human cultural arena. Indeed, much of what people—experts of one sort or another—have said about animals can only be explained in this context. Thus, the foregoing examples from the recent history of primatology suggest how social or political ideology can determine the research agenda of scientists. But these examples may seem too easy. After all, despite the explicit professional commitment of primatologists not to anthropomorphize the animals they study, those creatures are of special interest exactly because of their closeness to humankind. They are obvious targets for projection, as are the extinct pongids and hominids whose fossil remains are interpreted by students of human origins.[10]

It is, however, possible to find evidence that the same intellectual and cultural preconceptions shape discourses that, on the face of it, look much less promising. One such discourse informs the literature of animal breeding that emerged in late eighteenth-century Britain and developed and flourished throughout the next century. The ostensible subjects of this discourse—horses, cattle, sheep, pigs, dogs, and cats—share far fewer characteristics with human beings than do apes, monkeys, and australopithecines; its participants were concerned with practical results, rather than with anything so abstract and potentially tendentious as the increase of knowledge or the development of theory.

The flavor of this literature—both its tone and its content—is more easily demonstrated by excerpts than by general characterization. The following selections touch in various ways on the relations between the sexes, a subject that was crucial to successful animal husbandry; they also make assertions that are difficult to understand with reference only to the exigencies of stock breeding. In 1828, the author of an article that appeared in the *Farrier and Naturalist*, a livestock-oriented journal, asked, "What is . . . the part of the female in the great act of reproduction?" He answered his own question, "When the male predominates by his vigour, his constitution, and his health, she is limited, in some measure, to perform the same office that the earth does for vegetables . . . nothing more than a receptacle, in which are deposited the seeds of generation."[11] A few years later, William Youatt, the most distinguished British veterinarian of the early Victorian period and a prolific writer on domestic animals, recounted the following story as an illustration of the need to control the imagination of "even so dull a beast as the cow": a certain cow "chanced to come in season, while pasturing on a field . . . out of which an ox jumped, and went with the cow, until she was brought home to the bull. The ox was white, with black spots, and horned. Mr. Mustard [the owner of the cow] had not a horned beast in his possession, nor one with any white on it. Nevertheless, the produce of the following spring was a black and white calf with horns."[12] Early in the twentieth century, Judith Neville Lytton, a prominent if iconoclastic and combative member of the toy dog fancy, suggested the following remedy for barrenness in prize bitches: "In desperate cases . . . try the old . . . recipe of breeding to a thorough cur. . . . If the bitch breeds to this connection . . . the next time the bitch is put to a thoroughbred dog she will almost certainly breed to him. . . . The more . . . highly bred the bitch is, the more likely this is to succeed."[13]

Each of these statements depended on assumptions not only obviously false in the light of modern science but also subject to persuasive contradiction on the basis of accumulated practical experience that was widely available in the nineteenth century. Each statement uses, applied to the activities of domestic animals, language ordinarily reserved to describe human social intercourse. Why, then, did experts—the very people who should have access to the most enlightened thought and the widest information—hold these opinions (or believe these facts, as they would have put it), and why did they express them in this way? It is likely that both the form and the content of these excerpts were determined by the exigencies of human gender stereotypes rather than by those of applied biology.

This was the case even though animal husbandry was a quintessentially earthbound pursuit, constrained by physicality and detail on every side. It had no obvious connection to the stakes at issue in any arena of human social discourse, including that of gender. Certainly, the techniques used to breed animals were very different from those used to breed people. The results of breeding were highly concrete, and they were usually presented to the general public in the stripped-down terms of cash value. Given all this, it would be reasonable to assume that breeders' understanding of their craft would be structured by empirical rather than rhetorical considerations. Yet what they said about their cattle, sheep, and dogs was strongly conditioned by their views about the nature of human beings, especially women.

This assertion may seem particularly surprising because, by the nineteenth century, the breeding of pedigreed animals had become a highly technical and specialized endeavor, whether it was carried on by professional agriculturalists interested in producing improved farm livestock or by self-professed amateurs who concentrated on dogs, cats, and such smaller animals as guinea pigs, rabbits, and poultry. It was crudely materialistic in its explicit aims. Since the primary goal of all breeders was to produce superior young animals, the crucial focus of their attention was the selection of healthy and appropriately endowed parents for the new generation. Several factors encouraged them to be as pragmatic as possible in their matchmaking decisions.

In the first place, mistakes were easy to spot. Stringent standards existed for almost every kind of animal that was frequently bred, and these standards were widely disseminated in handbooks, prints, and periodicals and vigorously enforced by show judges and by the marketplace in which animals were bought and sold by knowledgeable fanciers. (There were occasional exceptions to this rule of consensus and conformity, the most notable being the pig, which seemed so gross and amorphous that breeders had trouble figuring out what an ideal animal should be like.)[14] These frequently reiterated standards meant that the inferiority of the offspring of ill-considered pairings would sooner or later become obvious—perhaps at birth, but certainly by the time they reached maturity. In addition, breeding was an expensive pursuit—absolutely expensive in the case of the larger animals, which could cost hundreds and even thousands of pounds to purchase and then to maintain in an appropriate style, and relatively expensive in the case of the smaller ones. Any pregnancy risked the life of the mother, and each successful pregnancy consumed a significant portion of her reproductive potential. Owners of valuable female animals had to expend this limited resource very carefully.

In the course of the eighteenth and nineteenth centuries, the expertise of breeders produced some impressive results. (This seems true even though recent historians have persuasively modified the most extravagant claims made by participants in the Agricultural Revolution and their subsequent admirers.)[15] The earliest and most celebrated achievement of English animal breeding was the modern thoroughbred racehorse, which appeared toward the beginning of the eighteenth century as the result of an infusion of Arabian blood into native English equine stock. The merit of such horses was easily measured on the track. By the middle of the eighteenth century, agriculturalists were applying the techniques developed by racehorse breeders to farm livestock, with consequent impressive increases in the size, most notably, of cattle and sheep but also of pigs and draft horses. And the nineteenth century saw a related explosion in the diversity of fancy animals. Most modern dog breeds originated then, despite the claims of greater antiquity made by some aficionados; the same was true for cats, rodents, and the diverse strains of pigeons that Darwin studied.

This record of serious animal husbandry in eighteenth- and nineteenth-century Britain thus seems to be one of straightforward, quantifiable, pragmatically oriented achievement. New methods were developed—albeit mostly through trial and error, rather than as a result of systematic theorizing—and carefully applied, with predictably impressive results. This was the way the master breeders themselves understood their accomplishments, as documented in their published reflections on their craft. Such reflections usually took one of two forms: advice to beginners or records of particular successes for the edification of posterity. Authors working in both genres suggested that the complex procedures they described could be rather mechanically applied either to the improvement of whole breeds by those at the forefront of husbandry or to the imitation of such results by breeders content to follow modestly in paths blazed by others. Thus, one early Victorian manual for sheep breeders confidently associated the method with the result, asserting that "there cannot be a more certain sign of the rapid advances of a people in civilization and prosperity, than increasing attention to the improvement of livestock"; in a related vein, an earlier agricultural treatise had assured readers that "the perfecting stock already well-bred is a pleasant, short and easy task."[16] At the end of the century, the author of a handbook for cat fanciers similarly suggested that good results would follow the methodical application of expertise: "[mating] requires . . . careful consideration, and . . . experience and theory join hands, while the knowledge of the naturalist and fancier is of . . . superlative value."[17] Pedigree charts, the ubiquitous schematic representations of the results of animal breeding, also corroborated this rather mechanical sense of what the enterprise involved.

When their discussions of animal breeding became more specific, however, the experts tended to retreat from their assertive self-confidence. Neither method nor knowledge, even when operating on cats of impeccable pedigree and robust health, could assure "anything like certainty," according to the expert just cited.[18] Manuals for breeders of cattle, sheep, and horses often warned novices not to attempt to produce the kinds of animals that won prizes at national shows, because of the difficulty, risk, and expense involved. Thus, when closely scrutinized, animal breeding no longer seemed merely a mechanical, if complex, technical procedure but was implicitly redefined as a more ambiguous and impressionistic activity. And the more precisely the instructions were articulated, the more confusing they became. Often experts raised issues or offered advice that was irrelevant to the achievement of their stated aims, or even counterproductive. Old and widely recognized canards were ritually chewed over for decades after they had been persuasively discredited.

An explanation might stress the unimaginative and derivative nature of many of these works, which occupied the borderline between technical and popular writing, or it might focus on the conservatism inherent in many fields of applied and popularized technology. And there is doubtless some truth to both of these possibilities. But the curious or anomalous elements in the discourse of animal breeding can be more fully explained if that discourse is also viewed as an arena for the discussion of human gender issues. In a way, it was an extremely obvious focus for such concerns. After all, the central task of breeders was to manage the sexual relations of their animals. This task often posed challenges beyond the merely intellectual problem of deciding which ones to pair up. The fact that the participants in this discourse were unaware of its double function merely allowed them to air their views and worries more directly.

In making their decisions about which animals to pair, breeders selected parents on the basis of both their individual quality (i.e., the extent to which they possessed the characteristics that were desired in their offspring) and a set of general notions about the way that the transmission of such characteristics took place. For most of the nineteenth century, there were few authoritative constraints on such ideas. Despite the claims of scienticity that agriculturalists had made since the beginning of the eighteenth-century vogue for improvement, few of them and even fewer breeders of small animals belonged to the scientific community; the works of popular natural history that they were most likely to encounter did not deal with the questions of reproductive physiology that engaged some elite biologists. And even if breeders had been aware of the most advanced contemporary research on reproduction, they could not easily have applied its results to their enterprise.

Although it was clear to scientists, as it was to breeders, that sexual intercourse was necessary if the higher animals were to reproduce, there was no expert consensus until late in the nineteenth century about why this was so.[19] That is, the modern understanding of the balanced contribution of sperm and egg to the development of a new organism was unavailable to eighteenth- and nineteenth-century animal breeders. Without this knowledge, they were free to predict and interpret the results of their breeding ventures with reference only to their own experience. That experience was vast and, indeed, considered extremely valuable by open-minded scientists like Charles Darwin.[20] It also turned out to include breeders' attitudes toward other people, as well as their observations of generations of animals.[21]

Many eighteenth- and nineteenth-century theories of reproduction presented it as the gradual enlargement and development of a tiny but complete seed, but scientists who adhered to this viewpoint were divided about whether that seed was contributed by the male or the female. Animal breeders, however, were of one mind about this question. Many, like the author of the *Farrier and Naturalist* article quoted earlier, defined the female parent as a mere receptacle. One expert, faced with explaining why, in this case, it was not "an easy thing to produce at once very perfect animals, provided that males of the right form could be obtained," preferred not to posit the mother as a significant source of variation. Instead, he had recourse to the fact that "the offspring will, to a greater or lesser extent, partake of the form and structure of the grandparents [i.e., the grandfathers]." And even if such an absolute assertion of male dominance needed modification in view of the obvious tendency of young animals to resemble both their parents, breeding experts still reserved the more vigorous genetic role for the stud. The imagery of activity and passivity remained useful in the modified case; it suggested, for example, that "the male gives the locomotive, and the female the vital organs."[22]

The preponderance of male influence never escaped the attention of writers on these subjects for long, even if they had been momentarily diverted by the need to comment on females. For example, a reminder that "without first class females the descendants will not shine . . . in the show yard" was predictably accompanied by the acknowledgment that "it must not be forgotten that the male has most influence in breeding."[23] The only situations in which it was generally considered that the female might disproportionately determine the results of procreation were those which introduced a different, and also powerful, cultural construct. Social superiority—that is, in the terms of animal husbandry, a more distinguished pedigree—might tip the scales in the direction of the female. As Youatt pointed out, the influence of "a highly bred cow will preponderate over that of the half-bred bull."[24] Since such exceptional circumstances could only result from extreme negligence or ignorance on the part of the breeder, however, they did not have to be incorporated into received wisdom. In general, breeders were advised to proceed on the assumption that "not only . . . is the male parent . . . capable of most speedily improving the breed of livestock . . . , but . . . *the male is the parent,* from motives of sense and sound polity, which we can alone look to for the improvement of our breed."[25]

Perhaps it was to maintain this strong differentiation in reproductive roles that cattle show judges were adjured to assess bulls "as males and not as females" and cows "as females and not as males." The telltale signs were admittedly difficult for even first-class judges to detect—not the obvious things but subtle variations in such unlikely features as the conformation of head and horns. But the stakes were considered high enough to justify the trouble, especially where bulls were concerned. According to one veteran cattle breeder, "effeminacy in the male must be shunned as the most deadly poison."[26]

The principles that guided the production of livestock animals were routinely applied to pet species. The author of a late Victorian cat breeding manual assured his readers that "the outward characteristics are in great measure transmitted by the male cat."[27] Nor did the advance of biological knowledge necessarily shake the faith of animal breeders in their time-tested principles. Instead, as it became available, the jargon of science could be appropriated to the service of the conventional understanding of animal reproduction. Everett Millais, one of the most prominent dog fanciers of the late nineteenth century, translated it into the new terminology as follows: "that the male . . . does influence the epiblastic and mesoblastic structures largely, and all out of proportion to the female is undoubted."[28]

So powerful was the influence attributed to at least some males, it was even believed that they could determine the character of offspring in the conception of which they had had no part. That is, they might gain access to the reproductive organs through the eyes of receptive females, as well as in the ordinary way. As a result, breeders anxious to preserve the purity and the quality of their stock had to guard the minds as well as the bodies of their impressionable female animals from such undesirable approaches. It went without saying that females would be both unable and disinclined to resist them. In short, females could not be trusted with the preservation of their own virtue, even on the level of imagination. Mr. Mustard's cow, referred to earlier, offered an extreme example of the feminine susceptibility posited by this view of relations between the sexes. The off-breed ox that jumped into her pasture when she was in heat was not even completely male—that is, he had been castrated and therefore rendered incapable of procreation—but, even so, he apparently left his mark on the calf she subsequently conceived after intercourse with the properly pedigreed bull selected by her owner.

If females of a relatively stolid species were so susceptible to the influence of random males, it was not surprising that female dogs, which were considered both more intelligent and more excitable, had to be guarded still more closely. Breeders agreed that the animals they termed maiden bitches were particularly vulnerable to such external stimuli and advised that "due influence should be exercised in the thorough isolation of bitches . . . or more than a temporary evil and disappointment may occur."[29] But more experienced bitches were also at risk, and beginning breeders were warned that "even very close intimacy between a bitch during oestrum and a dog she fancies may influence the progeny, although the dog has not warded her."[30]

The struggles between bitches and breeders were described in terms that evoked stubborn daughters in romantic narratives who refused to accept their fathers' choice of suitors. Hugh Dalziel, who wrote about a variety of Victorian dog breeds, once owned a Dandie Dinmont terrier whose wayward emotions made her useless for breeding; she "became enamoured with a deerhound, and positively would not submit to be served by a dog of her own breed." Even bitches who were more compliant might defeat their owners' purposes. Delabere Blaine, sometimes known as "the father of canine pathology," had a pug bitch whose constant companion was a white spaniel. All her litters were sired by pedigreed pugs, and all consisted of undeniably pug puppies, but one in each batch was white, a color that was rare and not desirable in that breed.[31]

Recognizing that it was useless to fight against such a predilection, one prolific breeder of dogs and cats who confessed that he would allow his champion studs to serve almost any female whose owner could pay the fee made one of his rare refusals in the case of a bitch that had "already formed an attachment to a dog of a meaner breed."[32] Such inclinations were fairly common among bitches, who were likely to implement them by stubbornly resisting their owners' prudent attempts to cloister them. The authors of manuals frequently warned novice breeders that bitches in heat would make unimaginably subtle and persistent attempts to escape from whatever quarters they were confined in. But it was necessary to persevere in thwarting them, because the stakes at risk in the preservation of female purity were high. A match with an inappropriate partner, especially in the case of a virgin animal, was held to have consequences far beyond the issue of that particular mating, as if a female's first sexual partner in some sense established a permanent proprietorship over her reproductive capacities.

Although it was, as one late-nineteenth-century kennel expert admitted, "an exceedingly rare phenomenon," which was difficult to verify, many breeders continued to believe in what was usually called "the influence of the previous sire" but was sometimes dignified by the scientific-sounding term "telegony."[33] The midcentury author of a scientific treatise on agriculture summarized this doctrine as follows: "The effect of the first male is so great as to cause all the animals that female shall afterwards give birth to, in a more or less degree, to resemble that by which the female was first impregnated." He chose to illustrate this doctrine with the story of a chestnut mare whose original mate was a quagga (a relative or variety of the zebra that became extinct late in the nineteenth century), and all of whose subsequent offspring were striped, even though all but the first resulted from her union with a black stallion.[34] The breeding literature teemed with similar examples of the dire consequences of letting females slip even once from the straight and narrow. The appearance of spotted puppies in a litter produced by two prize fox terriers was explained by the fact that the sire of the bitch's previous litter had been a dalmatian.[35] Of kittens of "a good Persian sire and dam" who nevertheless appeared "remarkably poor specimens . . . what might be called half-breeds," a late Victorian cat fancier said that "I can only attribute this to the blue female having twice strayed from the paths of virtue previous to the attentions of the prize-winning Persian."[36]

Despite their frequent appearance in the breeding literature, instances of the influence of the previous sire seemed to occur only at widely spaced intervals in real life. The cases just recounted, for example, were thirdhand at best. Even in the earlier literature, therefore, authors sometimes gingerly noted that there might be grounds on which to question this principle. The more scientists discovered about how reproduction actually worked, the harder it became for breeders to identify a mechanism that would account for such anomalies. They nevertheless clung tenaciously to this doctrine, perhaps because, weak though it might be as a predictor of the results of unsanctioned animal unions, it precisely expressed the metaphorical consequences of such lapses by human females. Even the most sophisticated experts hesitated to dismiss completely the possibility of influence or, as it might be more forthrightly expressed, contamination or infection by a female animal's first mate. At most, they might suggest that such occurrences were sufficiently rare that breeders did not need to worry about them. Thus, Neville Lytton, ordinarily impatient with the shibboleths of her fellow fanciers, conceded that "I am inclined to think [it] does occasionally happen," but she asserted that "it happens so seldom that no one has ever been able to collect evidence enough to prove. In any case it would only affect isolated individuals, and probably only as to a single character, . . . [and so] . . . I do not think breeders need trouble themselves about so small a matter as the possible influence of a previous sire on a single puppy."[37]

In addition to jeopardizing the quality (or legitimacy) of future offspring, the tendency of female animals to follow their own sexual inclinations was perceived to pose less concrete but perhaps equally troublesome threats. Although an occasional authority might compassionately recommend indulging the desires of bitches that were "highly fed . . . [and] living luxuriously, as a means of using up their excess stock of material," an interest in sex for its own sake rather than as a means to procreation was considered an indication of depraved character.[38] The behavior of bitches, in particular, confirmed the worst male fears about female proclivities. Although a single copulation might have sufficed for pregnancy, bitches would wantonly continue to accept new partners as long as they were in heat; connected with this unseemly pursuit of pleasure was a culpable indifference to its provider. One early nineteenth-century sportsman complained that "no convincing proof of satiety is ever displayed . . . and she presents herself equally to all," with the result that the largest of her suitors "is generally brought into action." He noted with some satisfaction, however, that oversexed bitches might pay for their failure to prefer refinement to brute strength; many died while bringing forth too-large puppies.[39]

According to other authorities, however, this unmatronly behavior might harm the offspring rather than the mother. In the dog, as in some other animals that routinely give birth to multiple offspring, it is possible for a single litter to have more than one father. Breeding authorities referred to this phenomenon as "superfoetation," a technical term that made it sound like an aberration or a disease. As even the possibility of this occurrence would jeopardize the pedigree of the resulting litter, aspiring breeders were strongly advised that "for at least a week after the bitch has visited the dog, the precautions for isolating her must not be relaxed, or all her owner's hopes may be marred."[40] But social stigma and unwelcome half-siblings were not the only ills that newly conceived pedigreed puppies might sustain as a result of their mothers' licentiousness. Dalziel suggested that during or after an unsanctioned and unnecessary second copulation, "excessive pain, terror, or other strong emotions, may affect the unborn pups."[41]

In other species, too, interest in copulation for its own sake signaled the weakness of female character. A late-eighteenth-century agriculturalist criticized the female ass for being "full as lascivious" as the male, which he claimed made her "a bad breeder, ejecting again the seminal fluid she has just received in coition, unless the sensation of pleasure be immediately removed by loading her with blows." Similarly, he condemned the sow, who "may be said to be in heat at all times; and even when she is pregnant she seeks the boar, which, among animals, may be deemed an excess." An edifying contrast, he pointed out, was offered by the demure behavior of cows, which, once pregnant, "will not suffer the bull to approach them."[42]

In males, however, eagerness to copulate was matter for praise. The he-goat was admired as "no despicable animal . . . so very vigorous . . . that one will be sufficient for above a hundred and fifty she-goats."[43] Breeders agreed that the only reason to curb the enthusiasm of studs was physical rather than moral, since too-frequent copulation was feared to undermine the constitution of both sire and offspring. Thus, one authority on horses complained that "our best stallions . . . cover too many mares in one season; and this is the reason why they get so few good colts"; another advised against pasturing a stallion with a herd of mares because in this situation "in six weeks, [he] will do himself more damage than in several years by moderate exercise."[44] Similarly, one expert on pedigreed dogs warned, "If you possess a champion dog . . . do not be tempted to stud him too much, or you may kill the goose which lays the eggs of gold. One bitch a fortnight is about as much as any dog can do, to have good stock and retain his constitution."[45]

Despite the need to practice such precise accounting, the sexual management of male animals was much simpler than that of females. In the company of a suitable partner, bulls, stallions, dogs, boars, and rams ordinarily did just what was expected of them. But even after breeders had presented their female animal to a suitable male in the required receptive and unsullied condition, their cares were not over. At that point, the female might decide to exercise an inappropriate veto power, offering an unmistakable challenge to the authority of her owner. After all, in an enterprise dedicated to the production of offspring, too much reluctance was as bad as too little, and resistance to legitimate authority was as unfeminine as proscribed sexual enjoyment.

The terms in which breeder described such insubordination expressed not only the anger it provoked but the extent to which that anger reflected worries about sexual subordination within their own species. Some categories of females were viewed with special suspicion. For example, bitches of the larger breeds, whose physical endowments commanded respect whether or not they were feeling refractory, had "to be taped or muzzled . . . to prevent either yourself or the dog from being bitten." Maiden bitches, too, were "generally a great annoyance from first to last." Their coyness might have to be counteracted with coercion, although breeders were cautioned to remember, "not too much."[46] But almost any kind of bitch might evince reluctance when confronted with a prospective mate not of her own choosing, in which case, she could be castigated as "troublesome," "morose," or even "savage."[47] The prescribed remedy was "hard exercise, until the bitch is thoroughly exhausted"; often this would "reduce a tiresome animal to submission." Bitches that refused to participate willingly at this point provoked their owners to severer measures—measures that again recalled the clichés of romantic fiction. They might be "drugged with some narcotic," or, in the most serious cases of insubordination, the male dog and the human breeder might cooperate in what was referred to as a "forced service."[48]

The technical discourse of animal husbandry clearly reflected contemporary concerns about human gender relations, even though the eighteenth- and nineteenth-century breeders of domesticated animals were not explicitly aware of this subtext as they shared their practical wisdom and rehearsed their triumphs. But they would not have made the same claims about the nature of their animals or used the same language to describe bovine and canine inclinations and behavior if they had not implicitly assumed an identity between human nature and animal nature—an identity they would certainly have denied if they had been asked about it directly. From the perspective of the late twentieth century, this particular conflation of the human social world with that of domestic animals is easy to criticize. Their projection of human social constructions onto animal mating habits led breeders astray in some practical senses, introducing inefficiency along with misunderstanding and error. And it expressed a view of gender relations that seems both incorrect and objectionable by contemporary standards. But it is hard not to feel that by placing people among the other animals, breeders also implicitly acknowledged an underlying truth, one that human beings have traditionally striven to deny, no less today than in the past.

NOTES

*I would like to thank Rosemarie Bodenheimer, Jonathan Dewald, Rita Goldberg, Ilona Karmel, Kathleen Kete, Jessica Marcus, and John Maynard for their helpful comments on earlier versions of this chapter.
    1. Genesis 2:20–22.

2. For an overview of attitudes toward animals in Western philosophy and theology, see John Passmore, "The Treatment of Animals," *Journal of the History of Ideas* 36 (1975): 195–218. Marc Shell offers an idiosyncratic and implausibly benign interpretation of those attitudes in "The Family Pet," *Representations* 15 (1986): 121–153. For another interpretation of the significance of pets, see Harriet Ritvo, "The Emergence of Modern Pet-keeping," in Andrew Rowan, ed., *Animals and People Sharing the World* (Hanover, N.H.: New England University Press, 1988), 13–32.

3. William Swainson, *On the Habits and Instincts of Animals* (London: Longman, Brown, Green, and Longmans, 1840), 74.

4. Charles Hamilton Smith, *Introduction to the Mammalia* (Edinburgh: W. H. Lizars, 1842), 74.

5. George John Romanes, *Mental Evolution in Animals* (London: Kegan Paul, Trench, 1883), inset.

6. Donald R. Griffin, *Animal Thinking* (Cambridge, Mass.: Harvard University Press, 1984), vii–viii.

7. Robert Nozick, "About Mammals and People," *New York Times Book Review,* Nov. 27, 1983; Tom Regan, *The Case for Animal Rights* (Berkeley, Los Angeles, London: University of California Press, 1983).

8. Stephen Kellert has worked out a typology of ten basic attitudes toward animals—naturalistic, ecologistic, humanistic, moralistic, scientistic, aesthetic, utilitarian, dominionistic, negativistic, and neutralistic. Only the first four admit the possibility of a categorization not based on the axiomatic division between humans and animals, and they by no means require such a reversal. For an overview of his analysis and the research that supports it, see Stephen R. Kellert, "Human-Animal Interactions: A Review of American Attitudes to Wild and Domestic Animals in the Twentieth Century," in Rowan, *Animals and People Sharing the World,* 137–176.

9. Donna Haraway, "Animal Sociology and a Natural Economy of the Body Politic, Part II: The Past Is the Contested Zone: Human Nature and Theories of Production and Reproduction in Primate Behavior Studies," *Signs: Journal of Women in Culture and Society* 4 (1978): 55–56; Sarah Blaffer Hrdy, "Empathy, Polyandry, and the Myth of the Coy Female," in Ruth Bleier, ed., *Feminist Approaches to Science* (New York: Pergamon, 1986), 119–146.

10. For an exploration of the relationship of twentieth-century paleoanthropology to twentieth-century cultural history, see Roger Lewin, *Bones of Contention: Controversies in the Search for Human Origins* (New York: Simon and Schuster, 1987).

11. M. Godine, "Comparative Influence of the Male and Female in Breeding," *Farrier and Naturalist* 1 (1828): 468.

12. William Youatt, *Cattle: Their Breeds, Management, and Diseases* (London: Baldwin and Craddock, 1834), 523. It should be remembered that oxen are castrated animals.

13. Judith Neville Lytton, *Toy Dogs and Their Ancestors, Including the History and Management of Toy Spaniels, Pekingese, Japanese and Pomeranians* (New York: D. Appleton, 1911), 194–195.

14. The struggles of breeders to determine the ideal form of the pig is elaborately chronicled in Julian Wiseman, *The History of the British Pig* (London: Duckworth, 1986).

15. For a thorough review of the breeding practices of eighteenth-century improvers in comparison with those of their predecessors, see Nicholas Russell, *Like Engend'ring Like: Heredity and Animal Breeding in Early Modern England* (Cambridge: Cambridge University Press, 1986). Less revisionist overviews include R. Trow-Smith, *A History of British Livestock Husbandry, 1700–1900* (London: Routledge and Kegan Paul, 1959), and Stephen J. G. Hall and Juliet Clutton-Brock, *Two Hundred Years of British Farm Livestock* (London: British Museum [Natural History], 1989).

16. Ambrose Blacklock, *A Treatise on Sheep* (Glasgow: W. R. McPhun, 1838), 67; John Lawrence, *A General Treatise on Cattle, the Ox, the Sheep, and the Swine* (London: H. D. Symonds, 1805), 30–31.

17. Harrison Weir, *Our Cats and All About Them* (Boston: Houghton Mifflin, 1889), 96.

18. Ibid., 96.

19. John Farley, *Gametes and Spores: Ideas About Sexual Reproduction 1750–1914* (Baltimore: Johns Hopkins University Press, 1982), chaps. 1 and 2. See also Frederick B. Churchill, "Sex and the Single Organism: Biological Theories of Sexuality in Mid-Nineteenth Century," *Studies in the History of Biology* 3 (1979): 139–177.

20. James A. Secord has discussed the contribution of pigeon fancying to Darwin's theory of evolution in " 'Nature's Fancy': Charles Darwin and the Breeding of Pigeons," *Isis* 72 (1981): 163–186. Darwin continued to make use of information supplied by animal breeders after he wrote *On the Origin of Species*, most notably, in *The Variation of Animals and Plants under Domestication* (1868).

21. Exposure to scientific data and theory would not necessarily have made any difference. At least some Victorian scientists shared breeders' inclination to identify women with other mammalian females, eagerly but without much evidence conflating the human menstrual cycle with the oestrus cycle of dogs and cattle. Thomas Laqueur, "Orgasm, Generation, and the Politics of Reproductive Biology," in Catherine Gallagher and Thomas Laquer, eds., *The Making of the Modern Body: Sexuality and Society in the Nineteenth Century* (Berkeley, Los Angeles, London: University of California Press, 1987), 24–35.

22. "The Physiology of Breeding," *The Agricultural Magazine, Plough, and Farmers' Journal* (June 1855): 17.

23. William M'Combie, *Cattle and Cattle-Breeders* (Edinburgh: William Blackwood, 1867), 153.

24. Youatt, *Cattle*, 524.

25. John Boswell, "Essay upon the Breeding of Live Stock, and on the Comparative Influence of the Male and Female Parents in Impressing the Offspring," *Farmer's Magazine* I, NS (1838): 248.

26. William M'Combie, *Cattle and Cattle-Breeders*, 118–119; Robert Oliphant Pringle, *The Livestock of the Farm*, ed. and rev. James MacDonald (Edinburgh: William Blackwood, 1886), 101–102.

27. John Jennings, *Domestic and Fancy Cats: A Practical Treatise on Their Varieties, Breeding, Management, and Diseases* (London: L. Upcott Gill, n.d.), 45.

28. Everett Millais, "Influence; with special reference to that of the sire," in *The Dog Owners' Annual for 1894* (London: Dean), 153.

29. Vero Shaw, *The Illustrated Book of the Dog* (London: Cassell, 1881), 525.

30. Hugh Dalziel, *The Collie: As a Show Dog, Companion, and Worker*, rev. J. Maxtee (London: L. Upcott Gill, 1904), 48.

31. Dalziel, *British Dogs: Their Varieties, History, Characteristics, Breeding, Management, and Exhibition* (London: "Bazaar," 1879–1880), 462–463.

32. Gordon Stables, *The Practical Kennel Guide; with Plain Instructions How to Rear and Breed Dogs for Pleasure, Show, and Profit* (London: Cassell Petter and Galpin, 1877), 121.

33. Millais, "Influence," 153. At an earlier period, this theory was occasionally applied to human matings as well. Thus, according to John Aubrey, the distinguished seventeenth-century doctor, William Harvey claimed that "he that marries a widow makes himself Cuckold." Quoted in Alan MacFarlane, *Marriage and Love in England, 1300–1840* (Oxford: Basil Blackwell, 1986), 232.

34. G. H. Andrews, *Modern Husbandry: A Practical and Scientific Treatise on Agriculture* (London: 1853), 163.

35. Millais, "Influence," 153.

36. Frances Simpson, *Cats and All About Them* (London: Isbister, 1902), 64.

37. Lytton, *Toy Dogs*, 195. Scientists took the notion of telegony more seriously than the scanty evidence would seem to justify, perhaps for the same reasons that made it appealing to animal breeders. Richard Burkhardt, Jr., "Closing the Door on Lord Morton's Mare: The Rise and Fall of Telegony," *Studies in the History of Biology* 3 (1979): 16–17.

38. Dalziel, *Collie*, 41.

39. William Taplin, *The Sportsman's Cabinet, or, A correct delineation of the various dogs used in the sports of the field* (London, 1803), I: 27–28.

40. Shaw, *Illustrated Book of the Dog*, 524.

41. Dalziel, *Collie*, 48.

42. John Mills, *A Treatise on Cattle* (London: J. Johnson, 1776), 271, 310, 401.

43. Ibid., 387.

44. George Hanger, *Colonel George Hanger, to All Sportsmen, and Particularly to Farmers, and Game Keepers* (London: George Hanger, 1814), 47.

45. Stables, *Practical Kennel Guide*, 125.

46. Ibid., 123–124.

47. Shaw, *Illustrated Book of the Dog*, 523.

48. C. J. Davies, *The Kennel Handbook* (London: John Lane, 1905), 66.

FOUR

Language and Ideology
in Evolutionary Theory:
Reading Cultural Norms
into Natural Law

Evelyn Fox Keller

In the mid-twentieth century, biology became a "mature science," that is, it succeeded, finally, in breaking through the formidable barrier of "life" that had heretofore precluded it from fully joining the mechanico-reductive tradition of the physical sciences. For the first time in history, the "secret of life" could credibly be claimed to have been solved: Living beings—presumably including man along with the rest of the animal kingdom—came to be understood as (mere) chemical machines.

But the chemical machine that constitutes a living organism is unlike machines of the eighteenth and nineteenth centuries. It is not a machine capable only of executing the purposes of its maker, that is, man, but a machine endowed with its own purpose. In short, it is a machine of the twentieth century, a cybernetic machine par excellence: absolutely autonomous, capable of constructing itself, maintaining itself, and reproducing itself. As Jacques Monod has explained:

> ... the entire system is totally, intensely conservative, locked into itself, utterly impervious to any "hints" from the outside world. Through its properties, by the microscopic clockwork function that establishes between DNA and protein, as between organism and medium, an entirely one-way relationship, this system obviously defies any "dialectical" description. It is not Hegelian at all, but thoroughly Cartesian: the cell is indeed a *machine*. (110–111)

The purpose—the sole purpose—of this machine is its own survival and reproduction, or perhaps more accurately put, the survival and reproduction of the DNA programming and "dictating" its operation. In Richard Dawkins's terms, an organism is a "survival machine," a "lumbering robot" constructing to house its genes, those "engines of self-preservation" that have as their primary property that of being inherently "self-ish." They are "sealed off from the outside world, communicating with it by tortuous indirect routes, manipulating it by remote control. They are in you and in me; they created us, body and mind; and their preservation is the ultimate rationale for our existence" (21). With this description, man himself has become a machine, but perhaps it might alternatively be said that the machine itself has become man.

The general question is this: To what extent can our contemporary scientific description of animate forms, culminating in the description of man as a chemical machine, be said to be strictly technical, and to what extent does it actually encode particular conceptions of man—conceptions that derive not so much from a technical domain as from a social, political, and even psychological domain? Have animate, even human, forms finally been successfully deanimated and mechanized, or have their mechanical representations themselves been inadvertently animated, subtly recast in particular images of man?

I suggest that traces of such images might be found in virtually all scientific representations of nature, but they are perhaps especially conspicuous in our descriptions of the evolution of animate forms—even in those representations that make the greatest claims to conceptual neutrality. It is no secret that evolutionary biology has provided a particularly fertile field for those who seek to demonstrate the impact of social expectations on scientific theory. Indeed, it might be said that it is precisely for this reason that modern evolutionary theorists have sought so strenuously to place their discipline on firm scientific footing. Population genetics and mathematical ecology are the two subdisciplines that have been constructed to meet this need—to provide a rigorous substructure for all of evolutionary biology. The general methodological assumption that underlies both of these subdisciplines can be described as atomic individualism, that is, the assumption that a composite property of a system both can and should be represented by the aggregation of properties inhering in the individual atoms constituting that system, appropriately modified by their pairwise or higher order interactions.[1]

As is conventional in biological discourse, I take the individual atom to be, alternatively, the organism or the gene. I shall, therefore, focus on the particular attributes customarily assumed to characterize the basic unit of analysis, the individual organism or gene.

But my focus will be on the practice rather than the principle of atomic individualism in evolutionary theory. Others have argued for an ideological load in the very assumptions of this methodological orientation (see, e.g., Wimsatt, Dupré), but here I wish to bracket such questions and focus instead on the lack of neutrality in its actual applications. In particular, I claim that properties of the "individual" that are generally assumed to be necessary are in fact contingent, drawn not from nature but from our own social and psychosocial heritage. More specifically, I will argue that much of contemporary evolutionary theory relies on a representation of the "individual"—be it the organism or the gene—that is cast in the particular image of man we might call the "Hobbesian man": simultaneously autonomous and oppositional, connected to the world in which it finds itself not by the promise of life and growth but primarily by the threat of death and loss, its first and foremost need being the defense of its boundaries. In psychological terms, we might say that such an individual betrays an idealized conception of autonomy: one that presupposes a radical conception of self and that simultaneously attributes to the relation between self and other an automatic negative valence, a relation, finally, not so much of independence as of dynamic opposition.

I claim that this psychosocial load is carried into evolutionary theory not by explicit intention but by language—by tacit linguistic conventions that privilege the autonomy of the individual at the expense of biologically constitutive interactions and, at the same time, obscure the logical distinction between autonomy and opposition. In this, they support the characterization of the biological individual as somehow "intrinsically" competitive, as if autonomy and competition were semantically equivalent, collapsed into one by that fundamentally ambiguous concept, self-interest. Accordingly, it is the language of autonomy and opposition in contemporary evolutionary theory that is the specific object of my concern.

DISCOURSE OF SELF AND OTHER

I begin with a relatively accessible example of actual confusion between autonomy and opposition that is found not in the theoretical literature per se but in a more general genre of scientific discourse, at once popularizing and prescriptive. Here the focus is not so much on the independence of one individual from another, of self from other, as on the independence of the most abstract other from self—of nature from man. Accordingly, the negative value that tacitly accrues to this relation attaches not so much to the self as to the other, that is, to nature.

With Darwin, evolutionary biology joined a tradition already well established in the physical sciences—a tradition that teaches that the laws of nature are, in Steven Weinberg's words, "as impersonal and free of human values as the rules of arithmetic" (Weinberg 1974). But this rhetoric goes beyond impersonality: nature becomes uncaring and "hostile," traits that are impersonal in a quite personal sense. To illustrate this tendency, consider, for example, Weinberg's own elaboration of his message:

> It is almost irresistible for humans to believe that we have some special relation to the universe, that human life is not just a more-or-less farcical outcome of a chain of accidents reaching back to the first three minutes. . . . It is very hard to realize that this all is just a tiny part of an overwhelmingly hostile universe. (Midgley, 88)

In much the same vein, Jacques Monod writes,

> If he accepts this message in its full significance, man must at last wake out of his millenary dream and discover his total solitude, his fundamental isolation, he must realize that, like a gypsy, he lives on the boundary of an alien world, a world that is deaf to his music, and as indifferent to his hopes as it is to his suffering or his crimes.[2] (Monod, 2)

The world we must steel ourselves to accept is a world of "uncaring emptiness," a "frozen universe of solitude" (173). The natural world from which animism has been so carefully expunged has become not quite neutral but "empty," "frozen," "overwhelmingly hostile," and "terrifying."

For the record, though, it was a poet, not a scientist, who gave us our most familiar metaphor conflating an absence of benevolence in nature with "overwhelming hostility." A nature that does not care for us becomes indeed a nature "red in tooth and claw"—callous, brutal, even murderous. It is a nature that cries, "I care for nothing; all shall go."

Mary Midgley suggests that such residual animism properly belongs to what she calls "the drama of parental callousness":

> First, there is the tone of personal aggrievement and disillusion, which seems to depend . . . on failure to get rid of the animism or personification which (these scientists) officially denounce. An inanimate universe cannot be hostile. . . . Only in a real, conscious human parent could uncaringness equal hostility. . . . Certainly if we expect the non-human world around us to respond to us as a friendly human would, we shall be disappointed. But this does not put it in the position of a callously indifferent human.[3] (1985: 87)

Midgley's explanation is persuasive—perhaps precisely because the slippage between an indifferent and a hostile nature so clearly does denote a logical error, once pointed out. But a similar problem surfaces in another set of contexts as well—where the move from a neutral to a negative valence in the conceptualization of self-other relations is less evidently a simple "mistake." Here it is not nature but the individual organism, the first rather than the second term of the self-other dichotomy, whom the insistently unsentimental biologist taxes with hostility.

I am referring in particular to the tradition among evolutionary biologists that not only privileges the individual descriptively but that also, in the attempt to locate all relevant causal dynamics in the properties intrinsic to the individual, tends to attribute to that individual not simply autonomy but an additional "intrinsic" competitive bent, as if independence and competition were inseparable traits. The very same move that defines self-interest and altruism as logically opposed makes independence virtually indistinguishable from competition. Michael Ghiselin is one of the most extreme representatives of this position and provides some particularly blatant examples of the rhetorical (and conceptual) conflation I am speaking of. To dramatize his position, he concludes:

> The economy of nature is competitive from beginning to end. . . . No hint of genuine charity ameliorates our vision of society, once sentimentalism has been laid aside. . . . Given a full chance to act for his own interest, nothing but expediency will restrain [an organism] from brutalizing, from maiming, from murdering—his brother, his mate, his parent, or his child. Scratch an "altruist" and watch a "hypocrite" bleed. (247)

Of course, Ghiselin's language is *intended* to shock us—but only to underscore his thesis. In this effort, he is counting on our acceptance, as readers, first, of the rule of self-interest as logically equivalent to the absence of altruism or charity, and second, of competitive exploitation as a necessary concomitant of self-interest. Our usual willingness to accept these assumptions, or rather, to allow them to pass unnoticed, is itself a measure of the inaccessibility of a domain where self-interest and charity (or altruism) conjoin and, correlatively, of a distinction between self-interest and competition. Unlike the previous example, where no one, if pressed, would say that nature "really is" hostile, Ghiselin's assumptions do seem to accord with the way things "really are." Because the difference between self-interest and competition is less obvious to most of us than the difference between impersonality in nature and hostility, the problem here is much more difficult. In other words, before we can invoke a psychosocial explanation of the conceptual conflation between radical individualism and competition, we need first to *see* them as different.

We can do this best by turning our attention from a prescriptive discourse that aims to set ground rules for evolutionary theory to an examination of uses of the same language in the actual working out of particular theoretical strategies. I want to look, therefore, at the technical uses of the language of individualism in mathematical ecology and population genetics—in the first case, on the language of competition, and, in the second, on the language of reproductive autonomy. In particular, I want to show how certain conventional interchanges, or trade-offs, between technical and colloquial language cast a blanket of invisibility, or rather, of unspeakability, over certain distinctions, categories, and questions. It is, I suggest, precisely through the maintenance of such an aura of unspeakability that social, psychological, and political expectations generally exert their influence, through language, on the actual structure and content of scientific theory.

COMPETITION AND COOPERATION
IN MATHEMATICAL ECOLOGY

One problem I want to examine arises in the systematic neglect of cooperative (or mutualist) interactions and the corresponding privileging of competitive interactions evident throughout almost the entire history of mathematical ecology. When we ask practitioners in the field for an explanation of this historical disinterest in mutualist interactions, their response is usually one of puzzlement—not so much over the phenomenon as over the question, How else could it, realistically, be? Yes, of course, mutualist interactions occur in nature, but they are not only rare, they are necessarily secondary.

Often it is assumed that they are in the service of competition: such phenomena have at times actually been called "cooperative competition." Indeed, the expectation of most workers in the field that competition is both phenomenologically primary *and* logically prior is so deeply embedded that the very question has difficulty getting airspace: there is no place to put it. My question thus becomes, What are the factors responsible for the closing-off of that space?

Part of the difficulty in answering this question undoubtedly stems from the massive linguistic confusion in conventional use of the term *competition*. One central factor can be readily identified, however, and that is the recognition that, in the real world, resources *are* finite and hence ultimately scarce. To most minds, scarcity automatically implies competition, both in the sense of "causing" competitive behavior and in the sense of constituting, in itself, a kind of de facto competition, independent of actual interactions between organisms. Indeed, so automatic is the association between scarcity and competition that, in modern ecological usage, competition has come to be defined as the simultaneous reliance of two individuals, or two species, on an essential resource that is in limited supply (see, e.g., Mayr 1963: 43). Since the scarcity of resources can itself hardly be questioned, such a definition lends to competition the same a priori status.

This technical definition of competition was probably first employed by Volterra, Lotka, and Gause in their early attempts to provide a mathematical representation of the effects of scarcity on the population growth of "interacting" species, but it soon came to be embraced by a wider community of evolutionary biologists and ecologists—partly, at least, to neutralize the discourse and so bypass the charge of ideologically laden expectations about (usually animal) behavior, in fact freeing the discourse of any dependence on how organisms actually behave in the face of scarcity. The term *competition* now covered apparently pacific behavior just as well as aggressive behavior, an absurdity in ordinary usage but protected by the stipulation of a technical meaning. As Ernst Mayr explains,

> To certain authors ever since [Darwin], competition has meant physical combat, and, conversely, the absence of physical combat has been taken as an indication of the absence of competition. Such a view is erroneous. . . . The relative rarity of overt manifestations of competition is proof not of the insignificance of competition, as asserted by some authors, but, on the contrary, of the high premium natural selection pays for the development of habits or preferences that reduce the severity of competition. (1963: 42–43)

Paul Colinvaux goes one step farther, suggesting that "peaceful coexistence" provides a better description than any "talk of struggles for survival." "Natural selection designs different kinds of animals and plants so that they *avoid* competition. A fit animal is not one that fights well, but one that avoids fighting altogether" (1978: 144).

But how neutral in practice is the ostensibly technical use of competition employed both by Mayr and Colinvaux? I suggest two ways in which, rather than bypassing ideological expectations, it actually preserves them, albeit in a less visible form—a form in which they enjoy effective immunity from criticism. So as not to be caught in the very trap I want to expose, let me henceforth denote competition in the technical sense as "Competition" and in the colloquial sense (of actual contest) as "competition."

The first way is relatively straightforward. The use of a term with established colloquial meaning in a technical context permits the simultaneous transfer and denial of its colloquial connotations. Let me offer just one example: Colinvaux's own description of Gause's original experiments that were designed to study the effect of scarcity on interspecific dynamics—historically, the experimental underpinning of the "competitive exclusion coexistence." He writes,

> No matter how many times Gause tested [the paramecia] against each other, the outcome was always the same, complete extermination of one species. . . . Gause could see this deadly struggle going on before his eyes day after day and always with the same outcome. . . . What we [might have] expected to be a permanent struggling balance in fact became a pogrom. (142)

Just to set the record straight, these are not "killer" paramecia but perfectly ordinary paramecia—minding their own business, eating and dividing, or not, perhaps even starving. The terms *extermination, deadly struggle,* and *pogrom* refer merely to the simultaneous dependence of two species on a common resource. If, by chance, you should have misinterpreted and taken them literally, to refer to overt combat, you would be told that you had missed the point. The Lotka-Volterra equations make no such claims; strictly speaking, they are incompatible with an assumption of overt combat; the competitive exclusion principle merely implies an avoidance of conflict. And yet the description of such a situation, only competitive in the technical sense, slips smoothly from "Competition" to genocide—much as we saw our neo-Tennysonians slip from impersonality to heartless rejection.

The point of this example is not to single out Colinvaux (which would surely be unfair) but to provide an illustration of what is, in fact, a rather widespread investment of an ostensibly neutral technical term with a quite different set of connotations associated with its colloquial meaning. The colloquial connotations lead plausibly to one set of inferences and close off others, while the technical meaning stands ready to disclaim responsibility if challenged.[4]

The second and more serious route by which the apparently a priori status of competition is secured can be explored through an inquiry into the implicit assumptions about resource consumption that are here presupposed and the aspects of resource consumptions that are excluded. The first presupposition is that a resource can be defined and quantitatively assessed independent of the organism itself; and the second is that each organism's utilization of this resource is independent of other organisms. In short, resource consumption is here represented as a zero-sum game. Such a representation might be said to correspond to the absolutely minimal constraint possible on the autonomy of each individual, but it is a constraint that has precisely the effect of establishing a necessary link between self-interest and competition. With these assumptions, apparently autonomous individuals are in fact bound by a zero-sum dynamic that guarantees not quite an absence of interaction but the inevitability of a purely competitive interaction. In a world in which one organism's dinner necessarily means another's starvation, the mere consumption of resources has a kind of de facto equivalence to murder: individual organisms are locked into a life and death struggle not by virtue of their direct interactions but merely by virtue of their existence in the same place and time.

It is worth noting that the very same (Lotka-Volterra) equations readily accommodate the replacement of competitive interactions by cooperative ones and even yield a stable solution. This fact was actually noted by Gause himself as early as 1935 (Gause and Witt 1935) and has been occasionally rediscovered since then, only to be, each time, reforgotten by the community of mathematical ecologists. The full reasons for such amnesia are unclear, but it suggests a strong prior commitment to the representation of resource consumption as a zero-sum dynamic—a representation that would be fatally undermined by the substitution (or even addition) of cooperative interactions.

Left out of this representation are not only cooperative interactions but *any* interactions between organisms that affect the individual's need and utilization of resources. Also omitted are all those interactions between organism and environment which interfere with the identification and measurement of a resource independently of the properties of the organism. Richard Lewontin (1982) has argued that organisms "determine what is relevant" in their environment—what, for example, *is* a resource—and actually "construct" their environment. But such interactions, either between organisms or between organism and environment, lead to pay-off matrices necessarily more complex than those prescribed by a zero-sum dynamic—pay-off matrices that, in turn, considerably complicate the presumed relation between self-interest and competition, if they do not altogether undermine the very meaning of self-interest.

Perhaps the simplest example is provided by the "prisoner's dilemma." But even here, where the original meaning of self-interest is most closely preserved, Robert Axelrod has shown that under conditions of indefinite reiterations, a ("tit-for-tat") strategy is generally better suited to self-interest than are more primitive competitive strategies.

Interactions that effectively generate new resources, or either increase the efficiency of resource utilization or reduce absolute requirement, are more directly damaging to the very principle of self-interest. These are exactly the kinds of interactions that are generally categorized as special cases: as "mutualist," "cooperative," or "symbiotic" interactions. Finally, interactions that affect the birth rate in ways not mediated by scarcity of resources, for example, sexual reproduction, are also excluded by this representation. Perhaps the most important of these omissions for interspecific dynamics is that of mutualist interactions, while for intraspecific dynamics, I would point to sexual reproduction, a fact of life that potentially undermines the core assumptions of radical individualism. In the last few years, there has been a new wave of interest in mutualism among not only dissident but even a few mainstream biologists, and numerous authors are hard at work redressing the neglect of previous years.[5] But in the sixty years in which the Lotka-Volterra equations have reigned as the principal, if not the only, model of interspecific population dynamics—even in the more genial climate of recent years—the omission of sexual reproduction from this model has scarcely been noted.

This omission, once recognized, takes us beyond the question of selective biases in admissible or relevant interactions between organisms. It calls into question the first and most basic assumption for the methodology of individualism in evolutionary theory, namely, that intrinsic properties of individual organisms are primary to any description of evolutionary phenomena.[6] To examine this argument, let us turn from mathematical ecology to population genetics, that branch of evolutionary theory that promises to avoid the practical difficulties of selective focus on certain interactions by excluding the entire question of competitive or cooperative interactions from its domain. In other words, traditional population genetics addresses neither interactions between organisms nor limitations in resources; it effectively assumes populations at low density with infinite resources.

However, one last problem with the language of competition must be noted lest it carry over into our discussion of individual autonomy in population genetics: the widespread tendency to extend the sense of "competition" to include not only the two situations we distinguished earlier (i.e., conflict and reliance on a common resource) but also a third situation[7] where there is no interaction at all, where "competition" denotes an operation of *comparison* between organisms (or species) that requires no juxtaposition in nature, only in the biologist's own mind. This extension, where "competition" can cover all possible circumstances of relative viability and reproductivity, brings with it, then, the tendency to equate competition with natural selection itself.

Darwin's own rhetorical equation between natural selection and the Malthusian struggle for existence surely bears some responsibility for this tendency. But contemporary readers of Darwin like to point out that he did try to correct the misreading his rhetoric invited by explaining that he meant the term *struggle* in "a large and metaphoric sense," including, for example, that of the plant on the edge of the desert: competition was only one of the many meanings of struggle for Darwin. Others have been even more explicit on this issue, repeatedly noting the importance of distinguishing natural selection from "a Malthusian dynamic." Lewontin, for one, has written,

> Thus, although Darwin came to the idea of natural selection from consideration of Malthus' essay on overpopulation, the element of competition between organisms for a resource in short supply is not integral to the argument. Natural selection occurs even when two bacterial strains are growing logarithmically in an excess of nutrient broth if they have different division times. (1970: 1)

However, such attempts—by Lewontin, and earlier and more comprehensively, by L. C. Birch (1957)—to clarify the distinction between natural selection and competition (what Engels called "Darwin's mistake") have done little to stem the underlying conviction that the two are somehow the same. In a recent attempt to define the logical essence of "the Darwinian dynamic," Bernstein et al. (1983) freely translate Darwin's "struggle for survival" to "competition through resource limitation" (192), thereby claiming for competition the status of a "basic component" of natural selection. Even more recently, George Williams (1986) describes a classic example of natural selection in the laboratory as a "competition experiment," a "contest" between a mutant and normal allele, in which he cites differential fecundity as an example of "the competitive interactions among individual organisms" that cause the relative increase in one population (114–115).

At issue is not whether overtly competitive behavior or more basic ecological scarcity is the rule in the natural world; rather, it is whether or not such a question can even be asked. To the extent that distinctions between competition and scarcity, on the one hand, and between scarcity and natural selection, on the other, are obliterated from our language and thought, the question itself becomes foreclosed. As long as the theory of natural selection is understood as a theory of competition, confirmation of one is taken to be confirmation of the other, despite their logical (and biological) difference.

While this clearly raises problems about the meaning of confirmation, my principal concern is with the dynamics by which such an oversight or confusion is sustained in the theory and practice of working biologists—with the internal conventions that render it effectively resistant to correction. Dynamics similar to those in the language of competition can also be seen in the language of reproductive autonomy, especially as employed in the theory and practice of population biology.

THE PROBLEM OF SEXUAL REPRODUCTION

In much of the discourse on reproduction, it is common to speak of the "reproduction of an organism"—as if reproduction is something an individual organism does; as if an organism makes copies of itself, by itself. Strictly speaking, of course, such language is appropriate only to asexually reproducing populations since, as every biologist knows, sexually reproducing organisms neither produce copies of themselves nor produce other organisms by themselves. It is a striking fact, however, that the language of individual reproduction, including such correlative terms as *an individual's offspring* and *lineage*, is used throughout population biology[8] to apply indiscriminately to both sexually and asexually reproducing populations. While it would be absurd to suggest that users of such language are actually confused about the nature of reproduction in the organisms they study (e.g., calculations of numbers of offspring per organism are always appropriately adjusted to take the mode of reproduction into account), we might nonetheless ask, what functions, both positive and negative, does such manifestly peculiar language serve? And what consequences does it have for the shape of the theory in which it is embedded?

I want to suggest, first, that this language, far from being inconsequential, provides crucial conceptual support for the individualist program in evolutionary theory. In particular, my claim is that the starting assumption of this program—that is, that individual properties are primary—depends on the language of individual reproduction for its basic credibility.[9] In addition, I would argue that, just as we saw with the language of competition, the language of individual reproduction, maintained as it is by certain methodological conventions, both blocks the perception of problems in the evolutionary project as presently conducted and, simultaneously, impedes efforts to redress those difficulties that can be identified.

The problems posed for evolutionary theory by sexual reproduction and Mendelian genetics are hardly new, and indeed, the basic theory of population genetics originates in the formulation of a particular method (i.e., the Hardy-Weinberg calculus) designed to solve these problems. The Hardy-Weinberg calculus (often referred to as "bean-bag" genetics) invoked an obviously highly idealized representation of the relation between genes, organisms, and reproduction, but it was one that accomplished a great deal. Most important, it provided a remarkably simple recipe for mediating between individuals and populations—a recipe that apparently succeeded in preserving the individualist focus of the evolutionists' program. One might even say that it did so, perhaps somewhat paradoxically, by tacitly discounting individual organisms and their troublesome mode of reproduction. With the shift of attention from populations of organisms to well-mixed, effectively infinite, pools of genes, the gap between individual and population closed. Individual organisms, in this picture, could be thought of as mere bags of genes (anticipating Richard Dawkins's "survival machines" [1976: 21])—the end product of a reproductive process now reduced to genetic replication plus the random mating of gametes. Effectively bypassed with this representation were all the problems entailed by sexual difference, by the contingencies of mating and fertilization that resulted from the finitude of actual populations and, simultaneously, all the ambiguities of the term *reproduction* as applied to organisms that neither make copies of themselves nor reproduce by themselves. In short, the Hardy-Weinberg calculus provided a recipe for dealing with reproduction that left undisturbed—indeed, finally, reinforced—the temptation to think (and to speak) about reproduction as simply an individual process, to the extent, that is, that it was thought or spoken about at all.

In the subsequent incorporation of the effects of natural selection into the Hardy-Weinberg model, for most authors in population genetics, the contribution of reproduction to natural selection fell largely by the wayside. True, the basic calculus provided a ready way to incorporate at least part of the reproductive process, namely, the production of gametes; but in practice, the theoretical (and verbal) convention that came to prevail in traditional population genetics was to equate natural selection with differential survival and ignore fertility altogether. In other words, the Hardy-Weinberg calculus seems to have invited not one but two kinds of elision from natural selection—first, of all those complications incurred by sex and the contingency of mating (these, if considered at all, get shunted off under the label of sexual, rather than natural, selection),[10] and second, more obliquely, of reproduction in toto.

I want to suggest that these two different kinds of elision in fact provided important tacit support for each other. In the first case, the representation of reproduction as gametic production invited confidence in the assumption that, for calculating changes in gene frequency, differential reproduction, or fertility, was *like* differential survival and hence did not require separate treatment. And in the second case, the technical equation of natural selection with differential survival which prevailed for so many years, in turn, served to deflect attention away from the substantive difficulties invoked in representing reproduction as an individual process. The net effect has been to establish a circle of confidence, first, in the adequacy of the assumption that, despite the mechanics of Mendelianism, the individual remains both the subject and object of reproduction, and second, in the adequacy of the metonymic collapse of reproduction and survival in discussions of natural selection.

The more obvious cost of this circle surely comes from its second part. As a number of authors have recently begun to remind us, the equation between natural selection and differential survival fosters both the theoretical omission and the experimental neglect of a crucial component of natural selection. Perhaps even more serious is the cost in unresolved difficulties that this equation has helped obscure.

One such difficulty is the persistence of a chronic confusion between two definitions of individual fitness: one, the (average) net contribution of an individual of a particular genotype to the next generation, and the other, the geometric rate of increase of that particular genotype. The first refers to the contribution an individual makes to reproduction, while the second refers to the rate of production of individuals. In other words, the first definition refers to the role of the individual as subject of reproduction and the second to its role as object. The disparity between the two derives from the basic fact that, for sexually reproducing organisms, the rate at which individuals of a particular genotype are born is a fundamentally different quantity from the rate at which individuals of that genotype give birth—a distinction easily lost in a language that assigns the same term, *birthrate,* to both processes.

Beginning in 1962, a number of authors have attempted to call attention to this confusion (Moran 1962; Charlesworth 1970; Pollak and Kempthorne 1971; Denniston 1978), agreeing that one definition—the contribution a particular genotype makes to the next generation's population—is both conventional and correct, while the other (the rate at which individuals of a particular genotype are born) is not. Despite their efforts, however, the confusion persists.[11] In part, this is because there remains a real question as to what "correct" means in this context or more precisely, as to which definition is better suited to the needs that the concept of fitness is intended to serve—in particular, the need to explain changes in the genotypic composition of populations. Given that need, we want to know not only which genotypes produce more but also the relative rate of increase of a particular genotype over the course of generations.

Not surprisingly, conflation of the two definitions of fitness is particularly likely to occur in attempts to establish a formal connection between the models of population genetics and those of mathematical ecology. Because all the standard models for population growth assume asexual reproduction, the two formalisms actually refer to two completely different kinds of populations: one of gametic pools and the other of asexually reproducing organisms. In attempting to reconcile these two theories, such a conflation is in fact required to finesse the logical gap between them. A more adequate reconciliation of the two formalisms requires the introduction of both the dynamics of sexual reproduction into mathematical ecology and a compatible representation of those dynamics into population genetics.

Counterintuitively, it is probably the second—the inclusion (in population genetics models) of fertility as a property of the mating type—that calls for the more substantive conceptual shifts. Over the last twenty years, we have witnessed the emergence of a considerable literature devoted to the analysis of fertility selection—leading at least some authors to the conclusion that "the classical concept of individual fitness is insufficient to account for the action of natural selection" (Christiansen 1983: 75).

The basic point is that when fertility selection *is* included in natural selection, the fitness of a genotype, like the fitness of a gene (as argued by Sober and Lewontin 1982), is seen to depend on the context in which it finds itself. Now, however, the context is one determined by the genotype of the mating partner rather than by the complementary allele. A casual reading of the literature on fertility selection might suggest that the mating pair would be a more appropriate unit of selection than the individual, but the fact is that mating pairs do not reproduce themselves any more than do individual genotypes. As E. Pollak has pointed out, "even if a superior mating produces offspring with a potential for entering a superior mating, the realization of this potential is dependent upon the structure of the population" (1978: 389). In other words, in computing the contribution of either a genotype or a mating pair to the next generation's population (of genotypes or mating pairs), it is necessary to take account of the contingency of mating: such a factor, measuring the probability that any particular organism will actually mate, incurs a frequency dependence that reflects the dependence of mating on the genotypic composition of the entire population.

Very briefly, the inclusion of a full account of reproduction in evolutionary theory necessitates the conclusion that natural selection operates simultaneously on many levels (gene, organism, mating pair, and group), not just under special circumstances, as others have argued, but as a rule. For sexually reproducing organisms, fitness in general is not an individual property but a composite of the entire interbreeding population, including, but certainly not determined by, genic, genotypic, and mating pair contributions. By undermining the reproductive autonomy of the individual organism, the advent of sex undermines the possibility of locating the causal efficacy of evolutionary change in individual properties. At least part of the "causal engine" of natural selection must be seen as distributed throughout the entire population of interbreeding organisms.

My point is not merely to argue against the adequacy of the individualist program in evolutionary theory but—like the point of my earlier remarks about competition—to illustrate a quite general process by which the particular conventions of language employed by a scientific community permit a tacit incorporation of ideology into scientific theory and, simultaneously, protect participants from recognition of such ideological influences. The net effect is to insulate the theoretical structure from substantive critical revision. In discussions of sexual reproduction, the linguistic conventions of individual reproduction—conventions embodying an ideological commitment to the a priori autonomy of the individual—both perpetuate that belief and promote its incorporation into the theory of evolutionary dynamics. At the same time, the conventional equation between natural selection and differential survival has served to protect evolutionary theory from problems introduced by sexual reproduction, thereby lending at least tacit support to the assumption of individual autonomy that gave rise to the language of individual reproduction in the first place. The result—now both of the language of autonomy and the language of competition—is to effectively exclude from the domain of theory those biological phenomena that do not fit (or even worse, threaten to undermine) the ideological commitments that are unspoken yet *in* language, built into science by the language we use in both constructing and applying our theories. In this way, through our inescapable reliance on language, even the most ardent efforts to rid natural law of cultural norms become subverted, and the machinery of life takes on not so much a life of its own as a life of our own. But then again, what other life could it have?

NOTES

1. The basic claim of atomic individualism can be schematically expressed as follows:

$$X = \sum_i X_i + \sum_{ij} X_{ij} + \Sigma_{ijk} + \Sigma_{ijkl} X_{ijkl} + \ldots.$$

(successive orders of interaction are represented by the terms *xij*, *xijk*, *xijkl*, etc.)

The actual implementation of this methodology depends, however, on three implicit assumptions:

1. The first term in the series is primary;
2. All relevant interactions are included in the subsequent summations; and finally, that
3. The series converges (i.e., there are no unexpected effects from neglected higher order terms).

Ultimately, it seems to me that the application of all three of these assumptions to evolutionary theory is subject to serious question. My particular focus here, however, is on the adequacy of the first two assumptions.

2. Although the actual words here are neutral enough, Monod's giveaway is in his use of the "gypsy" simile, for the world on the margins of which the gypsy lives is first and foremost a human world, a society, whose indifference is, in fact, rejection.

3. Midgley's manifestly psychological explanation is at least congruent with my own more explicitly psychological account of another, perhaps related, rhetorical and conceptual conflation—namely, that between objectivity and domination seen in a number of traditional attempts to describe (and prescribe) relations of mind to nature (see Keller 1985, chap. 6).

4. See Keller (1988) for a discussion of Hardin's use of the same slippage in arguing for the universality of the "competitive exclusion principle" (1960).

5. Douglas Boucher (1985) has even suggested a new metaphor: in place of "nature red in tooth and claw," he offers "nature green in root and bloom."

6. That is, it raises a question about the adequacy of the third assumption of my schematic account of the methodology of individualism—that in which the essential (or existential) autonomy of the individual organism is assumed.

7. Which is, in fact, the situation of population genetics.

8. Including both population genetics and mathematical ecology.

9. For example, in the absence of other organisms, the fitness of a sexually reproducing organism is, strictly speaking, zero.

10. Darwin originally introduced the idea of sexual selection—always in clear contradistinction to natural selection—in an effort to take account of at least certain aspects of reproductive selection. For many years thereafter, the idea was neglected. Its recent revival in the theoretical literature is of interest, but it ought not be taken to indicate an integration of reproductive dynamics into the central project of evolutionary theory. Rather, it indicates a shift in that project. In my view, the recent interest in sexual selection among sociobiologists is a direct consequence of the final, and complete, abandonment of the individual organism as a theoretical entity. Genic selection theories, it could be said, complete the shift of attention away from organisms begun by the Hardy-Weinberg calculus. Sexual reproduction is a problem in this discourse only to the extent that individual organisms remain, somewhere, an important (even if shifting) focus of conceptual interest.

11. See Keller (1987) for details.

REFERENCES

Axelrod, Robert. *The Evolution of Cooperation.* New York: Basic Books, 1984.

Bernstein, H., H. C. Byerly, F. A. Hopf, R. A. Michod, and G. K. Vemulapalli. "The Darwinian Dynamic," *The Quarterly Review of Biology* 58 (1983):185–207.

Birch, L. C. "Meanings of Competition." *American Naturalist* 91 (1957): 5–18.

Boucher, Douglas. *The Biology of Mutualism.* Cambridge: Oxford University Press, 1985.

Charlesworth, B. "Selection in Populations with Overlapping Generations. 1: The Use of Malthusian Parameters in Population Genetics," *Theoretical Population Biology* 1, 3 (1970): 352–370.

Christiansen, F. B. "The Definition and Measurement of Fitness," in B. Shorrocks, ed., *Evolutionary Ecology: B. E. S. Symposium* 23. Oxford and Boston: Blackwell Scientific Publications, 1984. 65–79.

Colinvaux, Paul. *Why Big Fierce Animals are Rare.* Princeton: Princeton University Press, 1978.

Dawkins, Richard. *The Selfish Gene.* Oxford: Oxford University Press, 1976.

Denniston, C. "An Incorrect Definition of Fitness Revisited," *Annals of Human Genetics, Lond.* 42 (1978): 77–85.

Gause, G. F., and A. A. Witt. "Behavior of Mixed Populations and the Problem of Natural Selection," *American Naturalist* 69 (1935): 596–609.

Ghiselin, Michael. *The Economy of Nature and the Evolution of Sex.* Berkeley, Los Angeles, London: University of California Press, 1974.

Keller, Evelyn Fox. "Reproduction and the Central Project of Evolutionary Theory," *Biology and Philosophy* 2 (1987): 73–86.

Keller, Evelyn Fox. "Demarcating Public from Private Values in Evolutionary Discourse," *Journal of the History of Biology* 21, 2 (1988): 195–211.

Lewontin, Richard. "Organism and Environment," in E. H. C. Plotkin, ed., *Learning, Development, and Culture.* New York: John Wiley and Sons, 1982.

———. "The Units of Selection," *Annual Review of Ecology and Systematics* (1970): 1–1B.

Mayr, Ernst. *Animal Species and Evolution*. Cambridge: Harvard University Press, 1963.

Midgley, Mary. *Evolution as a Religion*. London and New York: Methuen, 1985.

Monod, Jacques. *Chance and Necessity*. New York: Random House, 1972.

Moran, P. A. P. "On the Nonexistence of Adaptive Topographies," *Annals of Human Genetics*, 27 (1962): 383–393.

Pollak, E. "With Selection for Fecundity the Mean Fitness Does Not Necessarily Increase," *Genetics* 90 (1978): 383–389.

Pollak, E., and O. Kempthorne. "Malthusian Parameters in Genetic Populations, II. Random Mating Populations in Infinite Habitats," *Theoretical Population Biology* 2 (1971): 357–390.

Sober, E., and R. Lewontin. "Artifact, Cause, and Genetic Selection," *Philosophy of Science* 47 (1982): 157–180.

Tennyson, Alfred Lord. *In Memoriam* LV–LVI.

Weinberg, Steven. "Reflections of a Working Scientist," *Daedalus* 103 (Summer 1974): 33–46.

Williams, George. "Comments," *Biology and Philosophy* 1, 1 (1986): 114–122.

FIVE

Human Nature and Culture: Biology and the Residue of Uniqueness

Melvin Konner

I

Since the question, "Is there such a thing as human nature?" continues to be posed, and to be answered by some in the negative, it seems necessary to begin by exploring the meaning of this question and showing why it cannot, in any meaningful form, have any but an affirmative answer. The question raises doubts about whether aspects of the human condition can be considered inevitable outcomes of biological elements in the human makeup. In extreme forms, such doubts are dubious. If I assert that it is human nature to require a diet supplying eight essential amino acids, to walk bipedally, and to speak a language containing nouns and verbs, there are only a few ways to question the validity of the claim.

For example, it is possible to point to a small number of individuals who, from birth onward, are poisoned by an amino acid essential to all others, or who are never able to walk or speak, but these observations— which might be called the "rare-defect objection"—do not detract from the power of the generalizations. Second, and somewhat more interesting, it is easy to show that great variability exists in the way these generalizations are fulfilled by individuals and groups and that most of this variability is due to cultural or environmental causes. But these observations, the "cross-cultural objection," do not address the point that there is, in each of the systems in question, a core of features that do not vary. Third, there is the "freedom-of-will" objections: some individuals perfectly capable of walking will choose never to do so, while others may learn to walk faster or more gracefully than anyone in the world, or even to walk on their hands.

There are several answers to this objection, but two are decisive. First, such freedom of will exists, but the rarity with which it is exercised, at least at the extremes of the distribution of behavior, is not irrelevant to the question at hand. This answer resembles the reply to the rare-defect objection but is directed to motivation rather than capability, and it implies that motivations as well as capabilities may be legitimately included in the definitional sphere of human nature, a point to which we will return.

Second, within the definable but admittedly broad band of variation in patterns of walking resulting from the exercise of freedom of will, it is possible to show lawful relations between human choices and physiological outcomes. After the choice has been exercised—for a given daily amount of walking, say—there follow predictable consequences for the structure and function of muscle, bone, and the cardiopulmonary organs. These, in turn, have consequences for behavioral capability, health, and life span. The laws relating the precise spectrum of choices to the predictable outcomes are also part of what is meant by human nature. (Here perhaps a counterobjection will be raised: "But that is just what I mean. Human behavior is flexible, so much so that biology itself is under the sway of human choices." Of course it is; but predictably so, and with thresholds and limits provided by human nature—by the genes—and not by human choices. Biological concepts such as facultative adaptation, range of reaction, and bounded learning, among others, have been developed to describe parallel phenomena in nonhuman species.)

Finally, the "so-what objection" holds that the sorts of characteristics legitimately subsumed under the rubric of human nature are trivial and uninteresting. "Of course everybody can walk; so what? It's the variations that are interesting." It might be pointed out that every person who can walk exhibits a relatively stereotyped heel-toe progression with synchronized alternate arm swinging, reflecting a very complex wired-in coordinating pattern involving many millions of neurons. Or that every child assumes the ability to walk within a narrowly defined age period because of the maturation of certain parts of the nervous system, the growth of which are under genetic control. But then each successive complexity pointed out becomes subsumed under the ho-hum or so-what rubric, so that as soon as it is shown to be biologically determined, it will be deemed uninteresting. "That's not what I mean by human nature" will retreat to encompass only that which has not yet been given a biological basis.

Of course, what most of us mean by human nature is not primarily the dependence on certain nutrients or the ability to walk and talk but the condition of being subject to certain patterns of motivation that seem to constrain human freedom, and to this extent, the so-what objection really does apply to the characteristics we have considered so far. I will insist in the end that human nature fairly includes, in fact must include, certain characteristically human—that is, genetically coded, wired-in—perceptions, cognitions, competencies, response systems, and motor action patterns as well as motivations. Indeed, it is doubtful whether motivation can meaningfully be defined so as to exclude such other psychological characteristics. But it is necessary at this point for us to leave the safe realms of amino acids and coordinated locomotion for the more treacherous realms of love, fear, sacrifice, selfishness, lust, and violence, which come most readily to the mind when the concept of human nature is invoked, and to establish the extent to which these realms are subject to the kinds of arguments applicable in the safer ones.

To do this properly requires a series of intellectual strategies directed at exploring the phylogenetic origins of the pattern; the evolutionary, principally selective forces that have operated and continue to operate on it; the cross-cultural and other variability in it (or lack thereof) and the lawful relationships between that variability and variations in the environment that might be expected to influence it; the immediate physiological antecedents of the pattern; the sequence of development of the pattern, including both the maturational and environmental components; and the genetics of the pattern, as explored through both classical Mendelian methods and the methods of molecular and developmental genetics.

Each of these intellectual strategies has progressed so far in the last two decades as to render suspect any opinion on human nature that does not give clear evidence of having kept abreast of their progress. It is not possible here to review their implications even in relation to one of the motivational patterns of interest. However, it is possible to touch on some of the highlights relevant both to human motivation in general and to a legitimate concept of human nature (Konner 1982b).

II

The fossil evidence for human and proto-human evolution has accumulated steadily for more than one hundred years so no one familiar with it doubts the reality and continuity of that evolution (Ciochon and Fleagle 1987). However, new discoveries are made each year which change the details of the picture, and during the past two decades, biochemical taxonomy has further altered our concept of human evolution. There is, therefore, little to be gained for our purposes in closely following each argument in human paleontology. But there is much to be gained from understanding the general higher primate background of human evolution; the environment of human evolutionary adaptedness, that of hunting and gathering; and the principles of evolutionary adaptation as applied to behavior and reproduction.

All higher primates without exception are social animals with great learning capacity and with the mother-offspring bond at the center of social life (Cheney, Seyfarth, and Smuts 1986). This bond is always prolonged, as is the anatomic and behavioral course of individual development, including each phase of the life cycle as well as the life span as a whole. Laboratory and field studies alike demonstrate the capacity for complex social cognition and social learning, up to and including "cultural" transmission of social rank, tool-using techniques, and knowledge of location of food sources. Play, especially social play, is characteristic of all primate species, particularly during development, and there are various reasons to believe it to be an important opportunity for learning. For example (MacLean 1985), the higher primate emphasis on both the mother-infant bond and on play represents an intensification of the pattern established by the early mammals and is essential to the understanding of the phylogeny of the limbic system and the emotions.

Primate groups generally include a core of genetically related individuals with associated nonrelatives. In most instances, the core is a matrilineage, stable over the life course of the individuals. In any case, the distribution of acts of social support and generosity is preferentially toward genetic relatives but not exclusively so. Monkeys and apes aid nonrelatives and can usually expect some aid in return. Cooperation is ubiquitous, but so is competition, and one of the major purposes of cooperation is mutual defense against other group members. Conflict is frequent, with both sexes participating but with males generally exhibiting more physical aggression than females.

Beyond these broad generalizations, great variation exists in social organization both between and within species (Napier and Napier 1985). Monogamy is present in some South American monkeys, in gibbons, and in one or two other forms, but in most species, larger group associations subsuming more temporary (although sometimes more than transient) associations between individual males and individual females are the rule. The causes of this variation in higher primate social organization remain obscure, but some relevant evolutionary principles will be considered below.

Although there are important species variations, it may be generally said that higher primates are sensitive to significant perturbations of the early social environment, such as isolation rearing or repeated involuntary mother-infant separation, and that these perturbations give rise to abnormalities of sexual, maternal, and aggressive behavior that in humans would be viewed as psychopathology (Harlow 1963, 1969; Arling and Harlow 1967; Sackett et al. 1981). In a number of species (though not all), isolation rearing gives rise to stereotyped behavior such as rocking and self-directed aggression, and mother-infant separation gives rise to symptoms usually described as protest followed by depression. Even deprivation of contact with peers during development has produced abnormal behavior in some experiments. Apparent human analogues of these causal relationships, although difficult to interpret, have encouraged the use of primate models. These experiments emphasize the extent to which the normal development and behavior in such animals has come to depend, in the course of evolution, on an intact social matrix.

Natural variation in stable individual behavior patterns ("personality") occurs in free-ranging monkey and ape groups (Smuts 1985) and extends to variants that would be considered pathological if seen in humans, such as hyperaggressive, isolative, phobic, or depressed behavior. It is rarely possible to explore the causes of such variants, but most are probably both genetic and environmental in origin. Some abnormalities, such as severe depression (as in the case of an eight-year-old wild chimpanzee after the death of his mother) may be incompatible with survival (Goodall 1986). Others, however, such as hyperaggressiveness (as in the case of two female chimpanzees that systematically and repeatedly killed the infants of other females) may actually enhance reproductive adaptation for the abnormal individual.

The above generalizations can be considered applicable to the social and psychological world of proto-human higher primate species for a period of approximately 40 million years. Against this background, hominids evolved during the last few million years, culminating in the emergence of our species within the last few hundred thousand years, and finally in the appearance of truly modern *Homo sapiens* within the last hundred thousand. Aside from the increase in intelligence, as indicated by increasing relative and absolute brain size as well as by increasing complexity of stone tools, one hallmark of the transition to hominids was an increasing reliance on hunting. All monkeys and apes are largely vegetarians and insect-eaters; instances of meat-eating are instructive but relatively infrequent.

Among the most technologically primitive humans, whether in the fossil record or in the ethnographic one, hunting is invariably of major importance (Lee and DeVore 1968, Dahlberg 1981). Most of the stone tools that have survived archaeologically were used in hunting or butchering, and the demands caused by this activity have long been held to be central to the emergence of human intelligence and social organization. Recent evidence has shown that the stone used for this purpose had to be traded over long distances, implying unexpectedly complex social networks among our ancestors before 2 million years ago. Furthermore, even chimpanzees share meat after a kill (but not plant foods), and among human hunter-gatherers, the following of elaborate regulations for such sharing of meat may be a life-and-death matter. Finally, with one noteworthy exception (the Agta of the Philippines, where women routinely hunt), all hunting and gathering societies in the ethnographic record have a division of labor by sex, with men doing almost all the hunting and providing meat for their families and women providing most of the vegetable foods. These features of society related to hunting had to have been grafted onto an already complex social life characteristic of nonhuman higher primates.

However, this traditional male-centered view gives at most half the story (Dahlberg 1981). In many hunting and gathering societies, plant foods gathered by women constitute more than half of the diet. Plant foods are shared in these societies (although not beyond the immediate family), while they are not shared in nonhuman primates. The early advent of upright posture may have had more to do with the need for females to carry plant foods as well as infants to a base camp than with any advantage upright posture conferred in hunting, and it may be that among the first tools invented were digging sticks and carrying devices for plants or infants—tools that, however crucial, would not be preserved in archaeological assemblages and that would most likely have been invented by women.

Psychodynamic theorist John Bowlby coined the phrase "the environment of human evolutionary adaptedness," which aptly describes the hunting and gathering way of life. The phrase correctly implies that this is, or was, the context for which natural selection prepared us and from which we have departed only in the past 10,000 years, a very short time in evolutionary terms. (The industrial revolution, in the same terms, happened only a moment ago.) From many studies of recent hunting and gathering peoples, combined with archaeological evidence of those of the distant past, it is possible to make certain generalizations about this context (Lee and DeVore 1968): social groups were usually small, ranging in size from fifteen to forty people related through blood or marriage; groups were nomadic, moving frequently to take advantage of changing subsistence opportunities, and flexible in composition, size, and adaptive strategies; daily life involved physical challenge, vigorous exercise, and occasional hunger but with a usually dependable food base from a moderate work effort and with a marked division of labor by gender; disease, mainly infectious rather than chronic, produced high rates of mortality especially in infancy and early childhood, with consequent frequent experience of loss; virtually all of life's activities were done in a highly social context with people one knew well, often the same people for different activities; and privacy was limited, but creative expression in the arts was frequently possible, and conflicts and problems were dealt with through extensive group discussions.

These generalizations describe the context in which most of human evolution and prehistory have occurred, so it is often said that we are, in effect, hunter-gatherers in skyscrapers. Simplistic observations about the consequences of this change are often made and are not helpful. Mental illnesses, both major and minor, are present in such societies. All of them experience some level of violent conflict, up to and including homicide. Other human behaviors usually considered undesirable, such as selfishness, deceit, adolescent rebellion, adultery, desertion, and child abuse, occur in such societies, and it is impossible to compare the rates of such behaviors to those in our own society. Although fluid in their way, life in such societies is restricted to a much smaller number of people than ours, and the lack of privacy and inability to get away from those people must constitute stresses, just as crowding and high levels of contact with strangers may constitute stress in advanced societies. The stresses of illness and mortality, as well as the stresses and uncertainties of the daily food quest, also must take their toll. A truly thoughtful set of observations and analyses of the differences between psychological conditions in our society and the kind of society in which we spent most of our history could be imagined but has not yet been made.

III

Since the late 1960s, there has been rapid emergence of an influential new field of evolutionary study known as neo-Darwinian theory or, more commonly, sociobiology (Wilson 1975, Trivers 1985). This new set of principles has been quickly adopted by most investigators who study animal behavior under natural conditions, including ethologists and behavioral ecologists, and has also influenced many anthropologists and psychologists. Briefly summarized, the principles are as follows (Trivers 1985):

An organism is, in essence, a gene's way of making another gene. Put more strictly, it is a way found by up to thousands of genes, through short- or long-term cooperation, to make copies of themselves. As long as it is admitted that there can be no forces operating in nature other than physicochemical ones, it must be admitted that continued membership in an ongoing germ plasm is the only goal served by any given gene. To the extent that a gene influences behavior, it can only continue in the germ plasm if it maintains or enhances, through the behavior, the number of copies of itself in the gene pool of the next generation. (Contrary to a frequently repeated confusion, the cohesiveness of the genome has only quantitative, not qualitative, bearing on the validity of this principle.)

Genes increase their number by enhancing reproductive success. Enhancing survival is only one way of doing this. Where the two goals, enhancing survival and enhancing reproductive success, are in conflict, as they often are, genes that enhance reproductive success will replace genes that enhance survival. The concept of fitness in evolutionary theory has no meaning except the relative frequency of characteristics and of the genes that influence them. It is a tautological description of reproductive success and has nothing necessarily in common with medical, social, or athletic definitions of fitness, all of which can be and often are achieved without an increase, or even with a decrease, in technically defined reproductive fitness.

Fitness is now best defined as *inclusive*. By *inclusive fitness* is meant the tendency of genes to influence their frequency not only through the survival and reproduction of the individual carrying them but also through the survival and reproduction of other closely related individuals who may be carrying the same genes through common descent. This is the concept introduced by Hamilton (1964) to account, using the mathematics of evolutionary genetics, for the existence of altruism in animals, which previously seemed something to be culled by the process of natural selection. Hence the need for a newly defined subprocess of natural selection, called kin selection. If I die to save my identical twin, then the frequency of any gene that helped predispose me to that action will (all else being equal) be unaffected by my death. In general terms, such genes, or any genes predisposing me to self-sacrifice for a relative, should be favored under conditions where the ratio of the recipient's benefit to the altruist's costs exceeds the inverse of the degree of genetic relatedness. This concept has been invoked to explain self-sacrifice of soldier ants for the colony, alarm calls of birds and ground squirrels, and nepotism in human beings, among many other phenomena of human and animal behavior. Other theories brought to bear on the problem of altruism have been reciprocal altruism and the prisoner's dilemma model of cooperation, neither of which requires that the altruist and the recipient be related.

As argued by Robert Trivers (1972, 1985) from a suggestion of Darwin's, in species with two sexes in which there is a physiological or behavioral difference in the energy invested in individual offspring, the sex that invests more will become the scarce resource over which the other sex competes. In mammals and in most birds, females exhibit greater investment, but direct male parental investment may be very high in some species. Species in which male parental investment is high tend to be those in which pair-formation of a breeding male with the breeding female is long lasting; sexual dimorphism, both morphological and behavioral, is low; male competition for females is low; and variability among males in reproductive success is low. These "pair-bonding" species, a category including 8,000 species of birds but only a minority of mammal species, may be contrasted with "lek" or "tournament" species, so called because they sometimes have annual seasonal breeding "tournaments" in which males compete fiercely for females. These species often have high sexual dimorphism for display or fighting (e.g., antlers or peacock feathers), low tendency for pair formation, low direct male parental investment in offspring, and high variability in reproductive success.

Human beings are considered to be near but not at the pair-bonding extreme of the continuum, as viewed from the perspective of sexual dimorphism, degree of direct male involvement in the care of offspring in a wide range of cultures, and the known distribution of human marriage forms (Daly and Wilson 1983, Murdock 1967). Polygyny, in which one man marries several women, is allowed or encouraged in 83 percent of known cultures in the anthropological record (708 of 849), while the converse arrangement, polyandry, is rare (4 of 849), and a double standard of sexual restriction is extremely common; still, most human marriages have probably been monogamous at least in intent.

A neo-Darwinian model of parent-offspring conflict advanced by Trivers (1974, 1985) has profound implications for the nature of the family. Weaning conflict is very common among mammals, and there are equivalent phenomena among birds, even including tantrum behavior on the part of the weanling. If the evolutionary purposes of mother and offspring were isomorphic, then they should "agree" (the use of this kind of language is shorthand for "should have been selected to act as if they agreed" and implies no conscious intent) that a given level and duration of investment is necessary and sufficient, after which attention should be turned by the mother to her next unborn offspring. A naive model of the nature of the family assumes that since it functions as a harmonious unit under ideal conditions, that is presumably how it was designed by evolution. However, it was not so designed. Like the breeding pair discussed above, it is an association among individuals with overlapping but distinct evolutionary purposes. Its members naturally pursue individual goals that are sometimes at odds with each other's ultimate (not merely temporary) purposes, and their relations are naturally conflictful rather than harmonious. This natural conflict is not the result of friction in what should be or could be a smoothly functioning system but is intrinsic.

Competition among *unrelated* individuals can be expected at times to be extreme. Virtually all animal species for which there is sufficient evidence have been seen to exhibit extremes of violent conflict, up to and including homicide, in the wild (Wilson 1975). The belief that human beings are rare among animal species in that we kill our own kind is erroneous, and more evidence to the contrary accumulates every year.

One particularly noteworthy phenomenon is *competitive infanticide,* already alluded to in relation to wild chimpanzees. The paradigmatic case is that of the Hanuman langur monkey of India, as observed by Sarah Blaffer Hrdy (1977), among others. Langur troops consist of a core of related females and their offspring, associated for a period of a few years or less with unrelated immigrant males. Occasionally, new males arrive and challenge the resident males. If they win and take over the troop, they drive the previous males away and proceed systematically to attack and kill resident infants under six months of age. The mothers of those infants then come into estrus again (much sooner than they would have if the infants had survived and continued to nurse) and are impregnated by the new males. Controversy has centered over whether this is normal behavior or a response to crowding or other social stress. Such controversy misses the point that the behavior enhances the reproductive success of the new males at the expense of the old ones and therefore can be expected to be favored by natural selection, whether or not we choose to call it normal. Furthermore, similar phenomena have now been observed in many species.

The delineation of universal features of human behavior is central to the elucidation of the effects of phylogeny. But natural selection operating on organisms ancestral to ourselves created not only individuals with certain needs, drives, and capacities but also equations—"if-then" statements—relating the environment to the social system, the social system to the individual, and so on. In a cross-cultural study of husband-wife intimacy (Whiting and Whiting 1975), it was shown that societies in which husbands eat, sleep, and care for children together with their wives are also those that are less belligerent. That is, phylogeny appears to have provided a system such that separating men from women and small children is associated with successful adaptation as warriors. This is not to say that they must be warriors or that they must be aloof from their wives but that choosing aloofness may increase effective belligerency and/or perhaps vice versa. The universal characteristic here is not a phenotypic characteristic at all but an underlying mechanism relating two sets of characteristics to each other. (An extended discussion of this conceptual framework may be found in Konner 1982*b*.)

In the past decade, the application of neo-Darwinian or sociobiological theory to ethnological materials has produced many findings that seem to bypass the complex questions of the relationships among society, culture, and individual development. For example, societies in which young men inherit land from their mothers' brothers are more lax about the prevention of female adultery than are societies in which young men inherit from their fathers (Kurland 1979); in societies in which polygyny is allowed, wealthier and more influential men tend to have more wives (Betzig 1986); and in small-scale societies in which adoption of children is common, it tends to follow patterns predicted by genetic relatedness (Silk 1987). Investigators making these findings usually declare that they do not claim any direct genetic basis for these variations in human behavior, and indeed some of the worst confusion about sociobiology stems from a failure to appreciate this distinction between the propositions of neo-Darwinian theory and those of traditional behavioral genetics or molecular genetics.

Even in a nonhuman species such as the red-winged blackbird, males singing on richer territories mate with several females instead of one (Harding and Follett 1979). But the mechanism of this flexible adaptive system—known as a facultative adaptation—must be quite different in blackbirds than the similar mechanism in human beings (although it would probably underestimate blackbirds to assume that in them the system is under tight genetic control). The wings of insects come from thoracic tissue, the wings of birds from forearm structures, the wings of bats from fingers, and the wings of humans from technology. These four adaptations to the problem of flight serve similar functions with extremely different provenance. The same will prove to be true of adaptations in social behavior (Konner 1982*b*).

Neo-Darwinian or sociobiological theory is sometimes presumed to carry value judgments as a necessary concomitant. This logic appears to suggest that whatever is, is right. An extension of this fallacy would hold that sickle cell anemia and thallasemia must be accepted because natural selection has maintained them through balanced polymorphism, the heterozygotes being at an advantage in malaria resistance; or that myopia should not be corrected because natural selection in favor of sharp vision has relaxed in the human population since the end of the hunting and gathering era. Human judgments about what is desirable are separate from and must take precedence over any observations or explanations of what exists in nature, although they may be enhanced by taking the facts of the natural world into account.

IV

The main enterprise of cultural anthropology has been the description and analysis of cross-cultural variation, but that enterprise has always had an inevitable, even if tacit, complement: the characterization of features of human behavior that do not vary or that vary relatively little. The concept of universals has, however, at least five different meanings: behaviors, such as coordinated bipedal walking or smiling in social greeting, that are exhibited by all normal adult members of every known society; behaviors that are universal within an age or sex class, such as the reflexes in all normal neonates or the ejaculatory motor action pattern in all postpubertal males; population characteristics that apply to all populations but not all individuals, such as the sex difference in physical aggressiveness; universal features of culture rather than of behavior, such as the taboos against incest and homicide, or the highly variable but always present institution of marriage, or the social construction of illness in attempts at healing; and, finally, characteristics that, although unusual or even rare, are found at some low level in every population, such as homicidal violence, thought disorder, depression, suicide, or incest.

The list of characters that fill these five categories is a very long one, much longer than the prominent anthropologists of the early heyday of cross-cultural study would have predicted (Eibl-Eibesfeldt 1988). The search for societies without violence, or without gender differences that go beyond childbearing, or without mental illness, or even without the ability to make and use fire has been a vain one, and although there is convincing documentation of variation in the incidence or context of expression of most human behaviors, the existence of such a large core of constantly present, if variable, features constitutes a demonstration of the reality of human nature and its validity as a scientific construct (Konner 1982*b*).

In the realm of psychosocial development, Freud postulated, and present-day child psychiatry continues to accept in altered and disputed forms, a universal sequence of emotional development on which the social environment of the family could be claimed to produce enduring traits of emotional disposition. Beyond some very general elements—the existence of infantile sexuality, the formation of an attachment to a primary caretaker who is usually the mother, the ubiquity of conflicts and jealousies within the family—this allegedly universal sequence has never found empirical support; hence the unresolvable disputes among different schools of psychoanalysis and the enduring skepticism of outsiders. Extensive cross-cultural studies of human behavioral and psychological development have not produced evidence relevant to these particular models, but they have produced extensive evidence supporting some more empirically grounded putative universals of psychosocial growth. In the absence of knowledge of neuropsychological development, psychoanalytic theory postulated a libidinal theory of this development (Freud 1920) that few take seriously today. However, the growing body of actual knowledge about neural and neuroendocrine development can now begin to serve a parallel function in relation to the more empirically grounded newer studies of psychosocial growth.

Among the well-established cross-cultural universals of psychosocial development, the following are the best supported and in many cases can be plausibly related to putative underlying neural events (Konner 1982*a*, 1991): the emergence of sociality, as heralded by social smiling, during the first four months of life, in parallel with the maturation of basal ganglia and cortical motor circuits; the emergence of strong attachments, as well as of fears of separation and of strangers, in the second half of the first year of life, in parallel with the maturation of the major fiber tracts of the limbic system; the emergence of language during the second year and after, in parallel with the maturation of the thalamic projection to the auditory cortex among other circuits; the emergence of a sex difference in physical aggressiveness in early and middle childhood, with males on the average exceeding females, a consequence in part of prenatal androgenization of the hypothalamus; and the emergence of adult sexual motivation and functioning in adolescence, in parallel with and following the maturation of the reproductive system at puberty, against the background of the previously mentioned prenatal androgenization of the hypothalamus. In addition, there are a number of apparent cross-cultural universals of cognitive development.

There are other probable cross-cultural developmental universals, such as increased babbling in the second half of the first year and possibly progress through the first three, or perhaps four, of the six stages in Lawrence Kohlberg's scheme of moral development in childhood. Although the underlying neuropsychology is at an early stage of elucidation, the cross-cultural universality of these traits is well established; in each case, there is extensive experimental evidence to support the maturational nature of the process in behavioral development. They constitute a first approximation of the true structural basis of psychosocial development, which Freud groped for with his crude theory of libidinal development in the nervous system.

They also constitute a firm basis for the future understanding of how variations in social experience, whether clinical or cross-cultural, act on the maturing psychosocial competence to produce potentially lasting variations. In each of the processes mentioned, cross-cultural differentiation of the maturing competence begins almost as soon as the maturation occurs. However, the acceptance and increasingly detailed and reliable description of the maturational constants underlying the variation in psychosocial growth will provide a steadily firmer place on which to stand while attempting to investigate the role of cultural and individual experience.

V

Within the last two or three years, there has emerged a new mode of inquiry in the study of human nature. The current revolution in molecular genetics is rapidly leading both to a molecular neurogenetics and to a molecular genetics of behavior and mind. Its established empirical base already extends from the simplest animal systems to the most complex functions of the human mind and from the earliest to the latest stages of the life cycle. Some highlights among its recent discoveries are the following:

1) a family of genes coded for a set of neuropeptides that, in turn, controls the stereotyped egg-laying behavior of the sea slug *Aplysia californica* (Scheller et al. 1984);

2) a *Drosophila* behavioral mutant has been explained as the result of known genes that alter the potassium channel of the neuronal membrane (Tanouye et al. 1986);

3) a single-gene form of human pseudohermaphroditism has been traced to deficiency in 5-alpha-reductase, which converts testosterone to dihydrotestosterone; affected individuals have an ambiguous or feminine body habitus and psychological disposition until puberty, when they become physically and psychologically masculine despite having been raised as girls (Imperato-McGinley et al. 1979, 1980);

4) Huntington's disease, a neuropsychiatric condition that presents in the thirties or forties (often beginning with psychiatric manifestations), has been shown to be caused by a dominant gene on the short arm of chromosome 4 (Gusella et al. 1984);

5) manic-depressive illness (bipolar affective disorder), a severe form of mental illness presenting in adulthood, has been shown in different kindreds to be caused in part by a gene on the X chromosome (Baron et al. 1987);

6) Alzheimer's disease, the most common form of late-life dementia, has been shown to be caused in some kindreds by a gene on chromosome 21; a DNA probe cloned from the amyloid protein long known to accumulate in the brains of affected people has been localized to the same chromosome section; and the same gene is duplicated in individuals with Down's syndrome—who develop early Alzheimer's—even in the absence of the usual chromosomal anomaly, a duplication of the whole chromosome (Tanzi et al. 1987; St. George-Hyslop et al. 1987; Goldgaber et al. 1987; Delabar et al. 1987).

These recent findings remove any doubt regarding the ability of genes to alter complex behavior through comprehensible biochemical pathways affecting the nervous system. They are not subject to any of the methodological criticisms always leveled at classical Mendelian behavioral genetics, especially at correlational human studies. Extreme skeptics will still claim that these findings have no bearing on the development of normal human behavior, but there is no reason to believe that they are right. On the contrary, it is likely that of the hundred thousand or so genes in the human genome, the ones most easily identified would be the ones with the most devastating effects and that subsequently it would become possible to identify genes affecting physiology and behavior within the normal range. We can expect such identifications within one or two decades.

Such findings, however, are not the end but the beginning of the development of the epigenetic—interactionist—approach to human nature. In the absence of other treatments, few would argue that we should refrain from "gene surgery" for Alzheimer's disease, but even with manic-depressive illness there will be serious ethical issues in tampering with the system, which may produce certain desirable personality variations and even exceptional creativity as well as serious mental illness. Within the normal range, the arguments for restraint would be even stronger. Nevertheless, from the viewpoint of analysis of the development of behavior, a technology of molecular genetics will provide insights that will transform our view of human nature. Already we have learned that both cognitive and emotional functions can be altered by specific genes and that genes can manifest themselves in the behavioral phenotype at almost any stage of life, sometimes without prior developmental manifestations of any kind. The question is, How will the environment prove to interact with genetic predispositions and vulnerabilities?

Phenylketonuria provides a valuable model. It is a simple genetic disorder with increasingly understood molecular genetics, yet with an environmental proximate cause and a solution that involves modification of one of the most mundane features of the environment, the diet. Such environmental modification essentially obviates the impact of the genotype. Drug treatments have also been tried, and in the not too distant future, a molecular genetic intervention in the germ line ("gene surgery") may be possible. At that point, there will be a full spectrum of treatment possibilities, making phenylketonuria a paradigmatic instance of the complex interactions of genotype, metabolism, and environment in the development of neural, behavioral, and mental phenomena. It is not difficult to imagine in broad outline the similar range of interpretations that will develop for a variety of other abnormalities of brain and behavior and indeed for some variations within the normal range.

In addition, there are likely to be many new discoveries about the way environment exerts its influence on the development of behavior, and some of these are likely to be surprising. Neuroembryological research has given new meaning to the concept of plasticity by showing the great importance of competition among neurons and connections for destination sites in the developing brain, and the process of selective pruning goes on postnatally as well as prenatally (Changeux 1985; Goldman-Rakic et al. 1983). Brain functions as crucial to psychology as laterality may depend on complex intrauterine mechanisms under indirect, rather than direct, genetic control (Geschwind and Galaburda 1987), and these mechanisms of plasticity were not only unexplored but unsuspected until a few years ago.

VI

In the eighteenth century, Goethe (Magnus 1949) posited the existence of a fundamental or archetypal form in plant life, a sort of key to the order of life itself in the largest sense, and perhaps even of the universe beyond the realm of the living. Indeed, he made his search for order a foil to that of Newton, which he considered too mechanical; he thought that even the fundamental ordering principles of the universe might be biological, not physical. Although in this he went too far, there is a sense in which the *Urpflanze*, Goethe's ultimate plant form, really does exist and in which it has become, two centuries after he posited it, as central to the enterprise of at least the life sciences as he believed it would be.

The Urpflanze is, of course, DNA, and with the scientific unraveling of its form has come, and will continue to come, a sense of order and power in the realm of biology that only a mind like Goethe's could have imagined. The extent to which the realm of behavior will also come under the sway of this intellectual order remains to be seen; but even the answer to this question will be largely provided by that order. Undoubtedly, the answer will involve mechanisms of epigenesis that include such phenomena as operant conditioning, sensitive periods, psychological trauma, cognitive maps, and symbol systems as well as diet, infection, and injury. But the way these phenomena operate—within the constraints provided by the human genome—to produce individual and collective behavioral patterns and tendencies is vastly more uncertain than the textbooks in the relevant fields allow, and the mutual contradictions of those textbooks underscore the uncertainties. That the delineation of how the environment affects the individual, beyond the hoary pieties of plasticity, remains a task almost completely for the future is perhaps the greatest discovery of the past twenty years.

Two further implications of recent advances in biology need to be emphasized. First, if neo-Darwinian principles of behavior and reproduction are even mostly correct, the fundamental metaphor of modern social science is in error. That metaphor, which is as venerable as social science itself, claims that society is an organism, with individuals as cells, specialized subgroups of individuals as tissues or organs, and conflict as a transient aberration, or pathology, the elimination of which restores the social organism to health. The basic weakness of the analogy is most starkly exposed each time an individual or group departs from the society and joins or forms another—something the cells or organs of an animal cannot do, of course—but in fact the weakness is evident in the ubiquity of social conflict even within the most intimately interdependent social relationships. Such conflict is not inadvertent friction in a system that should, by design, function smoothly but is an inherent and inevitable expression of the purposes of social life itself.

Second, the motivational portions of the brain, particularly the hypothalamus, have functional characteristics relevant to the apparent chronicity of human dissatisfaction. Animal experiments on the lateral hypothalamus suggest that the motivated condition is to some extent nonspecific, with the internal state responsive to but not geared for the particular external circumstances. A continuum between attentiveness or alertness and intense drive states ensures that responsiveness will never be long delayed but also that it will not always be appropriate and, more important, that the organism's chronic internal state will be a vague mixture of anxiety and desire—best described perhaps by the phrase "I want," spoken with or without an object for the verb. This insight of physiological psychology about the internal motivational states of animals like ourselves fits well with the more recent insights of sociobiology about the conflictful external relations entered upon by the same and similar animals and also with the failure of the organismal model of societal coherence.

One consequence of these insights is that the view of life current in behavioral biology bears more resemblance to the view taken in the time-honored traditions of the humanities than either does to the canons of social science. Henry James once described life as "slow advance into enemy territory" and wrote, "Life *is*, in fact, a battle. Evil is insolent and strong; beauty enchanting, but rare; goodness very apt to be weak; folly very apt to be defiant; wickedness to carry the day; imbeciles to be in great places, people of sense in small, and mankind generally unhappy" (Zeibel 1951). Similar sentiments have been common in the literary traditions of many societies from the earliest religious and epic sagas to novels and plays completed this morning. Religious traditions of varied character recognize the reality of a deeply, even tragically, flawed human nature, but they exhort against it, while literary artists seem satisfied to describe it. In either case, it is viewed, sadly, as all too real, and these vividly brilliant classic observations of it fit well with Darwin's remark to Joseph Hooker: "What a book, a Devil's Chaplain might write on the clumsy, wasteful, blundering low and horribly cruel works of nature!"

Of course, that nature also includes an equally inherent ethical component that derives from the necessity for cooperation and altruism, the potential for responsibility, decency, love, even happiness. These capacities, too, are shared by many other animals, and we can take encouragement from the fact that they are so widespread in nature. But for them to prevail requires the kind of collective attention that is possible only in the framework of human culture. In this framework, reflection on the outcomes of natural tendencies results in judgments that restrain or modify those tendencies. It is full of deceptions, but it is much better than nothing, and it exceeds the capabilities of any other animal for similar restraint and modification.

The evolutionary, biological view of human nature provides many parallels with that of animal natures and only a few clear distinctions. Traditionally and presently, distinctions between ourselves and animals have emphasized the primacy and complexity of human rational faculties. But in recent years, the development of artificial intelligence has duplicated a surprising number of those same faculties, and in the community of people who think about the implications of this fact, it is common to distinguish humans from machines by referring to the human emotional faculties—precisely those we share in common with animals. It would seem that we are sorted to a pulp, caught in a vise made, on the one side, of the increasing power of evolutionary biology in explaining the emotions and, on the other, of the relentless duplication of human mental faculties by increasingly subtle and complex machines. So, what is left of us?

What is left is that only we combine the emotions and the life cycle drama of the animal world with a fully empowered reflective and communicative faculty. No other animal has that faculty, and no machine has an animal bodily life. Other animals can communicate, but they do not exchange views on the rightness or wrongness of their emotions. Machines can network and think, but they cannot discuss their fear of dying. What religious people think of as the soul or spirit can perhaps be fairly said to consist of just this: the intelligence of an advanced machine in the mortal brain and body of an animal. And what we call culture is a collective way of using that intelligence to express and modify the emotions of that brain, the impulse and pain and exhilaration of that body. Both the intelligence and the impulse, the communicative capability and the pain, are components of human nature, and the way they interact is the unique feature of that nature. Without conceding the existence of human nature, without describing it as forthrightly and richly as possible, we will never fully exercise that crucial feature, which alone holds the prospect of an admittedly limited but absolutely imperative transcendence.

REFERENCES

Arling, G. L., and H. F. Harlow. "Effects of Social Deprivation on Maternal Behavior of Rhesus Monkeys," *Journal of Comparative and Physiological Psychology* 64 (1967): 371–377.

Baron, M., N. Risch, R. Hamburger, B. Mandel, S. Kushner, M. Newman, D. Drumer, and R. H. Belmaker. "Genetic Linkage between X-chromosome Markers and Bipolar Affective Illness," *Nature* 326 (1987): 289–292.

Barry, H., III, and L. Paxson. "Infancy and Early Childhood: Cross-cultural Codes," 2. *Ethnology* 10 (1971).

Betzig, L. L. *Despotism and Differential Reproduction: A Darwinian View of History.* New York: Aldine, 1986.

Bowlby, J. *Attachment and Loss.* 3 vols. London: Hogarth Press, 1969–1977.

Changeux, J.-P. *Neuronal Man: The Biology of Mind.* New York: Oxford University Press, 1985.

Cheney, D., R. Seyfarth, and B. Smuts. "Social Relationships and Social Cognition in Nonhuman Primates," *Science* 234 (1986): 1361.

Ciochon, R. L., and J. G. Fleagle, eds. *Primate Evolution and Human Origins.* New York: Aldine de Gruyter, 1987.

Dahlberg, Frances, ed. *Woman the Gatherer.* New Haven: Yale University Press, 1981.

Daly, Martin, and Margo Wilson. *Sex, Evolution, and Behavior.* 2d ed. Boston: Willard Grant, 1983.

Delabar, M., D. Goldgaber, Y. Lamour, A. Nicole, J. Huret, J. De Grouchy, P. Brown, D. C. Gajdusek, and P. Sinet. "b Amyloid Gene Duplication in Alzheimer's Disease and Karyotypically Normal Down Syndrome," *Science* 235 (1987): 1390–1392.

Eibl-Eibesfeldt, I. *Human Ethology.* New York: Aldine Press, 1988. (Translation of *Die Biologie des Menschlichen Verhaltens: Grundriss der Humanethologie.* Munich: Piper, 1984.)

Freud, S. *A General Introduction to Psychoanalysis.* New York: Washington Square Press, 1920.

Galaburda, A. M., and T. L. Kemper. "Cytoarchitectonic Abnormalities in Developmental Dyslexia: A Case Study," *Ann. Neurol.* 6 (1979): 94–100.

Geschwind, N., and A. M. Galaburda. "Cerebral Lateralization: Biological Mechanisms, Associations, and Pathology: A Hypothesis and a Program for Research, Pts. I, II, III. *Arch. Neurol.* 42 (1985): 428–459, 521–552, 634–654.

———. *Cerebral Lateralization.* Cambridge: MIT Press, 1987.

Goldgaber, D., M. I. Lerman, O. W. McBride, U. Saffiotti, and D. C. Gajdusek. "Characterization and Chromosomal Localization of a cDNA Encoding Brain Amyloid of Alzheimer's Disease," *Science* 235 (1987): 877–880.

Goldman-Rakic, P. S., A. Isseroff, M. L. Schwartz, and N. M. Bugbee. "The Neurobiology of Cognitive Development," in P. H. Mussen, M. M. Haith, and J. J. Campos, eds., *The Handbook of Child Psychology. Vol. 2: Infancy and Developmental Psychobiology.* New York: John Wiley & Sons, 1983, 281–344.

Goodall, J. *The Chimpanzees of Gombe: Patterns of Behavior.* Cambridge: Harvard University Press, 1986.

Gusella, J. F., R. E. Tanzi, M. A. Anderson, W. Hobbs, K. Gibbons, R. Raschtchian, T. C. Gilliam, M. R. Wallace, N. S. Wexler, and P. M. Conneally. "DNA Markers for Nervous System Diseases," *Science* 225 (1984): 1320–1326.

Hamilton, W. D. "The Genetical Evolution of Social Behavior, I & II," *Journal of Theoretical Biology* 7 (1964): 1–16, 17–52.

Harding, C. F., and B. K. Follett. "Hormone Changes Triggered by Aggression in a Natural Population of Blackbirds," *Science* 203 (1979): 918–920.

Harlow, H. F. "The Maternal Affectional System," in B. M. Foss, ed., *Determinants of Infant Behavior.* Vol. 2. London: Methuen, 1963.

———. "Age-mate or Peer Affectional System," in D. Lehrman, R. Hinde, and E. Shaw, eds., *Advances in the Study of Behavior.* Vol. 2. New York: Academic Press, 1969.

Hrdy, S. B. *The Langurs of Abu: Female and Male Strategies of Reproduction.* Cambridge: Harvard University Press, 1977.

Imperato-McGinley, J., R. E. Peterson, T. Gautier, and E. Sturla. "Androgens and the Evolution of Male-Gender Identity among Male Pseudohermaphrodites with 5a-Reductase Deficiency," *The New England Journal of Medicine* 300 (1979): 1233–1270. Also in S. Chase and A. Thomas, eds., *Annual Progress in Child Psychiatry and Child Development.* New York: Brunner/Mazel, 1980.

Kagan, J. "The Uses of Cross-Cultural Research in Early Development," in T. H. Leiderman, S. R. Tulkin, and A. Rosenfeld, eds., *Culture and Infancy.* New York: Academic Press, 1977.

———. *The Nature of the Child.* New York: Basic Books, 1984.

Kagan, J., and R. E. Klein. "Cross-Cultural Perspectives on Early Development," *American Psychologist* 28 (1973): 947–961.

Konner, M. J. "Evolution of Human Behavior Development," in R. L. Munro, R. Munro, and B. Whiting, eds., *Handbook of Cross-Cultural Development.* New York: Garland Press, 1981.

———. "Biological Aspects of Mother-Infant Bond," in R. Emde and R. Harmon, eds., *Development of Attachment and Affiliative Processes.* New York: Plenum, 1982a.

———. *The Tangled Wing: Biological Constraints on the Human Spirit.* New York: Holt, Rinehart, Winston, 1982b. (Harper & Row paperback, 1983.)

———. "Universals of Psychosocial Growth in Relation to Brain Myelination," in A. Petersen and K. Gibson, eds., *Brain Development and Social Behavior.* New York: Aldine-DeGruyter, 1991.

Kurland, J. A. "Paternity, Mother's Brother, and Human Sociality," in N. A. Chagnon and W. Irons, eds., *Evolutionary Biology and Human Social Behavior.* North Scituate, Mass.: Duxbury, 1979, 145–180.

LeBoeuf, B., and R. S. Peterson. "Social Status and Mating Activity in Elephant Seals," *Science* 163 (1969): 91–93.

Lee, R., and I. DeVore. *Man the Hunter.* Chicago: Aldine, 1968.

Maccoby, E. E., and C. N. Jacklin. *The Psychology of Sex Differences.* Stanford: Stanford University Press, 1974.

MacLean, P. D. "Brain Evolution Relating to Family, Play, and the Separation Call," *Arch. Gen. Psychiatry* 42 (1985): 405.

Magnus, R. *Goethe as a Scientist.* New York: Henry Schuman, 1949.

Mason, A. J., J. S. Hayflick, R. T. Zoeller, W. S. Young, III, H. S. Phillips, K. Nikolics, and P. H. Seeburg. "A Deletion Truncating the Gonadotropin-Releasing Hormone Gene Is Responsible for Hypogonadism in the hpg Mouse," *Science* 234 (1986): 1366–1371.

Mason, A. J., S. L. Pitts, K. Nikolics, E. Szonyi, J. N. Wilcox, P. H. Seeburg, and T. A. Stewart. "The Hypogonadal Mouse: Reproductive Functions Restored by Gene Therapy," *Science* 234 (1986): 1372–1378.

McKusick, V. *Mendelian Inheritance in Man.* 7th ed. Baltimore: Johns Hopkins University Press, 1986.

Munroe, R. H., R. L. Munroe, and B. B. Whiting. *Handbook of Cross-Cultural Human Development.* Chicago: Garland STPM Press, 1981.

Murdock, G. P. *Ethnographic Atlas: A Summary.* Pittsburgh: University of Pittsburgh Press, 1967.

Napier, J., and P. H. Napier. *The Natural History of the Primates.* Cambridge: MIT Press, 1985.

Nemiah, J. "Chapter 20: The Neuroses," in H. Kaplan and B. Sadock, eds., *Comprehensive Textbook of Psychiatry.* 4th ed. Baltimore: Williams and Wilkins, 1985.

Plomin, R., J. C. DeFries, and G. E. McClearn. *Behavioral Genetics: A Primer.* San Francisco: Freeman, 1980.

———. *Development, Genetics, and Psychology.* Hillsdale, N.J.: Lawrence Erlbaum Associates, 1986.

Sackett, G. P., G. C. Ruppenthal, C. E. Fahrenbruch, and R. A. Holm. "Social Isolation Rearing Effects in Monkeys Vary with Genotype," *Developmental Psychology* 17 (1981): 313–318.

Scarr, S., and K. K. Kidd. "Developmental Behavioral Genetics," in P. H. Mussen, M. M. Haith, and J. J. Campos, eds., *The Handbook of Child Psychology. Vol. 2: Infancy and Developmental Psychobiology.* New York: John Wiley & Sons, 1983, 345–433.

St. George-Hyslop, P. H., R. E. Tanzi, R. J. Polinsky, J. L. Haines, L. Nee, P. C. Watkins, R. H. Myers, R. G. Feldman, D. Pollen, D. Drachman, J. Growdon, A. Bruni, J. Foncin, D. Salmon, P. Frommelt, L. Amaducci, S. Sorbi, S. Placentini, G. D. Stewart, W. J. Hobbs, P. M. Conneally, and J. F. Gusella. "The Genetic Defect Causing Familial Alzheimer's Disease Maps on Chromosome 21," *Science* 235 (1987): 885–890.

Scheller, R. H., R. Kaldany, T. Kreiner, A. C. Mahon, J. R. Nambu, M. Schaefer, and R. Taussig. "Neuropeptides: Mediators of Behavior in Aplysia," *Science* 225 (1984): 1300–1308.

Shostak, M. *Nisa: The Life and Words of a !Kung Woman.* Cambridge: Harvard University Press, 1981.

Silk, J. "Adoption and Fosterage in Human Societies: Adaptations or Enigmas?" *Cultural Anthropology* 2 (1987): 39–49.

Smuts, B. *Sex and Friendship in Baboons.* New York: Aldine, 1985.

Stoller, R. J., and G. H. Herdt. "Theories of Origins of Male Homosexuality," *Arch. Gen. Psychiatry* 42 (1985): 399.

Tanouye, M. A., C. A. Kamb, L. E. Iverson, and L. Salkoff. "Genetics and Molecular Biology of Ionic Channels in Drosophila," *Annual Review Neuroscience* 9 (1986): 255–276.

Tanzi, R. E., J. F. Gusella, P. C. Watkins, G. A. P. Bruns, P. St. George-Hyslop, M. L. Van Keuren, D. Patterson, S. Pagan, D. M. Kurnit, and R. L. Neve.

"Amyloid b Protein Gene: cDNA, mRNA Distribution, and Genetic Linkage near the Alzheimer Locus," *Science* 235 (1987): 880–884.

Trivers, R. L. "Parental Investment and Sexual Selection," in B. Campbell, ed., *Sexual Selection and the Descent of Man, 1871–1971*. Chicago: Aldine, 1972.

———. "Parent-Offspring Conflict," *American Zoologist* 14 (1974): 249–264.

———. *Social Evolution*. Menlo Park: Benjamin Cummings, 1985.

Whiting, J. W. M., and B. B. Whiting. "Aloofness and Intimacy between Husbands and Wives," *Ethos* 3 (1975): 183.

Wilson, E. O. *Sociobiology: The New Synthesis*. Cambridge: Harvard University Press, 1975.

———. *On Human Nature*. Cambridge: Harvard University Press, 1978.

Zeibel, Morton, ed. *The Portable Henry James*. New York: Viking, 1951, 27.

SIX

Reflections on Biology and Culture

John Dupré

I shall concentrate here on Melvin Konner's essay (chap. 5) for a reason perhaps embarrassingly characteristic of professional philosophers: I disagree with a great deal of it. However, Arnold Davidson, Harriet Ritvo, and Evelyn Fox Keller all help to illustrate central points underlying my dissent from some of Konner's claims, so I shall briefly try to bring out some of these general points before turning to my main task of dissent.

Let me begin with some very general remarks that apply to both Ritvo's and Davidson's contributions. As a general theoretical proposition, it would now be quite widely agreed that how we understand both ourselves and nature must depend considerably on our general theoretical beliefs. Despite major differences in subject matter and approach, I take both Ritvo and Davidson to be offering, among other things, more specific illustrations of this general truth.

But it is not just the understanding of, or, in the case of Davidson's subject matter, the affective response to, phenomena that is liable to such influences but even what we take to be the phenomena themselves. Many of Davidson's monsters, I take it, were quite widely supposed to actually exist, and their existence offered a variety of explanatory etiologies. The unpleasant demise of Davidson's masturbators is not merely asserted but described in amazing detail. In Ritvo's sources, the importance of bovine virtue is not merely assumed, detailed "factual" reports of the alarming consequences of its absence are offered. The "telegonic" effects of previous sexual partners on female animals are illustrated with numerous anecdotal instances.

These observations provide a useful background for my main focus: How far do such historical observations mandate skepticism about our current theories and even alleged facts? In particular, how much skepticism is properly suggested about our current theories about animals and the consequences of these for our theories of ourselves as animals? The answer, I shall suggest later, is a good deal.

Ritvo's essay not only suggests the appropriateness of such skepticism but also indicates a particular ground. The tendency to see views of ourselves reflected in nature, the "projections" she so clearly documents, has also been suggested for more contemporary theories—as, indeed, we can see in Keller's essay, to which I shall return shortly.

There are obvious difficulties in relating historical lessons to critiques of contemporary beliefs. The opinions that Ritvo and Davidson recount strike us as ludicrous and either comical or grotesque. We have our own theories that we take to be if not amply demonstrated, at least sufficiently so to reveal the complete untenability of these historical views. Consequently, the conclusion that these views are projections of prejudices about ourselves onto animals has no serious contender. When we come to consider contemporary beliefs, however, particularly those that carry our highest epistemological honorific, "scientific," we have no such alternative and accepted standpoint from which to launch such a critique.

But as Keller has persuasively illustrated, this does not mean that clear grounds for such a critique cannot, nevertheless, be provided. I think there is considerable force to the objections Keller raises to contemporary evolutionary theory. Since I cannot possibly recapitulate the intricacies of her argument here, I shall make just one further observation in support of her conclusion. Contemporary theorists of the evolution of social behavior often assert that the central problem in their field is, or if they believe it to have been solved, was, the possibility of altruism. (Needless to say, altruism is a concept like competition that allows considerable equivocal play between technical and colloquial usages.) There are, of course, compelling reasons internal to evolutionary theory for perceiving altruism as a major problem. Nevertheless, if one is at all inclined to skepticism about the absolute objectivity of scientific theory, this must surely add plausibility to the contention that evolutionary theory recapitulates a traditional image of Hobbesian man.

There remain major questions that, I think, Keller's account raises but does not answer. In particular, I have in mind questions about the exact source of the individualistic ideology Keller describes. More specifically, I see two rather different, though perhaps not incompatible, sources of this individualism. Keller's main suggestion, in line with a point emphasized earlier in these remarks, is that we project views of human society onto the animal world; views, that is, of Hobbesian man or now, perhaps, *Homo economicus var. Chicagoensis*. However, the individualism she describes is also an example of what I take to be a more general methodological prejudice in science. I have in mind reductionism, or the general belief that the behavior of complex entities must be understood wholly in terms of the properties of their constituent parts.[1] Perhaps this methodological assumption should itself be understood as a more far-reaching projection of social philosophy onto the entirety of nature. If not, the relation between these positions is something that will require further exploration for a fuller understanding of these issues.

Keller, to return to my main thread, provides strong evidence that the dangers of projection of social ideology onto the natural world have relevance to our evaluation of contemporary as well as historical ideas. Konner, by contrast, has a very different kind of project embodying a more complacent view of science: he encourages us to understand ourselves better by applying to ourselves the lessons that we have learned from our study of other animals. Since I take it we may all agree that we are, among other things, animals, this suggestion surely has something to commend it. However, the work of Ritvo and Keller should make clear a major danger inherent in such a project. To whatever extent our understanding of animals does involve a projection onto them of antecedent views about ourselves, the attempt to understand ourselves by applying our knowledge of animals will complete a small and unilluminating circle. (I think there is a close analogy here with Terry Winograd's cautions about the use of machines as a route to understanding ourselves.) In fact, I believe that it is just this methodological problem, rather than the often very confused debate about the existence of "human nature," that is central to the accusation that human sociobiology, the most conspicuous contemporary attempt to illuminate human nature by appeal to more general biological theory, functions, in large part, as a rhetorical device for the defense of conservative ideology.[2]

As I have already confessed, I disagree with a good deal of Konner's argument. Even if this reflects no more than my own ideological biases, that itself would provide some evidence that even the evaluation of up-to-date scientific ideas is susceptible to such bias. Konner presents his views with subtlety and sophistication, and I certainly cannot hope, in the space of these comments, to give a comparable defense of an opposing position. What I shall do, however, is briefly indicate three major points at which I disagree strongly with the views he expresses.

First, Konner asserts at the outset that "an organism is in essence a gene's way of making another gene." This is, of course, an extreme instance of the reductionism I mentioned above in discussing Keller's contribution.[3] I also think it is profoundly misleading, even false. The issues here are complex and somewhat technical, and I can do the least justice to this part of my dissent. I take the fundamental error to be the assumption that a gene, or even, for that matter, an organism (as Keller has argued), can be adequately characterized in isolation. Or more accurately, the gene that is characterized in terms of molecular biology cannot also be adequately described in terms of its phenotypic effects. Put simply, this is because the development of an organism involves enormously complex interactions between genes and with the environment, such that the question, what is the developmental upshot of a particular piece of DNA (such as an aquiline nose, or criminal tendencies)? is thoroughly ill-conceived.[4]

Konner is, of course, aware of these difficulties and remarks parenthetically that it is a confusion to suppose that the cohesiveness of the genome—that is, the enormously complex set of interactions between different genes and the environment in the development of an organism—has any but a quantitative bearing on the validity of this reductionistic premise. I believe he is mistaken. One way of seeing why this is so is to observe that given the incommensurability of the chemical and functional descriptions of genes, it is unclear that there is any interpretation of the term *gene* which could serve for an elaboration of Konner's Butlerian statement of the essence of an organism. As a matter of fact, this reductionistic slogan is generally offered as a consequence of speculations about the evolutionary process. But I think it is clear that if it cannot even be given ontogenetic sense, it has no chance at all of having a correct phylogenetic interpretation.[5] And finally, even if it were correct from both a developmental and an evolutionary perspective, there is a great deal more to an organism, especially a human one, than its ontogeny and phylogeny. I shall take up this remark again briefly at my conclusion.

My second main point ultimately concerns the role of language in science stressed by Keller and brings us back once more to the circle of projections with which I began this part of my commentary. Konner offers as support for the importance of biological considerations in understanding human behavior the claim that cultural anthropology has already discovered numerous cross-cultural universals. I suggest, on the contrary, that these divide exhaustively between the highly dubious and the irrelevant. In the latter category, I include examples such as coordinated bipedal walking and the reflexes of neonates. Certainly, I do not want to deny that human behavior is built on a substrate of (moderately) universal biological capacities. What are clearly more interesting are the universalistic claims about complex behaviors, and such claims I take to be uniformly dubious.

Let me illustrate the central problem with just one of Konner's examples. While admitting that the form is variable, he suggests that one significant universal—and hence presumably one that is to be taken to be grounded in biology—is the existence of marriage. But the variability of form, surely, is just the point. The question that needs to be asked is,

What is meant here by the word *marriage*? Certainly for us, in modern Western society, the term is weighed down with social, economic, and affective connotations. Without a clear statement of which of these are, and which are not, included in the alleged anthropological universal, such a claim can do nothing but mislead. Any sense of the word *marriage* thin enough to make the claim even approximately true will have, I suspect, very little to do with what we mean by the term.[6] (One is here not so far from—or at least on a slippery slope toward—the crude sociobiology that claims to observe "rape" in mallards or scorpionflies and concludes that rape must be "natural" for us.)[7] I would argue that *all* the interesting claims of this kind depend on just such oversimplistic uses of terms for complex social phenomena.

Third, and finally, I must take issue with the claims Konner makes about the genetic control of human behavior. At times, I must admit to being a little uncertain what these claims are. That there are "complex interactions of genotype, metabolism, and environment in the development of neural, behavioral, and mental phenomena" would be difficult to dispute. Yet I take it that the descriptions he offers of increasing scientific knowledge of genetically mediated mental disorders must be intended to show more than this. That these findings "remove any doubt regarding the ability of genes to alter complex behavior" suggests, if it does not strictly imply, that Konner has in mind the possibility of genetic control of complex behavior.[8]

At any rate, my objective here is not exegesis of Konner's essay. What does seem worth emphasizing is the utterly unsurprising character of the phenomena Konner draws to our attention and the absolute lack of any interesting conclusions about the determination of human behavior which follow from them. Like Konner, I think that "phenylketoneuria provides a valuable model." This, it will be recalled, is a genetic disorder that, in the absence of a specially controlled diet, results in massive toxicity to the brain and consequent psychological dysfunction. Apart from the banal fact that people with damaged or seriously abnormal brains are likely to behave strangely, it is very difficult to see what could follow from this. In particular, I cannot see that it tells us anything whatsoever about the relation between the genetically mediated development of the brain and mature human behavioral dispositions. To claim the contrary seems rather like concluding from the severe behavioral consequences of hitting someone over the head with a hammer that behavior must be determined to some important extent by an internal mechanism involving the action of miniature hammers. At the very least, not a shred of support is offered for hypotheses such as that there are genetic causes for, say, a predisposition to marriage.

Let me conclude on a more constructive note. I mentioned above that there was more to an organism, especially a human one, than phylogeny and ontogeny. In the human case, I cannot state better, or probably as well, what this is than Bernard Williams has done for us. The nature of a species, including our own, centrally includes its ethology; and the most striking and fundamental feature of human ethology is its existence within culture.

Without espousing some of the more excessive statements of cultural relativism, I think that the above fact requires that we take culture much more seriously than sociobiologists and their followers and apologists are generally prepared to do. A possible way of stating the consequences of so doing is the following.

We are inclined to suppose that because *Homo sapiens* is undoubtedly a perfectly respectable biological species, its universal properties must provide the fundamental insight into the nature and behavior of its members. But such taxonomic paralysis is just a form of essentialism, a traditional philosophical view almost uniformly rejected by contemporary theorists of biology.[9] If we reject essentialism, it is open to us to conclude, from the centrality of culture to human ethology and the great variability of culture, that for most purposes, *Homo sapiens* is much too broad and coarse a category for understanding human beings. We might more usefully think of humans not primarily as constituting one biological species but rather as composing many, no doubt overlapping, cultural species.[10]

NOTES

1. Reductionism, in the relevant sense, is described and defended at length by R. L. Causey in *The Unity of Science* (Dordrecht: D. Reidel, 1977). For further discussion and criticism, see my paper, "The Disunity of Science," *Mind* 92 (1983):321–346.

2. The currently definitive and most detailed demolition of human sociobiology is Philip Kitcher's *Vaulting Ambition: Sociobiology and the Quest for Human Nature* (Cambridge: Bradford Books/MIT Press, 1985). A good sense of the current state of scientific debate on the subject can be gleaned from the various comments on this work and Kitcher's replies in *Brain and Behavioral Sciences* 10 (March 1987). This also includes a précis of Kitcher's book.

3. The *locus classicus* for the defense of taking this slogan seriously is Richard Dawkins, *The Selfish Gene* (Oxford: Oxford University Press, 1976).

4. For the complexity of genetic interactions and the significance of this complexity, see Richard Lewontin, *The Genetic Basis of Evolutionary Change* (New York: Columbia University Press, 1974).

5. For a critique of "genetic selectionism," the idea that evolution should be conceived of as fundamentally concerned only with differential selection of genes, see E. Sober and R. C. Lewontin, "Artifact, Cause, and Genic Selection," *Philosophy of Science* 47(1982):157–180.

6. As his more extended presentation in *The Tangled Wing: Biological Constraints on the Human Spirit* (New York: Holt, Rinehart, Winston, 1982) makes clear, Konner is perfectly well aware of the facts of cultural variation. Our disagreement, I suppose, has to do entirely with how such facts are to be interpreted.

7. See, especially, David Barash, *The Whisperings Within* (London: Penguin, 1979). For a devastating critique of these arguments, see Anne Fausto-Sterling, *Myths of Gender: Biological Theories about Men and Women* (New York: Basic Books, 1985), esp. chap. 6.

8. Again, Konner's book *The Tangled Wing* confirms that his views on this topic are quite complex and sophisticated. But both here and there, he seems inclined to draw general conclusions that, to my mind, are entirely unwarranted by the kinds of facts he adduces.

9. See, e.g., David L. Hull, "The Effect of Essentialism on Taxonomy: 2000 Years of Stasis," *British Journal for Philosophy of Science* 15 (1965):314–326, 16 (1965):1–18; for a more general critique of essentialism, see my "Sex, Gender, and Essence," *Midwest Studies in Philosophy,* 11 (1986):441–457.

10. This suggestion is developed in more detail in my paper, "Human Kinds," in J. Dupré, ed., *The Latest on the Best: Essays on Evolution and Optimality* (Cambridge: Bradford Books/MIT Press, 1987).

PART TWO

Humans and Machines

SEVEN

Introduction

James J. Sheehan

There has always been a metaphorical connection between technology and nature. People have often looked to the natural world for images to help them understand social, political, and cultural developments, just as they have often imposed on nature images taken from human affairs. The character of natural and mechanical metaphors has changed over time. The boundary between nature and machine has sometimes been redrawn. But it is only recently that we have been able to imagine machines complex enough to be like humans and humans predictable enough to be like machines.

In the ancient and medieval worlds, what David Bolter calls the "defining technology" was not a mechanical device but rather some fairly simple form of manual production. When Plato looked for a metaphor to describe the way the universe functions, he spoke of a "spindle of necessity" with which the fates spin human destiny into the world. In the *Timaeus,* he compared the creator of the universe to a carpenter and a potter. Only in the seventeenth century, with the rise of a new cosmology, did the most important technological metaphors become mechanical rather than manual. The clock replaced the carpenter's lathe or the potter's wheel as a way of understanding how the universe operated. Like a clock, the universe was thought to be at once complex and comprehensible, a mechanism set in motion by a divine maker who, quite unlike the potter at his wheel, gave his creation the power to operate without his constant supervision.[1]

Just as the Greeks sometimes imagined that the gods had made living things from clay, so people in the mechanical age thought that some living things were no more than complex machines. This view was given

135

its most influential formulation by Descartes, who stands at the intersection of humanity's changing relationship to animals and machines. As we saw in the introduction to Part I, Humans and Animals, Descartes believed that animals were merely automata made of flesh. Even human activities that were not guided by reason could be seen as mechanical: "the beating of the heart, the digestion of our food, nutrition, respiration when we are asleep, and even walking, singing, and similar acts when we are awake, if performed without the mind attending to them." Such opinions would not, Descartes continued, "seem strange to those who know how many different automata or moving machines can be made by the industry of man." But, of course, Descartes did not think that humans were merely mechanical. The possession of reason opened a fundamental gap between humanity and machines—as well as between humanity and animals.[2]

In the eighteenth century, at the same time that some thinkers had begun to wonder if the gap between humans and animals was as fundamental as Descartes insisted, others called into question the basic distinction between humans and machines. The classic expression of this position was *L'Homme machine*, published by Julien Offray de La Mettrie in 1747. As his title suggests, La Mettrie believed that humans were no less machinelike than animals. "From animals to men," he wrote, "the transition is not extraordinary." In blunt, provocative language, La Mettrie argued that mind and body were equally mechanical: "the brain has muscles to think, as the legs have to walk." But he did not have much to say about how mental mechanisms actually worked. His epistemology, which emphasized the power of imagination, had little connection with his notion of brain muscles. In effect, *L'Homme machine* was what one scholar has called "a picturable analogy" of the mind, a "*modus cognoscendi*, designed to promote scientific inquiry, rather than any ultimate knowledge about the nature of things."[3]

In the nineteenth century, a great deal was learned about the body's physiological mechanisms. Research on chemistry and biology enabled scientists to understand how the body functioned like a steam engine—the machine that had replaced the clock as the era's "defining technology." Researchers believed that this knowledge of physiological mechanisms was part of a single scientific enterprise that would embrace the study of all matter, living and nonliving. "Physiology," Wilhelm Wundt maintained, "thus appears as a branch of applied physics, its problems being a reduction of vital phenomena to general physical laws, and thus ultimately to the fundamental laws of mechanics." Such laws, some maintained, explained mental no less than physical phenomena. Edward Youmans, for example, an American disciple of Herbert Spencer, regarded the First Law of Thermodynamics as extending from the farthest galaxies into the hidden recesses of the mind:

> Star and nerve-tissue are parts of the system—stellar and nervous forces are correlated. Nay more; sensation awakens thought and kindles emotion, so that this wondrous dynamic chain binds into living unity the realms of matter and mind through measureless amplitudes of space and time.

The chain of being, once a hierarchy of existence forged by divine decree, thus becomes a unified domain subject to the same physical laws.[4]

Within certain limits, the nineteenth century's mechanical metaphors were useful tools for understanding physiological phenomena like respiration and digestion. But these metaphors worked much less well when applied to the mind. To be sure, experimental psychologists learned to measure some kinds of perceptions and responses, and neurologists did important work on the structure of the brain; but it was difficult to imagine mechanisms complex and versatile enough to approximate mental activities. Nor could anyone come close to building a machine that could perform anything but the most rudimentary calculations. In the 1830s, for example, Charles Babbage failed in the attempt to manufacture an "analytical engine" that would be able to "think" mathematically. Because he did not have the technological means to perform the functions he had ingeniously contrived, Babbage remained "a brilliant aberration, a prophet of the electronic age in the heyday of the steam engine."[5]

Until well into the twentieth century, those who believed that the brain functioned mechanically had great difficulty describing just how these mental mechanisms worked. One product of these difficulties was behavioralism, perhaps the dominant school of empirical psychology in the early twentieth century, which denied that the nature of mental states was knowable and concentrated instead on studying behavioral responses to stimuli. In the 1920s, when a new controversy erupted over the concept of "l'homme machine," it was fought out on largely biological rather than psychological grounds. Joseph Needham, who took the La Mettrian position in this debate, acknowledged that his mechanistic view of human nature was no more than a "methodological fiction," even though he believed that "in science, man is a machine; or if he is not, then he is nothing at all." Given the sort of machines that Needham could imagine in 1928, it is not surprising that he could not find one that much resembled the mental world of human beings.[6]

All this changed with the coming of the computer. The theoretical and technological basis for the computer was laid in the 1930s by Alan Turing and others, but it was only after the Second World War that these machines moved from the realm of highly technical speculation to the

center of both scientific research and popular culture. Computers, unlike the crude calculating machines of the past, seemed fast, complex,
and supple enough to approximate real thought. The gap between mind
and machine seemed to be narrowing. For example, in 1949, Norbert
Wiener published his influential work on "Cybernetics," which he defined as "the entire field of control and communication theory, whether
in the machine or in the animal." That same year, John von Neumann,
who had built a rudimentary computer in Princeton, pointed out the
similarities between the computer and the brain. Two years later, in an
essay entitled "Computing Machinery and Intelligence," Turing predicted that within fifty years there would be machines that could perfectly imitate human intelligence.[7]

So swiftly did the use of computers spread that by the 1960s, they had
become our "defining technology," as fundamental to the way we view
ourselves and our worlds as Plato's crafts or Descartes's clockwork mechanisms had been to theirs. We now live in the era of "Turing's Man,"
whose relationship with machines Bolter summarizes in the following
telling phrase: "By making a machine think as a man, man re-creates
himself, defines himself as a machine."[8]

Computers played an essential role in the formulation of cognitive
science, which Howard Gardner defines as the "empirically based effort
to answer long-standing epistemological questions—particularly those
concerned with the nature of knowledge, its components, its sources, its
development, and its deployment." In the last two decades, this way of
looking at the mind has tended to replace behavioralism as the most
vigorous branch of empirical psychology. In the light of what computer
scientists claimed about the way their machines worked, the behavioralists' self-imposed refusal to talk about mental states no longer
seemed either necessary or desirable. As George Miller, who observed
the shift away from behavioralism, recalled,

> The engineers showed us how to build a machine that has memory, a
> machine that has purpose, a machine that plays chess, a machine that can
> detect signals in the presence of noise, and so on. If they can do that, then
> the kind of things they say about machines, a psychologist should be permit-
> ted to say about a human being.

Cognitive scientists insisted that they could open the so-called black box,
which behavioralists believed concealed the mental connection between
stimulus and response. Within this box, many were now convinced, they
would find something very much like a computer.[9]

Research on what came to be known as "artificial intelligence" began
during the exciting early days of the computer revolution, when the
technology's potential seemed without limit. The following statement,

from an article published in 1958 by Herbert Simon and Allen Newell, provides a good example of the style and tone with which the new field was announced:

> It is not my aim to surprise or shock you. . . . But the simplest way I can summarize is to say that there are now in the world machines that think, that learn and that create. Moreover, their ability to do these things is going to increase rapidly until—in a visible future—the range of problems they can handle will be coextensive with the range to which the human mind has been applied.

La Mettrie had declared that humans were machines but could say little about how these machines worked. Nineteenth-century physiologists could imagine the human body as a "heat engine," which converted fuel into growth and activities. To the advocates of artificial intelligence, the computer finally provided a mechanism comparable to the mind: to them, "intelligent beings are semantic engines—in other words, automatic formal systems with interpretations under which they consistently make sense." Marvin Minsky put the matter much less elegantly when, in what would become an infamous phrase, he defined the mind as a "meat machine."[10]

Artificial intelligence draws on several disciplines and contains a variety of different elements. It is, in the words of one of its practitioners, "a field renowned for its lack of consensus on fundamental issues." For our purposes, two intradisciplinary divisions seem especially important. The first is the difference between "strong" and "weak" artificial intelligence. The former (vigorously exemplified by Newell's essay in this volume) argues for the potential identity of mind and machine; the latter is content with seeing computers as models or metaphors for certain kinds of mental activities. The second division is rather more complex since it involves two different ways of thinking about and building intelligent machines. The one (and again, Newell is a fine example) seeks to define a sequential set of rules through which the computer can approximate— or duplicate—the workings of the mind. This perspective, which draws its philosophical inspiration from Descartes's belief in the possibility of defining certain rules of thought, builds on concepts first developed by Turing and von Neumann. Sherry Turkle calls the other approach to artificial intelligence "emergent AI," which includes "connectionist" models as well as models based on the idea of a "society of mind." Modeled on assumptions about neural operations in the brain, this approach emphasizes parallel operations rather than sequences, the storing and manipulation of individual pieces of information rather than the formulation of general rules. While both branches of artificial intelligence developed at about the same time, the former became dominant in the 1970s and early 1980s, while the latter seems to have become increasingly influential after 1984.[11]

Like sociobiology, artificial intelligence has been attacked from several directions—as philosophically naive, methodologically careless, and politically dangerous. Terry Winograd's essay suggests some of these criticisms, to which we will return in the conclusion. Critics like Winograd argue that fulfilling the promises made during the early days of cognitive science has turned out to be much more difficult than Turing and his contemporaries had believed. Changing the scale and broadening the scope of what a computer can do have involved conceptual and technological problems few of the pioneers envisioned. Nevertheless, no one doubts that computer scientists have made great progress on a number of fronts. Moreover, given the unpredictable course of scientific progress, it is hard to say what is and what is not possible. After all, as two scientists have recently written, computer experts have "the whole future" in which to show that intelligent machines can be created. Doubts about the feasibility of artificial intelligence, therefore, can lead to skepticism, not categorical rejection.[12]

A categorical denial that it will ever be possible to build machines that can think like humans can rest on two foundations. The first requires a belief in some spiritual attribute that separates humans from machines—and in Western culture at least, from animals as well. The second is based not on our possession of a soul but rather of a body: according to this line of argument, which is suggested in Stuart Hampshire's concluding remarks to this section, being human is inseparable from the feelings and perceptions that come from our physical existence. Without that knowledge of our own birth and death, a knowledge central to our conceptions of past, present, and future, any intelligence, no matter how skilled at solving certain sorts of problems, must remain essentially and unalterably different from our own. Melvin Konner makes this point by comparing the machines of the future to the gods of ancient Greece: "incredibly powerful and even capable of many human emotions—but because of their immortality, ineligible for admission into that warm circle of sympathy reserved exclusively for humans."[13]

NOTES

1. J. David Bolter, *Turing's Man: Western Culture in the Computer Age* (Chapel Hill: University of North Carolina Press, 1984), 11, 22.

2. Anthony Kenny, *Descartes: A Study of his Philosophy* (New York: Garland, 1968), 200–201.

3. Aram Vartanian, *La Mettrie's 'L'homme machine': A Study in the Origins of an Idea* (Princeton: Princeton University Press, 1960), 14, 16, 22, 25.

4. Cynthia Russett, *Sexual Science: The Victorian Construction of Womanhood* (Cambridge: Harvard University Press, 1989), 106–107.

5. Bolter, *Turing's Man*, 33.

6. Vartanian, *La Mettrie's 'L'homme machine,'* 132–134.

7. Howard Gardner, *The Mind's New Science: A History of the Cognitive Revolution* (New York: Basic Books, 1987), 20.

8. Bolter, *Turing's Man*, 13.

9. Gardner, *Mind's New Science*, 6; Miller quoted by Sherry Turkle, "Artificial Intelligence and Psychoanalysis: A New Alliance," in Stephen Graubard, ed., *The Artificial Intelligence Debate: False Starts, Real Foundations* (Cambridge: MIT Press, 1988), 242.

10. Hubert L. Dreyfus and Stuart E. Dreyfus, "Making a Mind versus Modeling the Brain: Artificial Intelligence Back at a Branchpoint," in Graubard, ed., *Artificial Intelligence Debate*, 19.

11. Gardner, *Mind's New Science*, 141. On shifting trends within AI, see the essays in Graubard.

12. Anya Hurlbert and Tomaso Poggio, "Making Machines (and Artificial Intelligence) See," in Graubard, ed., *Artificial Intelligence Debate*, 238.

13. Konner, "On Human Nature: Love Among the Robots," *The Sciences* 27 (1987): 14.

EIGHT

The Meaning of the Mechanistic Age

Roger Hahn

The late Eduard J. Dijksterhuis of Utrecht coined the term "Mechaniza-tion of the World Picture" to characterize the nature of the intellectual revolution that emerged triumphant in the seventeenth century. In his pathbreaking work, written close to forty years ago, he repeatedly re-fuses to provide a static definition for his central conception, choosing instead to describe it by showing how it emerged from a rediscovery and recombination of certain key strands of Greek natural philosophy in the late Renaissance and how it was centrally shaped by the success of Galileo and Kepler's new astronomy, Descartes's and Huygens's new philosophy of physics, and Newton's grand synthesis at the end of the century.

Conceptions of the world picture since the seventeenth century have admittedly never been the same. The Aristotelian universe of essential qualities and goal-directed forms apparently was displaced by the new mechanistic philosophy. For the last forty years, that transformation, known to historians by the shorthand label of the Scientific Revolution, has been chronicled, its origins have been established, and its character has been the subject of dozens of major monographs. Curiously enough, the issues Dijksterhuis broached but refused to settle have never been fully analyzed from a modern perspective. My concern is to offer some suggestions for finding a meaning for this Mechanistic Age which rests on historically sound grounds. That meaning requires special attention because "mechanistic" is the common epithet hurled at "reductionists." They are often crudely charged with a desire to eliminate the study of living beings by grounding them exclusively on the physical sciences. If we proceed with a historical analysis, we will see that the label "mechanis-tic" carries with it other substantial implications.

Perhaps the biggest obstacle to arriving at a full appreciation of the notion is in fact for us to remain captive of too strict a chronological view. Historians of science—and I must include myself among the guilty ones—have, through their decades of refining the meaning and arguing about the temporal limits of the Scientific Revolution, locked themselves into a much too narrow identification of the Mechanistic Age with this movement. It behooves us first to clear away these constricting and ultimately misleading views of the Scientific Revolution to permit reaching for a more encompassing meaning.

The current notion of the Scientific Revolution, though it has a history that would take us back to the eighteenth century, is in fact the by-product of a set of lectures given at Cambridge in 1948 by the late Sir Herbert Butterfield, eventually published under the title, *The Origins of Modern Science*. That notion was successfully elaborated by a group of major scholars that includes the aforementioned Dijksterhuis and my teachers and colleagues Alexandre Koyré, Marie Boas, her husband, A. Rupert Hall, Paolo Casini, I. Bernard Cohen, Thomas Kuhn, and most recently, Richard S. Westfall. They and their followers all suffer from a common historic myopia, namely, the unitary identification of the momentous Revolution with the "Mechanical Philosophy" and the conviction that its culmination came in the person of Sir Isaac Newton, whose *Philosophiae Naturalis Principia Mathematica* is justly hailed. As a consequence of this shortsighted view, historians have too rigidly equated the Scientific Revolution with the advent of a Mechanistic Age and struggled to confine its development to the seventeenth century, principally in an English context appropriate to Sir Isaac.

An oversimplified view of their argument runs somewhat as follows. Following on the almost simultaneous discovery in 1609 by Kepler of the ellipticity of planetary orbits and by Galileo of the physical imperfections of celestial bodies like the Moon and Jupiter seen in his telescope, progressive natural philosophers were forced one by one to abandon Aristotelian and Ptolemaic dicta concerning the cosmos. In the next decades, the old order was shattered beyond repair by a flood of opinions that included a devastating critique of Peripatetic concepts about the closed universe structured around a central point and its attendant terrestrial physics based on the idea that motion was determined by essential qualities residing in substance. The separation of the cosmos into a world of heavenly perfection and earthly imperfection which mirrored Christian beliefs, and of the correspondence between the microcosm of man and the macrocosm of the universe, was recognized as obsolete and jettisoned as misleading. Critical philosophers like Bacon and Descartes ridiculed assumptions about the erroneous grounds on which the older epistemology was based and began to proclaim a new philosophic order.

By the 1630s, its building blocks had been individually assembled: a new philosophy of mathematical cogency, often coupled with experimental confirmation; the postulation of a corpuscular ontology that focused on quantifiable elements and mechanisms immediately apprehended by the eye and the mind; infinite, isotropic space that was indifferent to the nature of the objects placed in it and hence stripped of hierarchical values taken for granted by traditional religious authorities. By the end of the seventeenth century, so the official line runs, all these pieces were brilliantly assembled into the Newtonian system of the world with its universal laws of motion, its new metaphysic of inert matter, absolute space and time, and the proclamation of a new progressive epistemology of the mathematical and experimental natural philosophy. Moreover, it is pointed out, Newton found it possible to incorporate a modified set of Christian values about the Lord into his mechanical and corpuscular system so that it would continue to reflect the harmony and power of the deity in the cosmos. Sir Isaac returned the favor of his prophetic birth on Christmas Day, 1642, by lending his genius to the Almighty to "save" the cosmos for Christianity. You will surely recall Pope's famous couplet that expresses the blessings Western civilization received when "Nature and nature's laws hid in night: / God said, let Newton be! and all was Light."

What is wrong with this interpretation from our perspective? It evades larger historic issues by giving a narrow, temporal, and geographic location to the Scientific Revolution, assuming it to coincide with the process of the mechanization of the cosmos. Ideas as profound and important as mechanisms have both roots and consequences that cannot be confined to seventeenth-century England. In saying this, I do not advocate the fashioning of a counterthesis, merely the decoupling of the concepts. Today as well as in the seventeenth century, in the world of Western civilization, whether it is found in Israel, Japan, or Merry Old England, we mainly operate with the assumptions of the Mechanistic Age. Let me elaborate.

The notion of the mechanical involves quite a few dimensions that, for the sake of analysis, I would like to display singly, keeping in mind that they are historically and conceptually interlinked.

First is the machine itself, with its internal workings displayed for all to apprehend. While it was principally articulated after the invention and with the help of printing, the machine was no newcomer to the Renaissance. Every civilization fashions more or less elaborate tools to cope with nature, but few had given them such a special place as did the Hellenistic Greeks and their Roman followers. Engines of war and construction were at first merely described with words and their principles laid down using terminology common to natural philosophers by major figures like Archimedes. Already in the third century B.C., it was axiomatic that their functioning was based on a geometric understanding of physical principles, in which number, proportion, size, and configuration were critical and for which the strength of materials and thermal forces responsible for expansion and contraction provided an essential explanatory component. Simple laws of leverage and the schemes for multiplying mechanical advantages by the use of the wedge, pulleys, and gears were well understood by engineers like Philo of Byzantium and Hero of Alexandria who used them to make sense of the common machines of antiquity.

But the Greeks also developed mechanical principles to serve quite different ends. They fashioned automata, that is, self-moving objects dressed up to resemble and imitate the operations generally ascribed to willful agents. One finds described singing birds activated by water pressure, temple doors that open in response to the lighting of fires, puppet shows representing shipyard workers, and mixing vessels that seem to be filled mysteriously as they are visibly being emptied. Such elaborate toys, popular in the Byzantine world, built to astound the spectator rather than enlighten him, are a testimony of the genius of ancient craftsmen.[1] But they also testify to the ancients' use of machines to glorify their own ability to penetrate nature's secrets and to mystify the gullible public by the fashioning of *mirabilia*. They are part of an ancient and tenacious thaumaturgic tradition. All the mechanisms to produce these effects are carefully hidden from view so as to increase the sense of the marvelous.

In ancient times, such automata were not built as mechanical models to *explain* living beings; they existed merely to imitate nature the way that an ancient artist would strive to copy and reproduce natural occurrences. A measure of the prowess of the artisan was his ability to reproduce in the most faithful way possible the natural processes we experience. Prior to the advent of Christianity, nature was worshiped because it encompassed such wonders; man's accomplishments would be measured by his ability to mimic life, not to make it serve his secular purposes. In the rare instances we know about, the Greek mechanist was proud to have outdone nature by feats of trickery, often executed by use of mirrors, by which the right and left might be transposed from their natural order or by which small objects might be magnified by placing them under a distorting glass object.

What differentiates this use of the mechanical artifact from the post-Renaissance version is the emphasis on secret processes, the reveling in the mysterious ways of nature. Mysterious at least to the public! The treatises from which we garner this picture of the Greek notion of machine were meant for the engineers, the few in society adept at understanding and imitating the cosmos. The mechanicians of ancient times were in this sense akin to the alchemists: by the use of secret means, the alchemist had meant to reproduce in the laboratory the complex procedures found in nature to grow metals in the telluric womb. The alchemical mahatma was the one who could imitate nature and perhaps speed up its natural processes. Man might coax nature along, but he never meant to dominate it.

The picture changes markedly as these ancient treatises are rediscovered and edited in the Renaissance, Hero, for example, in 1575. The spellbinding character of the mechanical contrivances is embraced by enthusiasts like Della Porta as part of the magical tradition, known to contemporaries as the secrets of nature. Knowledge about them was shared among the adept as an initiation rite for entrance into his Neapolitan *Accademia Secretorum Naturae*. But alongside the older approach to machines, a new tradition had already found favor with the other, more practically minded artisans. Agricola, for example, despite his humanistic training, focused on the actual description of machines employed by miners in his *De Re Metallica* (1556). Like his contemporaries, Biringuccio and Ercker, he took his mission to be to assemble a handbook of mining based directly on practices he observed in Saxon mines, and he strove to make them immediately accessible, though in the language of Columella and in the accompanying illustrations. He was not alone in this genre. Indeed, so many texts describing the arts of sailing, cartography, architecture, fortifications, gunnery, hydraulics, bridge building, and so on, often presented in the vernacular and accompanied by numerous diagrams, were published in the late sixteenth century that they provoked the compilation of encyclopedic treatises that became an immediate printing success. Jacques Besson's *Theatre des instrumens mathematiques et mechaniques* (1578), Agostino Ramelli's *Le Diverse e artificiose machine* (1588), and Vittorio Zonca's *Novo teatro di machine et edificii* (1607) all have in common the exaltation of machines as human inventions, downplaying the notion of artisans as mere imitators of nature. These compilers share the goal of spreading new knowledge to the multitudes. Even the illiterate artisans were permitted to profit from them, merely by studying the sumptuous illustrations.

Machines were now directly linked to the expectation of progress through mechanical improvement, a phenomenon that was widespread in the increasingly commercial and urbanized society of early modern Europe.[2] The same mood has continued unabated to our present day and is the most important root of the Mechanistic Age in which we operate.

What was gained through this dimension for the making of the Mechanistic Age is not just publicity and progress and its concomitants, democratization and the material improvement of society. The visual representation of machines forever stripped them of secret recesses and hidden forces.[3] The learned reader now expected to see for himself how things worked, no longer depending solely on classical authorities for confirmation. In his preface to *De Re Metallica,* Agricola assures us he personally went into the mine itself. In 1600, William Gilbert similarly dedicated his *De Magnete:* "to you alone, true philosophizers, honest men, who seek knowledge not from books only but from things themselves."[4]

The new style of philosophizing, preferring things to books and concrete, visually reliable instances to rhetorical systems of thought, was of course at one with the new experimental philosophy embraced by Galileo, Bacon, and even, to some extent, Descartes. Galileo sets the debates between his interlocutors in his *Discorsi* in the Venetian Arsenal where deeds speak louder than words. In a clear sense, the theoreticians of the Scientific Revolution borrowed a frame of mind from the artisan traditions displayed in the "theatre of machines" literature. Scientists' new preference for the palpable is evident not only in their prefaces but in their defense of demonstrations and experiments as the new arbiter among competing theories. It is no accident that all of the important discussion groups of the seventeenth century, from Gresham College to the Berlin Academy, owned scientific equipment and hired demonstrators. The tone of the new science was to displace the occult by the visible, the mysterious by the palpable.

Here one comes to the second important way by which we may analyze the meanings of the Mechanistic Age. It is characteristic of philosophical discussions of the era to reject occult forces whenever possible and to substitute for them self-evident principles much like one sees when watching a simple machine in operation.

According to the new mechanical philosophers, Aristotelian reliance on essential qualities as the central explanatory device in physics was the major weakness blocking the growth of understanding. To explain change by referring to an immaterial form that "informs" matter was quite unproductive. The charge was advanced, for example, that asserting an object falls to the center of the universe because its essence is heaviness is as illuminating as Molière's medical student who explains the power of opium to put patients to sleep as the result of a *virtus dormitiva* (opium is a soporific because it contains a dormitive power).[5] Peripatetic strategy seemed to obfuscate by substituting words for real causes. When asked further why earthy matter was heavy or opium soporific, the answer invariably was circular: because it was "in the nature" of the object to act in this fashion. How could progress ensue when playing such a dead-end rhetorical game?

Historians of the Scientific Revolution customarily claim that the introduction of the mechanical philosophy broke this impasse by providing a solution to this philosophic dilemma. If visible, palpable mechanisms of change were substituted for the hidden, occult forms, the future of natural philosophy might be ensured. And none seemed more intelligible than action through direct contact. The immediacy of understanding that comes from watching a stationary billiard ball move when struck by another, or how power is transmitted from one gear to another, or even how blood gushes from an opened artery when the heart contracts had a dramatic impact on the mind confused by Peripatetic verbosity. Even the seemingly complicated functions of animate beings were rendered more understandable by assumptions that their members—the hand or arm, for instance—operated as did machines, with levers, gears, pulleys, and gates, following the commands of the mind.[6] In the late seventeenth and early eighteenth centuries, bodily parts were pictured as individual mechanisms. The structural correspondence between man-made machines and living entities was adopted because it promised a new degree of intelligibility. The new scientists of the seventeenth century could readily give up on the old metaphysics when they juxtaposed the mechanical world of their era with the scholastic auditorium in universities, one vital, illuminating, and progressive, the other stultifying, fruitless, and tautological.

What principles did they propose instead? The new rule adopted was to ground all explanations on the idea of matter in motion. The corpuscular philosopher, who unashamedly borrowed from ancient atomists, found new psychological satisfaction in reducing the complexity of nature to the simplicity of corpuscles capable of motion and causing change by impact only. To the mind troubled by the older verbiage, they were surely preferable to Peripatetic forms and qualities. For Descartes, the principal systematic proponent of this view, matter was the analogue of extension, in the same way space was defined by the objects that occupied it. Common sense as well as logic showed us with undeniable reality that things are composed of matter and that next to impenetrability, matter was principally characterized by its location. Motion, too, was grounded on irrefutable visible existence. Neither was hidden or occult. Both were, as Descartes enjoyed repeating, clear and distinct and, to his mind, ultimately real. The mechanical philosopher reveled in having found an ontologically satisfying basis for apprehending nature, one that was not merely true by virtue of what the senses and the mind perceived but that could also be manipulated by mathematical symbols rather than scholastic terminology. Adopting the mechanical philosophy brought in its wake the ascendancy of mathematical language that purportedly guaranteed that proper logic would be observed and clarity maintained. It seemed to answer all the criticism laid at the door of the ancients and to offer a hope for deepening our understanding.

To a considerable extent, the mechanical philosophy provided a much-desired new ideology that brought success to many seventeenth-century natural philosophers. It had all kinds of advantages. For Descartes, as it had for Galileo earlier and was to have later for Locke, it permitted the separation of primary from secondary causes into the fundamental quantitative and the derivative qualitative realm. As a well-taught paradigm, it served to focus generations of scientists on specific riddles of nature—for example, the nature of the vacuum, the production of colors—that required experimental elucidation. But it would be a gross historical simplification to suppose that this new philosophy solved all the old problems and earned Descartes universal acclaim.

Practitioners of the new philosophy realized all too quickly that Descartes had substituted a new ontology for the old one—the quantifiable for the qualitative—but it was itself metaphysical. Instead of relying directly on tangible experience, it proposed principles, different from those of Aristotle but principles nonetheless. Scholastic debate was by no means absent from discussion centers where Descartes's philosophy was taught and applied. Was extension coterminous with matter? How divisible were corpuscles, and how many kinds of matter were there? How was movement transmitted and its total quantity in the universe to be measured? How could one verify by palpable, visual experiments the submicroscopic explanations for the action of the lodestone, or the production of colors? Leaving aside for a moment the immense problems posed by living matter for Descartes, how could one fully understand the motion of the heavenly bodies in elliptical paths? The new mechanical philosophy seemed to have created as many new problems as it resolved. Some of the solutions offered clearly reintroduced into our language the very occult terms that Descartes and his followers had thought to have repudiated. A major group of thinkers, particularly in England and including Sir Isaac, sought the answer to the mechanical philosophers' weak points in the nature of the deity, or by postulating universal gravitation and short-range affinities of an electric, magnetic, or even alchemical sort. It is particularly because of this historic turn of events that I urge a decoupling of that which has led us too casually to equate the Mechanistic Age with the Scientific Revolution. By following the intellectual path chosen by Newton too exclusively, as most of my colleagues have done, they have made us lose sight of the continuing agenda of those who instituted the Mechanistic Age.

A third and very subtle aspect of the Mechanistic Age was the change in emphasis traditionally given to the notion of causality from what Aristotle called formal and final causes to efficient and material ones. Indeed, many who embarked on this path found themselves holding a nominalist position that went so far as to deny causality altogether—witness David Hume's mid-eighteenth-century critique. The detailed history of this change has yet to be written, but its main stages within the history of science are clearly evident and provide a major ground for later criticism of the mechanistic philosophy.[7] By diminishing the importance of first causes, or even denying the possibility of reaching them, the mechanistic scientist has abandoned a task natural philosophers originally assumed for themselves: to make complete sense out of the world and to provide an explanation for it by attributing a goal for nature and its creator. The Mechanistic Age completed the process of displacing teleology in favor of a search for laws that link phenomena in regular, repeatable patterns of behavior. Note that the historical trajectory that takes us from Plato to the positivists of the nineteenth century passes through the Scientific Revolution but is not restricted by it. Conversely, all the actors of the Scientific Revolution were not equally committed to the abandonment of final causes. Moreover, leaving out Hume, the main proponents of this constituent lived on the Continent and operated next to the mainstream of the traditional Scientific Revolution: Pascal, Malebranche, d'Alembert, Buffon, Laplace, Bernard, and Du Bois-Reymond. There is insufficient space to carefully map this path, so I will confine myself to illustrating it mainly with Laplace, for it was in his hands that this aspect of the Mechanistic Age found its most assertive and pregnant outcome, the principle of strict mechanical determinism.

As is well known, both Plato and Aristotle drew on *telos* as the central concept for explaining the world. Not only were structures of living beings best understood through their function but all physical change was expressed in terms of a process analogous to substances fulfilling their natural destiny. Aristotle had specifically singled out the atomists for criticisms because their system left events to chance. For him, all satisfactory explanations required an overdetermined set of causes that left no room for fortune. When atomist notions were refurbished in the seventeenth century and were adopted for the establishment of a cogent mechanical philosophy, the charge of impiety was added to the discomfort evidenced over the belief that all could ultimately be made intelligible by the fortuitous interplay of invisible material elements. But there were devout Christians like Pascal and Malebranche who took refuge in the idea that even though the natural philosopher could never divine the real intentions of God, he could at least note nature's regularities and establish the phenomenal laws under which they operated. Like other nominalists, they radically separated God's omniscience from man's limited abilities to reach essences and to fathom purposes.

It is no accident that such developments took root precisely at the time when the scientific community began to organize and define itself against the older natural philosophic tradition. Not only did scientists of the second half of the seventeenth century develop communication networks and produce works collectively sanctioned but they also sought out a rationale for a separate existence which offered them a differential role in the world of intellectuals. In effect, scientists like Pascal and Malebranche acknowledged the existence of a sphere of activity in which scientists had little to contribute, namely, theology, but proclaimed the special ability of colleagues to study nature directly and extract from it ever more precise regularities.

Those familiar with the English tradition in natural religion, in which Sir Isaac Newton participated, will notice what a radical turn this Continental path represents, a point that once more underscores my admonition to stray from the straight and narrow path mapped out by traditional historians of the Scientific Revolution.

Yet in another important sense, the followers of this Continental path shared with their colleagues across the Channel a distrust of essential qualities. At about the same time, but on different occasions, d'Alembert and Buffon, who were each accused of anti-Christian leanings, were annoyed by the continued fascination their contemporaries displayed for claiming to apprehend nature's true being. Buffon argued for an empirical system of natural classification to describe the realm of natural history; d'Alembert argued for a redefinition of the elusive concept of what we now call energy conservation, to avoid having to ground his physics on an essentialist understanding of gravitational forces. Both of them justified their stand by narrowing the territory in which scientists with their current methods could reasonably expect to make headway. Although religious authorities failed to interpret it this way, nominalist scientists retreated from the impenetrable domain of final causes, cheerfully turning it over to the ecclesiastic community, while asserting their authority to speak about the empirically based laws of nature with self-assurance. That position is still fashionable today and continues to constitute a major argument in defense of science's autonomous right to know regardless of its consequences in other domains of culture.

Laplace's major contribution to this component of the Mechanistic Age was to demonstrate with heavy scientific artillery in probability theory, celestial mechanics, and physics that such a specialized, professional approach, far from diminishing the extent and richness of the scientist's domain, helped him focus on what it was reasonable for man to understand and to dream constructively about what might be possible. He did this on several occasions.

In a classic paper on heat written with Lavoisier in 1783, he argued that the ultimate truth of competing theories about its nature (kinetic vs. materialist) was best set aside in favor of the establishment, with careful experiments, of the behavior of thermal phenomena.[8] To that end, Laplace invented the ice calorimeter to measure heat exchanges in combustion and respiration and derived tables pointing to laws for the expansion of metals on heating. For us, it matters little that his efforts were easily bested by the next generation of physicists. What is noteworthy, considering his great authority in the scientific community, was his explicit disregard for quiddity as long as some progress could be achieved by empirical means. Laplace laid great store in what we call an operational or instrumentalist view of science, one that favors the knowable mechanisms of nature, studied mathematically, over its deeper and less evident aspects. He preferred the palpable to the speculative. In discussing respiration, for example, Laplace and Lavoisier confined themselves to statements about the oxygen consumed and the heat produced, leaving aside all reflections on the relationship between the nature of life and vital heat, a commonplace subject in their epoch.[9]

We legitimately ask if this conscious choice was merely a stratagem to disarm nettlesome religious or philosophic critics or a conviction about the special nature of the scientists' occupation.[10] Undoubtedly both. Beyond this, and for personal reasons, Laplace also preferred epistemological certainty to ontological profundity. In one of those paradoxical events that befalls so many in their lifetime, his conventional career choice of the priesthood had been shattered by a conversion experience brought about by the discovery of the beauty and power of the analytic versions of Newtonian astronomy practiced in France. Laplace, moreover, fashioned a new mathematical tool, the a posteriori calculus of probabilities (statistical inference) that he assumed would lead with ineluctable power from observed phenomena to laws of nature and from laws to causes. The most remarkable by-product of his efforts was his massive five-volume *Traité de Mécanique Céleste,* which offered a thorough analysis of the Newtonian astronomical world, using the new language of calculus but entirely stripped bare of the theological and metaphysical concerns Newton prized so dearly.

Like Newton, Laplace shunned unfounded hypotheses. A particularly clear instance of his reluctance to accept speculative theory when no direct evidence was available was his reaction to a clever but bizarre hypothesis proposed by the Genevan Le Sage to explain universal gravitation.[11] This completely mechanistic theory involved numerous tiny ultramundane particles traveling at great speed through space in a random fashion. In this model, attraction was the result of the mutual shielding effect solid bodies would have when in proximity to each other, an effect that would increase greatly as the distance between them decreased. Laplace demanded to know what speeds and masses the hypothesis entailed. When they turned out to be larger than the speed of light, he lost interest. Le Sage's particles were a clever but vacuous hypothesis that could not be tested directly with apparatus at hand and hence were not worthy of the concern of a practicing mechanistic scientist. The Mechanistic Age demanded tangible evidence rather than unsupported models, even when these turned out to be based on the principles of matter in motion.

It must not be assumed from this that such a positivist stance, which favored fact over fancy, ruled out hypotheses, or altogether blocked their use. It merely distinguished between pure conjecture and imaginative solutions that were testable. Laplace's postulation of the nebular hypothesis to account for the origins of the solar system is an apt illustration of this. Using probability theory, he argued that there must be a physical cause responsible for the planet's orbiting around the sun in a plane close to the ecliptic, all in the same direction and with nearly circular paths. His hypothesis, though thoroughly speculative, was nonetheless testable and fruitful, hence acceptable until it was refuted. Clearly, the philosophy of what we might call phenomenological positivism did not constitute an obstacle to the scientist's imagination. On the contrary, none is more visionary than Laplace's mechanistic assertion of determinism:

> The present state of the system of nature is evidently a result of what it was in the preceding instant, and if we conceive of an Intelligence who, for a given moment, embraces all the relations of being in this Universe, It will also be able to determine for any instant of the past and future their respective positions, motions, and generally their affections.
>
> Physical astronomy, that subject of all our understanding most worthy of the human mind, offers us an idea, albeit imperfect, of what such an Intelligence would be. The simplicity of the laws by which celestial bodies move, the relationship of their masses and their distances allow us to follow their motions through analysis, up to a certain point: and in order to determine the state of the system of these large bodies in past or future centuries, it is enough for the mathematician that observation provide him with their position and speeds at any given instant.
>
> Man owes this advantage to the power of the instrument he uses and to the small number of relations he employs in his calculations; but ignorance of the diverse causes that produce the events and their complexity, taken together with the imperfection of analysis, prevent him from making assertions with the same certitude on most phenomena.[12]

It is clear from this remarkable credo that Laplace expected future progress in science to depend on a patient but correct adaptation of the methods of astronomy to the unsolved problems of nature in other realms. On different occasions, he expressed this vision specifically for crystallography, chemistry, and psychology. In an unpublished manuscript, he repeated this conviction for biology. But we would be mistaken if we assumed his philosophy of astronomy depended on the adoption of specific axioms about matter—for example, that it be inert rather than self-activating—any more than if we assumed he refused to consider alternate theories of heat and light to the corpuscular ones favored in his day.

For him, as for many of the biological reductionists of the nineteenth century, it was the proper scientific approach to problem solving that counted more than the specific character of the theory employed. The epistemological virtue of the "mechanistic" approach mattered more than its materialistic ontology.

The physiologist Magendie, who was Laplace's disciple, and his famous student Claude Bernard accepted the notion that living beings could not transgress the laws of the inorganic world but maintained they were additionally held to laws of the organic realm.[13] Du Bois-Reymond, who belonged to the group that signed a reductionist manifesto in 1846, also adhered to this notion and recommended that only physical and chemical tools be employed to analyze physiological phenomena. He did so principally because their operations were intelligible, not because physics and chemistry were ontologically more reliable or prior.

It seems to me a major historical misunderstanding to argue that the philosophy of biological reductionism turned on a temperamental philosophic preference for the physical over the life sciences. The record, as it is now being unfolded by historians of the nineteenth century, shows that it was the example provided by the physical sciences more than their principles that impressed researchers in biology.[14] Most of the great figures received training and developed their ideal picture of what a solid science might be from experience with astronomy, physics, and chemistry. In one way or another, they all took to heart messages like the one offered by Laplace that, with sufficient persistence, the life sciences would soon arrive at a stage of maturity that gave them the kind of power of penetration reached by followers of Newtonian astronomy. We now know that their optimism was perhaps a bit premature. In their enthusiasm, they may have failed to count on the almost limitless variety that exists in the natural world and the complexity of living processes. Yet the faith in progress through the adoption of experimental science is still the driving force behind today's research programs. In that sense, the effects of the Mechanistic Age are still with us.

Ultimately, the critical by-product of the Mechanistic Age was to have provided examples of how nature could be apprehended by men of science. To be acceptable, as we have seen, any new science had to reveal the mechanism of its theories to the eye, to be grounded on verifiable evidence, to adopt an unambiguous vocabulary for the sake of clarity, to argue cogently (preferably employing a logically reliable language), and to concern itself with immediate rather than distant causes, in any case, causes that could be tested. In short, the Mechanistic Age offered a philosophy for scientific understanding that had proven to be effective and remarkably productive.

There are other features that our rapid historic survey may have enabled us to have glimpsed, though they are more implied than made manifest. It is perhaps most evident in the Laplacean credo. Whereas in ancient times, man and the universe were considered first as the by-products of a creator to be contemplated and imitated, since at least the nineteenth century, the scientifically informed mind has been prepared to substitute his mental prowess for that of God. Laplace's Intelligence could just as easily be a perfected human calculator as the Supreme Being. Thus it is that the modern scientist is potentially in as good a position to construct the universe and manipulate it according to his cumulative insights as he is to analyze a universe created by a deity. In the modern era, understanding has become a means of control. Man is now the mechanic, the maker of the machine: What Vico implied by asserting the identity of *verum* and *factum,* what man makes, he is able to know.[15]

The Laplacean credo of determinism not only offered the potential of prediction, and hence a measure of control, but it also promoted man to the rank of a lesser god. That message was well understood by many of the biological reductionists who were uneasy with its implications. Du Bois-Reymond was the most explicit spokesman who raised doubts about the ultimate power of the scientific mind. In a series of popular addresses on science over a century ago, he explicitly set limits to the power of science, maintaining that despite the likelihood further research would dissolve some of our ignorance, there were issues that would never be settled by science.[16] He listed seven impenetrable riddles of nature that would forever remain beyond our ken. What is significant about them is that they included issues dear to physical scientists as well as his biological colleagues. They are not canonical enigmas, but his list nonetheless illustrates the kinds of metascientific issues he considered beyond the limits of the wisdom of scientists: the essence of force and matter; the origin of movement; the origin of life; the purposeful character of nature; the nature of simple sensations; the origins of intelligence and language; and the riddle of freedom of the will.

Despite the remarkable progress of science, the nineteenth century was also the period in which doubts about the implications of the Laplacean credo emerged. It is a measure of the ambiguity with which his message was greeted that Du Bois-Reymond reminded his listeners that man was not omniscient. Perhaps he should also have reminded us that he is not omnipotent either. I have always been impressed that Goethe's *Faust* and Shelley's *Frankenstein* appear on the historic scene just as the Mechanistic Age is in its full glory. Does this not suggest that issues of this magnitude are never settled?

As stated at the outset, the modern age was nonetheless irretrievably transformed by the establishment of a philosophy of mechanism that showed how much understanding could be enlarged by adopting its tenets. True, modern man could not expect to equal the prowess of the deity simply by the use of his new secular instrument, but he could now hope to deepen his grasp on nature with considerably more confidence.

NOTES

1. See Pierre Maxime Schuhl, *Machinisme et Philosophie* (3d ed.; Paris: Presses Universitaires de France, 1969). Jean Pierre Vernant, "Remarques sur les formes et les limites de la pensée technique chez les Grecs," *Revue d'Histoire des Sciences et de leurs Applications* 12 (1957): 205–225 (translated in his *Myth and Thought Among the Greeks* [London: Routledge & Kegan Paul, 1983]); and Bertrand Gille, *Les Mécaniciens Grecs: La Naissance de la Technologie* (Paris: Seuil, 1980).

2. Alex Keller, "Mathematical Technologies and the Growth of the Idea of Technical Progress in the Sixteenth Century," *Science, Medicine and Society in the Renaissance: Essays to Honor Walter Pagel* (New York: Neal Watson, 1972), 11–27.

3. William Eamon, "Technology as Magic in the Middle Ages and the Renaissance," *Janus* 70 (1983): 171–212.

4. William Gilbert, *De Magnete* [On the Magnet], trans. Silvanus P. Thompson (London: Chiswick Press, 1900), ii, verso.

5. John L. Heibron, *Elements of Early Modern Physics* (Berkeley, Los Angeles, London: University of California Press, 1982), 17 *et seq.*

6. Gérard Simon, "Les machines au XVIIe siècle: Usage, typologie, résonances symboliques," *Revue des Sciences Humaines* 58 (1982): 9–31.

7. Léon Brunschvicg, *L'Expérience Humaine et la Causalité Physique* (Paris: Félix Alcan, 1922); and Leszek Kolakowski, *The Alienation of Reason: A History of Positivist Thought* (Garden City, N.Y.: Doubleday, 1968).

8. Lavoisier and Laplace, *Memoir on Heat*, trans. Henry Guerlac (New York: Neal Watson, 1982).

9. Frederic Lawrence Holmes, *Lavoisier and the Chemistry of Life: An Exploration of Scientific Creativity* (Madison: University of Wisconsin Press, 1985).

10. Roger Hahn, "Laplace and the Mechanistic Universe," in *God and Nature: Historical Essays on the Encounter between Christianity and Science* (Berkeley, Los Angeles, London: University of California Press, 1986), 256–276.

11. See Laplace's unpublished correspondence with Le Sage and Prévost listed in Roger Hahn, *Calendar of the Correspondence of Pierre Simon Laplace* (Berkeley: Office for History of Science and Technology, 1982).

12. Quoted in Hahn, "Laplace and the Mechanistic Universe," 268–269.

13. G. June Goodfield, *The Growth of Scientific Physiology* (London: Hutchinson, 1960).

14. Roger Hahn, "Science in the Early 19th Century: Another View," *Acta Historiae Rerum Naturalium Necnon Technicarum*, special issue 13 (1981): 59–74; Frederick Gregory, *Scientific Materialism in Nineteenth-Century Germany* (Dordrecht: D. Reidel, 1977); Timothy Lenoir, *The Strategy of Life: Teleology and Mechanics in Nineteenth-Century German Biology* (Dordrecht: D. Reidel, 1982); and John E. Lesch, *Science and Medicine in France: The Emergence of Experimental Physiology, 1790–1855* (Cambridge: Harvard University Press, 1984).

15. Nikhil Bhattacharya, "Knowledge 'per caussas': Vico's Theory of Natural Science," in Giorgio Tagliacozzo, ed., *Vico: Past and Present* (Atlantic Highlands, N.J.: Humanities Press, 1981), I: 182–197; and the articles by Badaloni, Belaval, and Berlin in Giorgio Tagliacozzo and Hayden V. White, eds., *Giambattista Vico: An International Symposium* (Baltimore: Johns Hopkins Press, 1969).

16. Emil Du Bois-Reymond, *Ueber die Grenzen des Naturerkennens: Die sieben Welträthsel* (2d ed.; Leipzig: Von Veit, 1884); also in his *Vorträge über Philosophie und Gesellschaft,* ed. Siegfried Wollgast (Berlin: Akademie Verlag, 1974).

NINE

Metaphors for Mind, Theories of Mind: Should the Humanities Mind?

Allen Newell

The outer frame of this essay is the computer revolution. The computer threatens to infiltrate the humanities and, indeed, all intellectual disciplines. There is much to the world besides disciplines, of course, and the computer has its effects on the larger stage of economics and war. But the disciplines provide a more than adequate frame for us. The computer—by which I mean the hardware, the software, and the algorithms, along with their underlying theory—is leading to a technical understanding of all intellectual operations. By taking intellectual operations to be the technology for processing information as represented in data structures, the computer is proceeding to transform them all. From word processors, to communication networks, to data bases, to data analysis, to theoretical calculations, to simulations, to automatic running of experiments, to preparation of scholarly papers, to scheduling appointments—all across the board, it transforms first this intellectual operation and then that one. The transformations are piecemeal, mostly commercially driven, and often attack the intellectually peripheral and the socially mundane. But, as with the locusts, one can hear the *munch, munch, munch* across the land.

Since we did not previously understand intellectual operations all that well, the sweep of this revolution is unclear and contentious. It is possible to believe that only certain intellectual operations will be transformed and that others will remain within a separate and sheltered realm. This is one reason the computer revolution is only a threat; the reality has only partly arrived, and it is unclear that the rest will ever come. Contentiousness arises because the lack of clarity extends even to whether it is a threat. Perhaps the metaphor of the locusts is false. Perhaps the arrival should be greeted with joy and hosannas. For it will bring with it not only the capability for intellectuals to engage in more intellectual operations per day but to do so with an immeasurably deepened understanding of what the intellectual operations themselves mean. The situation is yet more complex. One of the insidious aspects of the computer revolution is that it arrives on wings of benefice—cost/benefice, it is true, but since the disciplines value funds as much as the world at large, and also find them in short supply, the infiltration of the computer is usually welcomed in the small, even while in the large, it is discussed in symposia, papers, and books.

So much for the outer frame. The theme of this volume is the location of humanity, and its method is to work along the boundaries between humanity and other things, such as beasts and machines. This connects it with the computer revolution, although in overlapping and partial ways. For the computer as machine touches this theme at more than one place: as an exemplar of the modern technological age, as a machine that deals in the root operations of intellectuals, and as something that mimics the human mind.

Which introduces the inner frame—computers and the mind. This is the aspect of the computer revolution that concerns us. Whenever the issue explicitly arises of how the computer locates our humanity, the answer invariably centers on what computers tell us about our mind. It is not clear that we are right in always moving to this focus. Other aspects of the revolution may in the long run be more important. But, as in much that is human, there is recursive self-fulfillment: we inquire about what is important, but our criteria for importance is largely how much we observe ourselves inquiring.

I accept this framing. Let us inquire once more about what the computer tells us about ourselves, as reflected in our minds. However, this inner frame is still too large. We must pick out a single thread within it. Nevertheless, at last we are ready to begin, although the framing is not quite ready to end.

METAPHORS FOR MIND

The computer is a *metaphor for the mind*. That is how it so often gets said. It does not even seem strange any more. Western society has always used the technologies of the time as metaphors for the human mind. For all I know, all other civilizations do the same. In any event, it is enough that we do.

We often trace the course of technological metaphors for mind from Descartes and the hydraulic fountains of his time, through the telephone switchboard, and on up to the computer. Rising above the sequence, by the sort of modest inductive capability natural to us all, we have often been assured that the leading metaphor for mind will move on with the next technological advance (holograms were once a favorite). Some truth resides in this, no doubt. Metaphor is a particularly disarming way of arriving at truth. It invites the listener to find within the metaphor those aspects that apply, leaving the rest as the false residual, necessary to the essence of metaphor. And since *within the metaphor* is always, by the linguistic turn (Toews 1987), *within the listener,* the invitation is to find within oneself some truth that fits. Having done that, it is difficult to argue against the truth that the metaphor reveals. Indeed, to fail to find any truth that applies seems to say more about the listener than about the metaphor; perhaps he is one of those who does not get jokes either. So there is truth in the computer as a metaphor for mind, though perhaps as much social truth as scientific truth.

This brings us to the final framing, which is personal. This pervasive use of computer as metaphor for mind has always somehow rankled. Always I experience a sense of discomfort in using it, or in hearing it, or in taking it as the right way of putting it. Maybe I do not get the joke. Maybe I do and do not like it. Maybe I like it but do not know how to do it. Maybe I think it is no metaphoring matter.

In any event, let us explore the issue. I shall expand on my William James Lectures at Harvard University (Newell 1987). Although those were a perfect place for a wider view, in fact, I focused strongly on matters internal to the science of cognition and did not address such issues as the computer metaphor.

I now believe, however, that I can answer the question of what disturbs me about the use of computer as metaphor for mind. It contrasts with a *theory of mind*. It distances the object, so to speak. If the computer is a metaphor for mind, it is by that same token no more about mind than a metaphor. Metaphors being clearly in the eye of the beholder, they leave the objects themselves untouched, or touched in only a literary way that does not derange the topic itself, because it is only commentary. Thus, to view the computer as a metaphor for mind is to keep the mind safe from analysis.

Science is not like that. At least science does not take itself as metaphorical. Acknowledging always the necessity of approximation and the inevitability of error, it still sees itself as attempting to describe its subject matter directly and not metaphorically. It has indeed become fashionable both to deconstruct science (Latour and Woolgar 1979) and to take all science as metaphorical—to take metaphor as a metaphor for science. This can be done, of course. As already noted, metaphor has a certain inevitability about it with respect to squeezing out some truth. A boa constrictor is not a bad metaphor for metaphor. But sometimes the bones crack. In particular, it is clearly wrong to treat science as metaphor, for the more metaphorical, the less scientific. In contrast to metaphors for mind, to understand the mind—what it is, how it can be, why it works, how far it reaches, whence it arises, and where it is located—requires a scientific theory of mind.

The metaphor for mind that the computer makes available for our use is available to us all already. It is unclear that it can or needs to be sharpened. It is already richer than might be imagined. It indicates mind as something mechanical, atomistic, context independent, slavishly rule following, repetitive, stereotypical, jerky, single minded [sic], quantitative, unchanging, rigid, unadaptive, powerful, compulsive, exhaustive, obsessed with detail, noncaring, a spindler/mutilator, passionless, formal, logical, errorless . . . Pull the plug! I am being too compulsive.

In fact, the computer as metaphor mixes many sources and changes before our eyes. The computer as computer continues to become different things at a rapid rate. Our exposure to it, in all its forms, increases correspondingly, both directly by personal experience and indirectly through both the advertising and public media and the technical and intellectual literature. One source goes back all the way to the computer as machine, in which the computer is all gears. But we have all seen enough to realize that the computer is clearly not a rolling mill or tick-tock clock. So the machine view gets overlaid with others that arise from the nature of programming and from the specialized nature of applications, such as the lean, clean, saturated color panels of computer animation or the whiz and abstract thrill and terror of interactive computer games. These different sources bear family resemblances, but they blur the metaphor and allow it to convey different things on different occasions. Good thing, in fact, for a metaphor, where the richer, the better. The computer metaphor can take care of itself very well, without any help from me. My purpose is to probe whether the way to treat what the computer can tell us about mind is as metaphor or as science.

THEORIES OF MIND

More effort needs to be spent explicating the nature of a scientific theory of mind. I prefer to do that at a specific level, not at the level of science in general. Still, something general needs to be said, if only because so much has been written and mused about the nature of science as it might pertain to humans and their societies and cultures, or whether in fact it could pertain at all. Again, the focus here is not to straighten out the notion of science per se. Rather, I want to be sure the notion of science that I use is clear.

By a *theory of mind*, I mean just what I would in talking about any scientific theory. I mean it in the same sense as in the theory of plate tectonics in geology, the theory of organic chemistry, the astronomical theory of the planetary orbits, the theory of the atom, and on and on. These examples are themselves not quite the same, but they all contain a solid common kernel. Society, in the body of the attending scientists, attempts to organize its knowledge of some body of phenomena. Its goal is to use the knowledge for prediction, explanation, design, control, or whatever. Theory is the symbolic organization of this knowledge.

Sciences all grow to look alike in many ways—the natural and biological sciences very much so, as well as bits and parts of the human sciences. They all develop bodies of solid fact and regularities and surround them with an explicit, if somewhat conventional, apparatus of evidential support. They all develop theories, which tend to mathematical and formal symbolic form. These theories tend to be mechanistic. That is, they posit a system or collection of mechanisms, whose operation and interaction produce the regularities. The theories of all the sciences all fit, more or less well, into a single theoretical fabric that is a stitched-together coherent picture of a single universe. An article of faith for a long time, this has become increasingly evident with the amazing emergence of biology to match in power and elegance the older physical sciences—and to be one with them in a seamless scientific web.

Some aspects of the sciences reflect the nature of the world, others the nature of the enterprise itself. That scientific theories are cast in terms of underlying mechanisms seems to reflect the nature of the world. Theories could be different and sometimes are. That theories have a formal and calculational character reflects the scientific enterprise. This quality makes the knowledge that is the science derivable from the theory and not from the theorist. To use a scientific theory requires both knowledge and skill, especially the latter. Hence, not everybody can take a theory and produce its results (or even reproduce them). But the results, when produced, are the results of the theory, not of the theorist—a matter of no small import, since humans themselves have (or contain, depending on your metaphor) bodies of knowledge. Humans can predict, explain, design, and control, all without benefit of science, much less theory. Perhaps what best characterizes science methodologically is its ability to get these activities into external symbolic artifacts, available to all who are "skilled in the art."

If science stayed outside the house of man, there would be nothing to consider in contrasting metaphors and theories of mind. But, of course, a scientific psychology does exist, and it is recognizably a family member of the science kin group. The contrast requires more than just a scientific psychology, however. The computer must underlie both the metaphor of mind (which it avowedly does) and the theory of mind. If this were not the case, the contrast would still amount only to the proverbial one hand clapping.

But the cognitive revolution has occurred (Gardner 1985). It is thirty years old. It has come to dominate individual psychology. New scientific upstarts now rail against it instead of against behaviorism. And this revolution has been dominated by the computer—or more correctly, by the abstract notions of computation and information processing that have emerged as the theoretical counterpart to the technological advance. Even the philosophers say so (Dennett 1988, Fodor 1983). The acceptance has moved to the creation of an umbrella interdiscipline called cognitive science. In some quarters, we can actually hear the clapping. There is indeed a contrast to consider.

Unified Theories of Cognition

My William James Lectures give some indication of what it might mean for there to be a theory of mind, in the sense we have been discussing.

> Psychology has arrived at the possibility of unified theories of cognition— theories that gain their power by having a single system of mechanisms that operate together to produce the full range of human cognition.

I did not say they are here yet, but I argued they are within reach and that we should strive to attain them. Nor did I claim there was a single such unified theory. Indeed, in my lectures I argued that in our current state of knowledge, there would be several theories. I did claim that enough was known to attempt unified theories and that they had immense benefits for cognitive science—bringing into one theoretical structure the constraints from the great store of empirical regularities that cognitive psychology has amassed, along with what we now understand about the mechanisms of cognition.

The lectures were built around the presentation of an exemplar unified theory, embodied in a system called Soar, developed by John Laird of the University of Michigan, Paul Rosenbloom of the Information Sciences Institute at the University of Southern California, and me (Laird, Newell, and Rosenbloom 1987). Soar provides an appreciation of what is required of a unified theory, what its yield might be, and how ready the field is to develop them. Soar is only an exemplar; there are others as well (Anderson 1983).

Figure 9.1 presents the elements of the theory of human cognition embodied in Soar. So far, I have taken care to say *theory embodied in Soar*. As we shall see, Soar is a specific kind of system—an architecture or machine organization.[1] We usually take a theory of some domain, here a theory of the mind, as being the assertions about the nature of that domain—here assertions about how the mind is structured, how it operates, how it is situated, and so on. So Soar, as a system, cannot literally be a theory. But the theory asserts that the central structure in mind is the

1. Controller-Perception-Cognition-Motor

2. Knowledge and Goals

3. Representation, Computation, Symbols

4. An Architecture plus Content

5. Recognition Memory (about 10 ms)

6. Decision Cycles—Automatic (about 100 ms)

7. Problem Spaces and Operators (about 1 sec.)

8. Impasses and Subgoals

9. Chunking (about 10 sec.)

10. Intended Rationality (100 sec. and up)

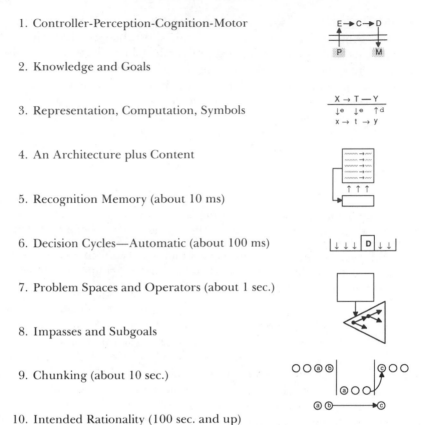

Fig. 9.1.   Soar as a unified theory of cognition

cognitive architecture, that humans have one and that its nature determines the nature of mind. The theory then specifies a lot about that architecture. Soar is a system that embodies these particular specifics. Because the architecture is so central and determines so much about the mind, it is convenient to slip language a bit and identify Soar with the theory of cognition it embodies.

Figure 9.1 enumerates the main mechanisms in Soar. The top four items are shared by all comprehensive cognitive-science theories of human cognition. Soar operates as a controller of the human organism, hence it is a complete system with perception, cognition, and motor components. This already takes mind in essentially functional terms—as the system that arose to control the gross movements of a mammal in a mammalian world. Soar is goal oriented with knowledge of the world, which it uses to attain its goal. That knowledge is represented by a symbol system, which means that computation is used to encode representations, extract their implications for action, and decode specific desired actions. Thus, Soar is an architecture—a structure that makes possible a hardware-software distinction. Most of the knowledge in such a system is embodied in the content that the architecture makes meaningful and accessible.

The rest of the items describe Soar from the bottom up, temporally speaking. Soar comprises a large *recognition memory*. This is realized by an Ops5-like production system (Brownston et al. 1985). A production system consists of a set of productions, each consisting of a set of conditions and a set of actions. At each moment, the conditions of all productions are matched against the elements of a temporary *working memory*, and those productions that are satisfied then execute, putting new elements into working memory. Human long-term memory comprises many productions, in the millions perhaps. A cycle of production execution also occurs very rapidly, around 10 milliseconds (ms).[2] Although in artificial intelligence (AI) and cognitive science, productions are usually taken to correspond to operators (deliberately deployed actions), in Soar they correspond to an associational memory. Thus, production actions behave like a memory retrieval: they only enter new elements into working memory and cannot modify or delete what is there. Also, there is no conflict resolution (of the kind familiar from Ops5); instead, each production executes independently, just like an isolated memory access and retrieval.

The next level of organization, which occurs within about 100 ms, consists of the *decision cycle*. This comprises a sequence of retrievals from long-term memory (i.e., a sequence of production firings) which assemble from memory what is immediately accessible and relevant to the current decision context. This sequence ultimately terminates when no more knowledge is forthcoming (in practice, it quiesces quickly). Then a *decision procedure* makes a choice of the next step to be taken. This changes the decision context, so that the cycle can repeat to make the next decision. At the 100 ms level, cognitive life is an endless sequence of assembling the available knowledge and using it to make the next deliberate choice.

The decisions taken at the 100 ms level implement search in *problem spaces*, which comprise the next level of organization, at the 1 second (sec.) level. Soar organizes all its goal-oriented activity in problem spaces, from the most problematical to the most routine. It performs a task by creating a space within which the attainment of the task can be defined as reaching some state and where the moves in the space are the operations that are appropriate to performing the task. The problem then becomes which operators to apply and in what order to reach a desired state. The search in the problem space is governed by the knowledge in the recognition memory. If Soar has the appropriate knowledge and if it can be brought to bear when needed, then Soar can put one operator in front of another, to step its way directly to task attainment. If the memory contains little relevant knowledge or it cannot be accessed, then Soar must search the problem space, leading to the combinatorial explosion familiar to AI research.

Given that the problem-space organization is built into the architecture, the decisions to be made at any point are always the same—what problem space to work in; what state to use (if more than one is available); and what operator to apply to this state to get a new state, on the way to a desired state. Making these choices is the continual business of the decision cycle. Operators must actually be applied, of course; life is not all decision making. But applying operators is merely another task, which occurs by going into another problem space to accomplish the implementation. The recursion bottoms out when an operator becomes simple enough to be accomplished within a single decision cycle, by a few memory retrievals.

The decision procedure that actually makes the choice at each point is a simple, uniform process that can only use whatever knowledge has accumulated via the repeated memory searches. Some of this knowledge is in the form of *preferences* about what to choose—that one operator is preferred to another, that a state is acceptable, that another state is to be rejected. The decision procedure takes whatever preferences are available and extracts from them the decision. It adds no knowledge of its own.

There is no magic in the decision cycle. It can extract from the memory only what knowledge is there, and it may not even get it all. And the decision procedure can select only from the options thereby produced and by using the preferences thereby obtained. Sometimes this is sufficient, and Soar proceeds to move through its given space. Sometimes— often, as it turns out—the knowledge is insufficient or conflicting. Then the architecture is unable to continue: it arrives at an *impasse*. This is like a standard computer trying to divide by zero. Except that, instead of aborting, the architecture sets up a *subgoal* to resolve the impasse. For example, if several operators have been proposed but there is insufficient information to select one, then a *tie impasse* occurs, and Soar sets up a subgoal to obtain the knowledge to resolve the tie, so it can then continue.

Impasses are the dynamo of Soar; they drive all its problem solving. Soar simply attempts to execute its top-level operators. If this can be done, Soar has attained what it wanted. Failures imply impasses. Resolving these impasses, which occurs in other problem spaces, can lead to other impasses, hence to subproblem spaces, and so on. The entire subgoal hierarchy is generated by Soar itself, in response to its inability to attain its objectives. The different types of impasses generate the full variety of goal-driven behavior familiar in AI systems—operator implementation, operator instantiation, operator selection, precondition satisfaction, state rejection, and so on.

In addition to problem solving, Soar learns continuously from its experiences. The mechanism is called *chunking*. Every time Soar encounters and resolves an impasse, it creates a new production (a chunk) to capture and retain that experience. If the situation ever recurs, the chunk will fire, making available the information that was missing on the first occasion. Thus, Soar will not encounter an impasse on a second pass.

The little diagram at the right of *chunking* in figure 9.1 sketches how this happens. The view is looking down on working memory, with time running from left to right. Each little circle is a data element that encodes some information about the task. Starting at the left, Soar is chugging along, with productions putting in new elements and the decision procedure determining which next steps to take. At the left vertical line, an impasse occurs. The architecture adds some elements to record the impasse, hence setting a new context, and then behavior continues. Finally, Soar produces an element that resolves the impasse (the element c at the right vertical line). Behavior then continues in the original context, because operationally resolving an impasse just is behavior continuing. The chunk is built at this point, with an action corresponding to the element that resolved the impasse and with conditions corresponding to the elements prior to the impasse that led to the resolution (the elements a and b). This captures the result of the problem solving to resolve the impasse and does so in a way that permits it to be evoked again to avoid that particular impasse.

Chunking operates as an automatic mechanism that continually caches all of Soar's goal-oriented experience, without detailed interpretation or analysis. As described, it appears to be simply a practice mechanism, a way to avoid redoing the problem solving to resolve prior impasses, thus speeding up Soar's performance. However, the conditions of the productions reflect only a few of the elements in working memory at the time of the impasse. Thus, chunks *abstract* from the situation of occurrence and can apply in different situations, as long as the specific conditions apply. This provides a form of *transfer* of learning. Although far from obvious, this mechanism in fact generates a wide variety of learning (Steier et al. 1987), enough to conjecture that chunking might be the only learning mechanism Soar needs.

Chunks get built in response to solving problems (i.e., resolving impasses). Hence, they correspond to activities at about the 1 sec. level and above. The chunk itself, of course, is a production, which is an entity down at the memory-access level at about 10 ms.

The higher organization of cognitive activity arises from top-level operators not being implementable immediately with the information at hand. They must be implemented in subspaces with their own operators, which themselves may require further subspaces. Each descent into another layer of subspaces means that the top-level operators take longer to complete, that is, are higher level. Thus, the time scale of organized cognitive activity climbs above what can be called the region of cognitive mechanism and toward the region of *intendedly rational* behavior. Here, enough time is available for the system to do substantial problem solving and use more and more of its knowledge. The organization of cognition becomes increasingly dictated by the nature of the task and the knowledge available, rather than by the structure of the architecture.

This rapid-fire tour through the mechanisms of Soar serves primarily to box its compass, to see the mechanisms that are involved. It is an architecture that spans an extremely wide range of psychological functions. Some limits of the range should be noted. Perception and motor behavior currently exist in the theory only in nascent form. Perhaps as important, the impasse-driven means-ends structure that builds up in a given situation is ephemeral. Long-term stable organization of behavior could hardly be held in place by the momentary piled-up impasse subgoal hierarchy. Soar does not yet incorporate a theory of what happens as the hours grow, disparate activities punctuate one another, and sleep intervenes to let the world of cognition start afresh each morning. All these aspects must eventually be within the scope of a unified theory of cognition. Soar's failure to include them shows it to be like any scientific theory, always in a state of becoming.

Our description of Soar contains a strong emphasis on *temporal level.* Soar models behavior from about 10 ms on up to about 1,000 sec. (30 min.). Soar, as a theory of human cognition, is tied strongly to the world of real time. Figure 9.2 provides a useful view of the time scale of human action. The characteristic time taken by processes fractionates our world into realms of distinct character. Neural systems take times of the order of 100 microseconds (μsec) to 10 ms to produce significant effects. Cognitive systems take times of the order of 100 ms to 10 sec. to produce significant effects. Beyond that, in the minutes to hours range, is something labeled the rational band. And up above that stretch time scales that are primarily social and historical, left blank because theories of unified cognition are initially situated in the lower bands, focused on the architecture.

These bands correspond to realms of scientific law. The neural band is within the realm of physical law, as we have come to understand it in

TIME SCALE OF HUMAN ACTION

Scale (sec.)	*Time Units*	*System*	*World* (theory)
10^7	months		
10^6	weeks		**SOCIAL BAND**
10^5	days		
10^4	hours	Task	
10^3	10 minutes	Task	**RATIONAL BAND**
10^2	minutes	Task	
10^1	10 seconds	Unit task	
10^0	1 second	Operations	**COGNITIVE BAND**
10^{-1}	100 milliseconds	Deliberate act	
10^{-2}	10 milliseconds	Neural circuit	
10^{-3}	1 millisecond	Neuron	**BIOLOGICAL BAND**
10^{-4}	100 microsec-onds	Organelle	

Fig. 9.2.   Time scale of human action

natural science. And it is physical law on down, although with a twist as it enters the realm of the very small and quantum indeterminacy. But the cognitive band, which is the structuring into a cognitive architecture, is the realm of what can be called representational law. By appropriate computational structuring, internal happenings represent external happenings. The computations obey physical laws; they are physical systems after all. But they also obey the laws of what they represent. From the internal tokens that represent two numbers, an addition algorithm fashions another internal token for a sum of the two numbers. To discover an addition algorithm is precisely to discover a tiny physical system that, while doing its physical thing, also produces situations that obey the laws of addition (given further encoding and decoding processes).

As computations operate in the service of the system's goals, the sys-

tem itself begins to behave as a function of the environment to attain its
goals. This is the realm of reason. No rigid laws hold here, because goal-
oriented computation is precisely a device to circumvent whatever is in
the way of goal attainment. In Aristotelian terms, this is the realm of
final causes, whereas the neural band is the realm of efficient causes, and
there was nothing in the Aristotelian scheme that corresponded to computation, which is the apparatus for moving between the two. A key
point in this is that it takes time to move away from the mechanics (the
architecture) and up into rational behavior. And, indeed, it never fully
happens, so that a longer but better term would be *intendedly rational
band*.

With the picture of figure 9.2, one can see that a unified theory of
cognition is primarily a theory of the cognitive band. It provides a
frame within which to consider the other great determiners of human
behavior—the structures of the task environments people work in and
the knowledge people have accumulated through their social worlds—
but it does not determine this. Rather, it describes how these determiners can be possible and what limits their expression.

Fragments of the Theory

Let me provide a few quick illustrations of the theory. These will be like
strobe-light exposures—a fragment here, a flash there. Still, I hope they
can bring home two critical points. First, Soar is a theory, in the same
mold as theories in the other sciences, a collection of mechanisms that
combine together to predict and explain empirical phenomena. The
predictions come from the theory, not the theorist. Second, as a unified
theory of cognition, Soar has a wide scope, both in types of behavior
covered and in terms of time scale. Though never as great as wishes
would have it, Soar can still stand for the possibility that unified theories
of cognition might be in the offing. Let us begin with immediate reactive
behavior, which occurs at a time scale of about 1 sec., and work up the
time scale of human action.

Stimulus-response compatibility   *Stimulus-response compatibility* is a phenomenon known to everyone, though perhaps not by that name. Anyone
who has arrived at an elevator to find the Up button located physically
below the Down button would recognize the phenomena. The Up button
should map into the direction of travel—*up* on top. This human sense of
should, in fact, translates into longer times to hit the button and greater
chances to hit the wrong button. Stimulus-response compatibility effects
are everywhere. Figure 9.3 shows another example, perhaps less obvious. A person at a computer editor wants to *delete* some word. The editor
uses abbreviations, in this case dropping the vowels to get *dlt.* Thus, the

Task: Intend to *delete* → Type *dlt* (vowel deletion)

		ms
Perceive.	Minimum	~40
Encode.	1 production/letter (6 letters)	~120
Attend.	1 operator	~60
Comprehend.	1 operator to verify	~60
Perception$_{bj}$ = 314		~280
Intend.	Get each syllable: 2 operators	~120
	Get spelling of syllable: 2 operators	~120
	Get each letter: 2 + 4 = 6 operators	~360
	Identify each letter: 2 + 4 = 6 operators	~360
	If consonant link to save: 3 operators	~180
	Issue command: Type letter: 3 operators	~180
Mapping$_{bj}$ = 66 × 25 = 1650		~1,320
Decode & move. Keystroke (can't split D&M): 3 × 180		~540
Motor$_{bj}$ = 203 × 3 = 609		~540
Totals: Total$_{bj}$ = 2,573, Obs avg = 2,400		~2,140

Fig. 9.3.   SRC example: Recall command abbreviation

person needs to get from *delete* to *dlt* to command the editor appropriately. Stimulus-response compatibility occurs here. On the more compatible side, the designer of the editor might have chosen *delete* itself, although it would have required more typing. On the less compatible side, the designer might have chosen *gro*, thinking of *get rid of*.

Figure 9.3 shows an accounting of how Soar would predict the time it takes a person to type *dlt*. First is the processing that acquires the word and obtains its internal symbol: *perceive* the sensory stimulus (in the experimental situation, the word was presented on a computer display); *encode* it (automatically) to obtain its internal symbol; *attend* to the new input; and *comprehend* it to be the task word. Second is the cognitive processing that develops the *intended* answer: getting each syllable; extracting each letter; determining if it is consonant; and, if so, creating the command to the motor system that constitutes the internal intention. Third is the motor processing: *decode* the command, and *move* the finger to hit the key (successively *d, l,* and *t*). The entire response is predicted to take about 2.1 sec. (2,140 ms), whereas it actually took 2.4 sec.

Soar is operating here as a detailed chronometric model of what the human does in responding immediately in a speeded situation. This does not fit the usual view of an AI-like system, which is usually focused on higher-level activities. But a theory of cognition must cover the full temporal range of human activity. In particular, if the theory of the architecture is right, then it must apply at this level of immediate behavior.

These operators and productions are occurring within the architectural frame indicated in figure 9.1. But Soar is not an original theory here. Lots of psychological research has been done on such immediate-response tasks, both theoretical and experimental. It has been a hallmark of modern cognitive psychology. In this case, the experimental work goes back many years (Fitts and Seeger 1953), and there is an extant theory, developed primarily by Bonnie John (1987), which makes predictions of stimulus-response compatibility. What is being demonstrated is that Soar incorporates the essential characteristics of this theory to produce roughly the same results (the numbers subscripted with *bj* are the predictions from John's theory).

Acquiring a task   Figure 9.4 shows a sequence of situations. At the top is a variant of a well-known experiment in psycholinguistics from the early 1970s (Clark and Chase 1972). In the top panel, a person faces a display, a warning light turns on, then a sentence appears in the left-hand panel and a picture of a vertical pair of symbols in the right-hand panel. The person is to read the sentence, then examine the picture and say whether the sentence is true or not. This is another immediate-response chronometric experiment, not too different in some ways from the stimulus-response compatibility experiment above. In this case, one can reliably predict how long it takes to do this task, depending on whether the sentence is in affirmative or negative mode, uses *above* or *below,* and is actually true or false. This experiment, along with many others, has shed light on how humans comprehend language (Clark and Clark 1977).

Our interest in this example does not rest with the experiment itself but with the next panel down in the figure. This is a set of trial-specific instructions for doing the task. A cognitive theory should not only predict the performance in the experiment but also how the person reads the instructions and becomes organized to do the task. The second panel gives the procedure for doing the task. Actually, there were two variants of the experiment, the one shown, and one where 4 reads "Examine the picture" and 5 reads "Then read the sentence." These are not the only instructions needed for doing the task. The bottom two panels indicate increasingly wider contexts within which a person does this task. These panels, written in simple language, are an overly homogeneous and systematic way of indicating these layers of context. In an actual experiment, the person would gather part of this information by observation, part by the gestures and behavior of the experimenter, and part by interaction directly with the experimental apparatus.

The experiment occurs

Plus is above star	+ *

1. Light turns on.
2. Display shows.
3. Subject reads, examines, and presses a button.

Prior trial-specific instructions

4. "Read the sentence."
5. "Then examine the picture."
6. "Press the T-button if the sentence is true of the picture."
7. "Push the F-button if the sentence is false of the picture."
8. "Then the task is done."

Prior general instructions

9. "At some moment the light will come on."
10. "After the light comes on, a display will occur."
11. "The left side of the display shows a sentence."
12. "The right side of the display shows a picture."

Introduction

13. "Hello."
14. "This morning we will run an experiment."
15. "Here is the experimental apparatus."
16. . . .

Fig. 9.4.   Acquiring a task

Soar does both the top two panels (but not the bottom two). Focusing on the second panel, as the interesting one for our purposes, Soar takes in each simple sentence and comprehends it. This comprehension results in a data structure in the working memory. Soar then remembers these specifications for how to behave by chunking them away, that is, by performing a task whose objective is to be able to recall this information, in the context of being asked to perform the actual task. On recalling the instructions at performance time, Soar performs the task initially by following the recalled instructions interpretively, essentially by following them as rules. Doing this leads to building additional chunks (since Soar builds chunks to capture all its experiences). On subsequent occasions, these chunks fire and perform the task without reference to the explicitly expressed rule. Soar has now internalized this task and performs it directly thereafter.

The point is that Soar combines performance and task acquisition in a single theory, as required of a unified theory of cognition. It shows one advantage of having unified theories. The theory of the performance task is not simply stipulated by the theorist (as Clark and Chase had to do) but flows, in part, from the theory of how the task instructions organize the person to do that performance.

Problem solving   Let us move up the time scale. Figure 9.5 shows a little arithmetical puzzle called cryptarithmetic. The words DONALD, GER-ALD, and ROBERT represent three 6-digit numbers. Each letter is to be replaced by a distinct digit (e.g., D and T must each be a digit, say D = 5 and T = 0, but they cannot be the same digit). This replacement must lead to a correct sum, that is, DONALD + GERALD =ROBERT. The figure shows the behavior of a subject solving the puzzle (Newell and Simon 1972). Humans can be given cryptarithmetic tasks and protocols obtained from transcripts of their verbalizations while they work. The subject proceeds by searching in a problem space; the figure shows the search explicitly, starting in the initial state (the upper left dot). Each short horizontal segment is an operator application, yielding a new state. When the search line ends at the right of a horizontal line, the subject has stopped searching deeper and returns to some prior state already generated (as indicated by the vertical line, so that all vertically connected dots represent the same state on successive returns). The subject often reapplies an earlier operator, as indicated by the double lines, so the same path is retrod repeatedly.

It takes the subject about 2,000 sec. (30 min.) to traverse the 238 states of this search, averaging some 7 sec. per state. Although a puzzle, it is still genuinely free cognitive behavior, constrained only by the demands of the task. This particular data is from 1960, being part of the analysis of problem solving by Herb Simon and me (Newell and Simon 1972). A unified theory of cognition should explain such cognitive behavior, and Soar has been organized to do so, providing detailed simulations of two stretches, lines 1–4 and 8–12. Figure 9.6 shows the more complex behavior fragment (lines 8–12), where the subject has trouble with column 5 of the sum (E + O =O) and thus goes over the material several times, a behavior pattern called *progressive deepening*. These two stretches are far from the whole protocol, but they still amount to some 200 sec. worth.

The reason for reaching back to old data is the same as with the stimulus-response compatibility and the sentence-comprehension cases. Initially, the most important element in a proposed unified theory of cognition is coverage—that it can explain what existing theories can do. One attempts to go further, of course. In the sentence case, it is getting the theory to cover the acquisition of the task by instruction. In the cryptarithmetic case, it is attaining completeness and detail.

Development   Finally, consider an attempt to understand how the development of cognitive functions might occur. This territory has been

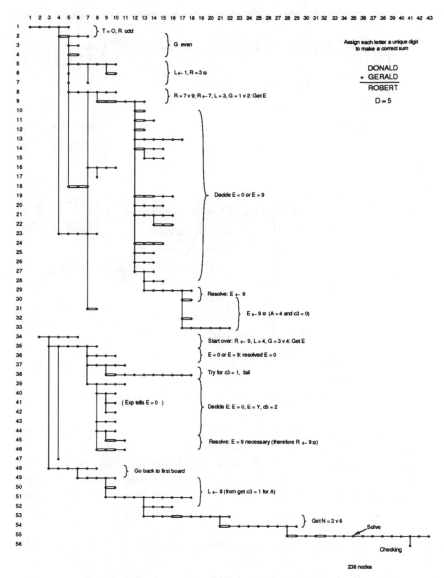

Fig. 9.5. Behavior of a person on the cryptarithmetic task

mapped out by Piaget, who gave us an elaborate, but imperfect and incomplete, theoretical story of stages of development, with general processes of assimilation and accommodation, oscillating through repeated equilibrations. Piaget also mapped the territory by means of a large and varied collection of tasks that seem to capture the varying capabilities of

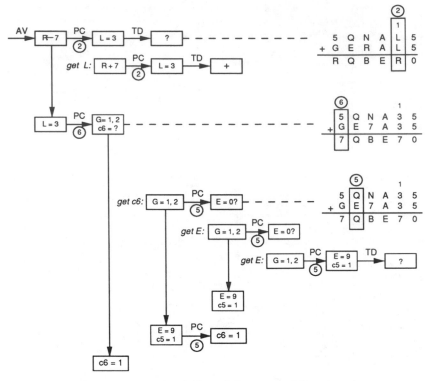

Fig. 9.6.   Soar simulation of the cryptarithmetic task

children as they grow up. Some are widely known, such as the conservation tasks, but there are many others as well.

This exploration with Soar uses the Piagetian task of predicting whether a simple balance beam (like a seesaw with weights at various distances on each side) will balance, tilt right, or tilt left with various placements of weights. As they grow up, children show striking differences in their ability to predict, only taking total weight into account (around 5 years), to considering both weights and distance, providing they are separable, to (sometimes) effectively computing the torque (by late adolescence). Developmental psychologists have good information-processing models of each of these stages (Siegler 1976), models that are consonant with cognitive architectures such as Soar. What is still missing—here and throughout developmental psychology—is what the transition mechanisms could be (Sternberg 1984). That, of course, is the crux of the developmental process. It will finally settle, for instance, whether there really are stages or whether cognitive growth is effectively continuous.

Soar provides a possible transition mechanism. It learns to move through the first two transitions: from level 1 (just weights) to level 2 (weights and distance if the weights are the same) to level 3 (weights, and distance if they do not conflict). It does not learn the final transition to level 4 (computing torques).[3] Soar predicts how the beam will tilt by encoding the balance beam into a description, then using that description to compare the two sides, and finally linking these comparisons to the three possible movements (balance, tilt-left, tilt-right). Soar has to learn both new encodings and new comparings to accomplish the transitions, and it does both through chunking. Figure 9.7 provides a high-level view of the transition from level 1 to level 2. It shows the different problem spaces involved and only indicates schematically the behavior within problem spaces. My purpose, however, is not to show these learnings in detail. In fact, both types of learning are substantially less rich than needed to account for the sorts of explorations and tribulations that children go through.

The above provides the context for noting a critical aspect of this effort to explore development with Soar. Soar must learn new knowledge and skill in the face of existing learned knowledge and skill, which is now wrong. In this developmental sequence, the child has stable ways of predicting the balance beam; they are just wrong. Development implies replacing these wrong ways with correct ways (and doing so repeatedly). That seems obvious enough, except that Soar does not forget its old ways. Chunking is a process that adds recognitional capability, not one that deletes or modifies existing capability. Furthermore, the essence of the decision cycle is to remain open to whatever memory can provide. Soar, as a theory of human cognition, predicts that humans face this problem, too, and there is good reason and some evidence on this score. Humans do not simply forget and destroy their past, even when proved wrong.

The solution within Soar is to create cascades of problem spaces. If an existing problem space becomes contaminated with bad learning, a new clean space is created to be used in its stead. That is, whenever the old space is to be used, the new one is chosen instead. Of course, when first created, this new space is empty. Any attempt to use it leads to impasses. These impasses are resolved by going back into the old space, which is still around, since nothing ever gets destroyed. This old space contains the knowledge necessary to resolve the impasse. Of course, it also has in it the bad learning. But this aspect can be rejected, even though it cannot be made to go away. The knowledge for this must come from a higher context, which ultimately derives from experimental feedback. Once an impasse has been resolved by appropriate problem solving in the old space, chunks are automatically formed (as always). These chunks transfer this knowledge into the new space. Thus, on subsequent occurrences

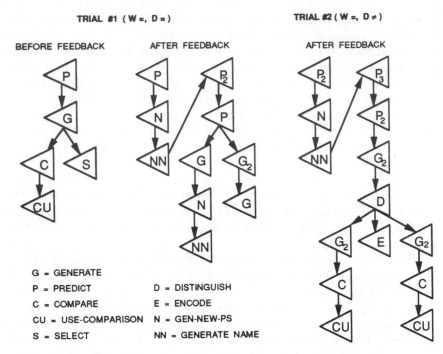

Fig. 9.7. Problem spaces used in learning about the balance beam

of using the new space, it will not have to return to the old space. It may do so for some other aspect, but then that too is transferred into the new space. Gradually, with continued experience, the new space is built up and the old space entered less and less often. But it always remains, because Soar never knows all the information that was encoded in the old space, nor could it evaluate its quality in the abstract. Only in the context of an appropriate task does such knowledge emerge.

The Scope of Soar

Soar addresses a significant range of other phenomena that surround central cognition. Figure 9.8 provides a summary list. Heading the list is the demonstration that Soar accounts for the ability to be intelligent. One of the reasons AI is closely related to cognitive psychology is that functionality is so important. A theory of cognition must explain how humans can be intelligent. But there seems no way to demonstrate this without constructing something that exhibits intelligent behavior according to the theory. Soar demonstrates this by being a state-of-the-art AI system (Laird, Newell, and Rosenbloom 1987).

Soar exhibits the qualitative shape of human cognition in many global

1. The ability to exhibit intelligence
2. Global properties of cognitive behavior
3. Immediate-response behavior
4. Simple discrete motor-perceptual skills
5. Acquisition of cognitive skills
6. Recognition and recall of verbal material
7. Short-term memory
8. Logical reasoning
9. Problem solving
10. Instructions and self-organization for tasks
11. Natural language comprehension
12. Developmental transitions

Fig. 9.8.   Cognitive aspects addressed by Soar

ways. For instance, it is serial in the midst of parallel activity and it is interrupt driven. Next, Soar provides a theory of immediate responses, those that take only about 1 sec. Stimulus-response compatibility was an example. Soar also provides a theory of simple discrete motor-perceptual skills, namely, transcription typing. In general, however, Soar is still deficient in its coverage of perceptual and motor behavior, with typing as close as we have gotten to these critical aspects.

Soar provides a plausible theory of acquisition of cognitive skills through practice. It also offers the main elements of a theory of recognition and recall of verbal material—the classical learning domain of stimulus/response psychology. Soar also provides some aspects of a theory of short-term memory, including a notion on how the plethora of different short-term memories (whose existence has been revealed experimentally) might arise. It provides a theory of logical reasoning, of problem solving, and of how instructions are converted into the self-organization for doing new immediate-response tasks. In addition, it implies a specific but still undeveloped theory of natural language comprehension. Finally, it has demonstrated an idea for a transition mechanism in developmental psychology.

Figure 9.8 presents the range of things that one candidate for a unified theory of cognition has addressed. It has done this with varying degrees of success, depth, and coverage. No claim is made for its superiority over existing cognitive theories. Indeed, Soar contains mechanisms that make it a variant of existing successful theories. The issue is not to demonstrate novelty but to show that a single unified theory can cover all these phenomena—that it is one architecture that does all of these tasks and does them in fair accord with human behavior on the same tasks. Finally, to come back to our main point, Soar is a genuine theory. It is not just a broad framework or a simulation language that provides a medium to express specific microtheories. One does calculations and simulations with Soar and reasons from the structure of the architecture to behavior. Above all, Soar is not a metaphor for mind.

SHOULD THE HUMANITIES MIND?

We have taken a brief tour of Soar. Should the humanities care? They could be fascinated, of course, or repelled, or bored, or mildly pleased at being informed about events across the intellectual river. But should they *care*?

Recall the contrast: metaphors for mind or theories of mind. The computer provides a metaphor for mind, to be used at will, for all that metaphor is good for. Soar represents the other side of the contrast. It is also the computer—a living representative of artificial intelligence and computer science, a state-of-the-art AI system realized as a computer program, employing many mechanisms historically central to AI. But Soar is also a theory of human cognition, a theory of mind. It is put forth not as metaphor but as a standard sort of scientific theory, analogous to, say, the valence theory of chemical compounds or the kinetic theory of gases in thermodynamics. Soar embodies much that has gone into the computer-derived theories of mind, which have played a central role in the cognitive sciences. Soar is not pure AI, whatever that might be, but the melding of cognitive psychology and AI.

What follows for the humanities if it turns out that the metaphorical stance cannot prevail and that, with greater or lesser speed, a theory of mind emerges? Is the mind likely to clank, if the computational view is sustained? Or will it make no difference, because it will simply become a new psychophysics that occupies some obscure scientific corner, while the great questions march on always as before? Or will it turn the humanities into a part of science? If such a transformation were to occur, would it be a good thing for the humanities? Would it finally give them power to deal with questions they have found it difficult to grapple with? Would they pose new questions? Would they start to accumulate knowledge as opposed to history? Or would it destroy them, by grinding them down into laboratory drudges focused only on small questions? Even if it could be maintained that the true, good, and beautiful still lay over the far horizon, would it raise so much havoc in the transition to not be worth the candle? And if it is not worth the candle, can it then be avoided? Or must it be suffered like the plague?

Such questions cannot be answered any more than history can be lived in advance. One way to approach them is by speculating from Soar as a unified theory of cognition. Suppose this is how a cognitive theory will look. Suppose, further, this theory is as right about humans as, say, the classical valence theory is about chemical reactions (which is not all that right, by the way, and much better approximations exist in orbital theory). What kinds of things might follow for the humanities? What would such a science tell them about the nature of mind, hence the nature of man, that they might find useful, interesting, or provocative?

I offer several such speculations. They must be taken as such. They can be appreciated, criticized, and used for further speculation. But they are not solid scientific claims. They attempt too much. Treat them as precursors, perhaps. But none of this makes them metaphorical—approximate, irrelevant, or downright wrong, perhaps, but not metaphorical.

Speculation 1. On being Logical and the Nature of Insight

The issue is familiar and easily stated. Are people logical? Why not? Do people follow rules? If so, do they do so on everything and always? Why is insight opposed to reason? What is insight anyway? These are not all the same question, but they all cluster in the same corner of our concern with our nature. Indeed, the computer metaphor for mind is itself part of this cluster, though here we use the computational theory of mind to explore the nature of the corner.

What does the theory say? Let us start with representation—the form in which knowledge about the world or task is encoded into internal data structures. Consider a situation with an apple, ball, and cap on a table, viewed by someone in passing (fig. 9.9). A moment later, when asked where the ball is, the person promptly answers that it is between the apple and the cap. The situation is simple, but prototypical, permitting the inference that humans have memory, containing knowledge of the external world, organized to permit the performance of tasks (in this case, answering a simple question about an observed situation).

Two broad classes of representations can be distinguished (among others). On the one hand are *propositions*. The statement, *the apple is to the left of the ball,* can serve as prototype, although it is necessary to abstract away from its specifically linguistic form to admit various graphlike and Lisp-like symbolic structures (and P1 of the figure is abstracted a little). On the other hand are *models*. The list (A B) in the figure at the right side (M1) can serve as prototype. An item is to the left of another if it occurs before it in a list.

Both representations are symbolic: they refer to something external, to (in this case) apples, balls, and their spatial relation, and they are realized in symbolic structures of a familiar kind. But they represent in different ways. Each requires different processes to encode knowledge into the representation and make use of it. Propositions involve the familiar apparatus of connectives, variables, predicates, functions, quantifiers, modalities, and rules of inference. Their processing is easily de-

Situation

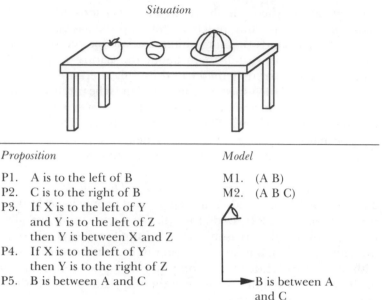

Proposition	Model
P1. A is to the left of B	M1. (A B)
P2. C is to the right of B	M2. (A B C)
P3. If X is to the left of Y and Y is to the left of Z then Y is between X and Z	
P4. If X is to the left of Y then Y is to the right of Z	
P5. B is between A and C	B is between A and C

Fig. 9.9. Propositions and models

limited and realized in many kinds of computer programs, for example, theorem provers. Models are also familiar. Their structures can be put in part-to-part correspondence with what they represent. Their processing is not quite so easily delineated, but it can be described as *matchlike*.

The difference is easily illustrated in figure 9.9 by what is required to answer the question of the whereabouts of the ball. On the propositional side, P1 and P2 encode the information about the table as acquired in passing. P3 and P4 are two general rules of inference, and by their appropriate application, the answer P5 is produced. On the model side, M2 encodes the information acquired in passing (being an augmentation of M1, the initial encoding), and then inspection of this representation (by the eye at the bottom) simply reads off the fact that the ball is between the apple and the cap. The reading-off process must, of course, embody the semantics of the encoding, which means it must have been formed especially for this encoding scheme (though not especially for this particular question).

Soar posits that humans always represent by models.[4] The eye of figure 9.9 is the recognition memory of figure 9.1. The construction of special recognizers for various classes of tasks is accomplished by chunking in response to initially working it through deliberately. There is a fair amount of evidence generally in the cognitive literature that humans do use models (Johnson-Laird 1983), although the case is not conclusive. It is difficult to be conclusive about representations since alternative representations can mimic one another in many ways.

But we are interested in what our theory says. Why might humans employ models? A prime reason is functional. A model is a representation that can be processed rapidly and with assurance by recognition (matchlike) processes. Two models of something can be seen to be the same (or different) just by putting them into part-to-part correspondence and checking each part locally. Not only are models fast but they can be relied on to be fast. Propositions, however, require general inference techniques—essentially the proving of theorems and the derivation of results. These are processes that can take an indefinite amount of time and that lead to combinatorial explosions. For a system built to operate in real time, under the necessity of rapid response, models are substantially more satisfactory than propositions. It might also be observed that models are a natural representation for recognition-memories such as Soar's; after all, the production system is the *eye* that surveys the model and *sees* its properties. But that is not a coincidence. Model and recognition are as yin and yang.

Models satisfy another function, namely, the relation of being the internal representation of the external situation with which the organism is in close-coupled sensory contact. To track and fixate a moving visual target requires an internal representational structure. Such a structure functions as a pointer-structure to permit the coordination of eye movements, occlusion, object permanence when the object disappears behind a tree, and so on. It has intense real time constraints, for continuous updating and for coordinated action. Phenomenally, it would be transparent—pipes through which attention reaches out to contact the moving scene. Models with their part-to-part correspondences are clearly fitted for this task—built like an optic fiber, with its multiplicity of channels, to stay with the pipe metaphor. It is a small (but real) leap to take the representations for all thought as being grounded structurally in the representations that are available for perceptual-motor purposes. But it is another reason to believe that human representations are models, to wit, they grew out of the operational models used in perceiving and acting.

As might be expected, a trade-off is involved. Models are not nearly as powerful a representation as propositions. In their pure form, they cannot deal with notions of disjunction, negation, or quantification. Even if augmented by various notations, such as a tag that a given model part is *not* in the real situation (which thus adds a local propositional element), they remain extremely limited. However, propositional representations, especially forms that are equivalent to quantified logics, have essentially unlimited representational power.

In terms of the theory, humans are not logical because models do not lend themselves to working with general situations. Models work well for situations such as that of figure 9.9. But human failings in reasoning are typically revealed by tasks such as syllogisms:

All bakers are golfers.
Some bakers are not cardplayers.
What follows necessarily about golfers and cardplayers?

It is difficult to represent such quantified situations with models. The expressions can represent a diversity of possible situations, which cannot be captured in any single model. To reason correctly requires generating all possible models and accepting as valid only what holds in all of them. But this requires elaborate and controlled processing, which humans find difficult to do in their heads.

That humans represent by models does not rule out their employing propositions mentally. They certainly hold internal dialogues with themselves and, no doubt, more complex reasonings as well. Within the theory, this occurs by working with *models of propositions*. The internal representation is a model of the propositional form, and the operators are rules of inference. They could be rules such as P3 and P4 in the figure, or even more basic ones such as modus ponens and substitution, which apply encoded forms of rules such as P3 and P4 to other propositions such as P1 and P2. This might seem to abolish the distinction between models and propositions. On the contrary, it reveals how different they are. For the cognitive system, working with a model is working directly in terms of what the model refers to. Thus, when it is working with propositions, it is working directly with propositions, all right, but therefore only indirectly—that is, at one remove—from what the propositions refer to. This is the basis, within the theory, for the fact that following rules is always cognitively remote, compared to directly grasping or seeing the facts themselves.

Insight is bound up with the modellike structure we have described. Seeing that the ball is between the apple and the cap in M2 of figure 9.9 is as close to direct appreciation as the organism comes. No application of rules mediates the process.[5] The recognition of the memory system is inner sight, so to speak. It is not a homunculus: it does not reason, and it does not reflect (that happens in the higher levels of decision cycles and problem spaces). It responds to patterns. The patterns it sees are not fixed in advance, say, by nature. Chunking adds continually new patterns. These can be highly specific, for example, involving the relationship of betweenness, as expressed in a given modellike representation.

Suppose all the above were true? Should the humanities care? It would seem so. The central point would be to make evident exactly why it is that humans fail to be logical or arrive at conclusions by applying rules versus seeing the matter directly. It would also make clear that this depends on specific features of the human architecture and why these features are part of the architecture. This would lead on to understanding that there could be intelligent systems with different architectural properties, which would be quite different—never showing insight, or always being logical on small reasoning tasks, or never being able to apply rules and only working by insight. Such a zoo of intelligences would let us understand our own humanity, with the liberation that comparative study always brings.

Speculation 2. On being Embedded in the Natural Order

The issue is the place of man in the universe. The background can start with the special version of this in our Western heritage—Greek and Hebrew roots, through Rome and up through the emergence of European civilization. A strand of this heritage is the uniqueness of man and his separateness from the other creatures of the world, even his hegemony over them. Not all cultural heritages have this particular homocentric focus, but ours certainly does. The scientific contribution to this heritage, at least in the received version of cultural history, is a succession of defeats for uniqueness and special position and a gradual realization that man is part of nature, not to be distinguished in kind and maybe only modestly in degree. Some of the major scientific revolutions are associated with such defeats (or victories, if you are rooting for the other side). Think of the Copernican revolution, which decentered man and his earth, the Darwinian revolution, which joined man firmly with the animals, and the Freudian revolution, which removed man's action from the control of his own conscious will.

One current battleground over human uniqueness seems to be the human mind—its intelligence, ability to use language, and so on.[6] The computer, itself, is one of the skirmish lines. For if humans were like a computer—whatever that might mean, given the diverse and multiple notions comprising the computer metaphor for mind—then humankind would no longer be unique. Or at least its mind would not, so that some other source of uniqueness would have to be found. And the supply is becoming a little lean.

What does the theory say? There is the obvious statement that a scientific psychology makes the human mind a part of the natural order. Indeed, a scientific biology does so almost as well. However, both could still leave the central claim of uniqueness essentially untouched. Instead, let us focus on the attempt to admit computers as capable of solving difficult tasks but to take them as doing so in an entirely different way than human intelligence. Thus, it is said, the computer solves problems by brute force. In the context of the grand battle above, such a move yields on functionality—solving difficult problems is not unique to humans—but preserves style and type. In the words of Monty Python's Flying Circus, any discussion of computer intelligence should be prefaced by, "And now for something completely different."

Figure 9.10 provides an analysis of this issue. It shows a space within which intelligent systems are located by the means they use to perform their task.[7] The vertical axis is *preparation*, the extent to which a system draws on what it has prepared in advance of the task. The horizontal axis is *deliberation*, the extent to which a system engages in processing once the task has begun. The curves represent equal-performance isobars. Different choices of how much to draw on prepared material and how much to compute once the task is set can yield the same performance—more preparation and less deliberation versus less preparation and more deliberation. Traveling out along the arrow moves from lower performance isobars to higher performance ones. Both axes represent knowledge—knowledge that comes from stored memory structures (what has been prepared) and knowledge that comes from computation during the decision process. The axes, however, are not measured in knowledge abstractly. Stored knowledge is measured in structures (number of rules or number of memory bits) and acquired knowledge is measured in situations searched or processed.

This trade-off is fundamental to information-processing systems. The structure of a system places it in a local region of this space, for it tends to treat all tasks similarly. The rough locations of various types of AI systems are shown in figure 9.10. The early AI systems were search oriented, with little knowledge (equivalent to a dozen rules) and modest search (hundreds of situations). Expert systems use more knowledge (up to about 10^4 rules currently) but do much less search. Indeed, they can be seen as an exploration into what can be gained by immediately accessible knowledge without appreciable search. Hitech, Hans Berliner's high-master chess machine (Berliner and Ebeling 1988) is way out at the extreme of deliberation, with about 10^7 situations examined per external move and with only about 10^2 rules. Hitech would certainly qualify as one of those systems that attains its results by brute force, that is, by massive search.

It is also possible to locate humans on this curve at least approximately. Taking chess as an example, humans can search only about 10^2 situations in deciding on a move. This rough estimate can be derived from Soar and is attested empirically. But humans have about 10^5 rules, as inferred from a Soar-like theory (Simon and Gilmartin 1973) to explain the empirical results of the well-known chess perceptions experiments (Chase and Simon 1973). Chess is only one area of expertise, of

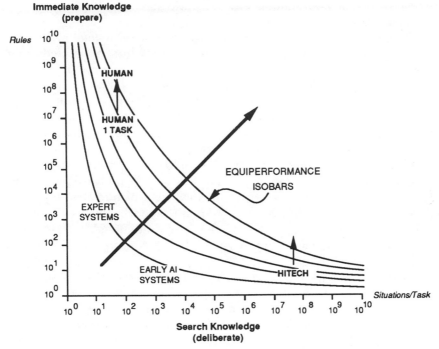

Fig. 9.10. The preparation vs. deliberation trade-off

course. The total knowledge that a human has available over all tasks would amount to many times this, although perhaps not by more than two orders of magnitude.

This space provides a fundamental view of how information-processing systems can differ and yet be related to one another. It tells us that systems, such as Hitech, are not completely different—not an unrelated way of attaining task performance (labeled say as *brute force*) but rather a different part of the total space of information-processing systems. The same considerations enter into systems such as Hitech as into other systems in the space. For instance, once the architecture of a system is fixed, whether for a human or Hitech, the amount of deliberation in a given time becomes essentially fixed. Then the system can improve only by vertical movement in the space (see the small vertical arrows in fig. 9.10). Indeed, Hitech has moved from a low expert to a high master entirely by adding recognition knowledge. For another instance, it is possible to have systems that move back and up along an isobar, that is, decreasing deliberation and increasing preparation. Soar, with its chunking, is such a system. It appears much more difficult to move in the other direction. In fact, I do not know any artificial systems that do so in any substantial way. To understand intelligence requires understanding the nature of this entire space.

Having located humans and brute force intelligent systems in the same space, can we push farther? Why, for instance, are humans located where they are?[8] The theory we are assuming (Soar) offers a clue and echoes the prior example. Human minds are controllers of real time systems. Their form as recognition-intensive rather than search-intensive systems is functional in that respect. Furthermore, their architecture is structured to learn continuously from experience, which continuously moves the system away from deliberation toward recognition.[9]

Suppose all the above were true? Should the humanities care? This analysis denies the separateness of machinelike, brute force intelligence from human recognition-intensive intelligence, which relates only to one aspect of whether the human mind is unique and what assures its unique role in the universe. Nevertheless, this is reason enough to care, given the long multistage battle on this topic, which has occupied such a secure place in Western thought.

There is, perhaps, another small yield. Such a view emphasizes that our minds are a technology—like other technologies in being a set of mechanisms for the routine solution of a class of problems. Technologies differ with respect to the features of the natural order they exploit and to the class of tasks they solve. But all technologies have much in common. This might join with our growing appreciation of other natural biological technologies—the biochemical technologies of metabolism, the macromolecular (DNA/RNA) technologies of replication and protein manufacture, and the cellular technologies of the immune system. We might come to realize the essential role of technologies in the scheme of all organized complex systems, whether natural or artificial. This might even lead us to accept technology as an essential part of what is human and therefore an essential part of a liberal and humanistic education. That also would be reason enough for the humanities to care.

Speculation 3. On Linking the Mundane and the Sublime
The issue is the nature of creativity, which occupies a special place in the humanities. There is confounding between the role of social worth, which introduces an unsettling relativity, and the role of individual talent, which is where we Westerners seem to want to ground creative action. However, too much of what the humanities celebrate—from great composers to great artists to great writers—is polarized by the matter of creativity. The topic remains special.

What does the theory say? There is a long history of attempts within cognitive psychology to describe creativity as just problem solving (Newell, Shaw, and Simon 1962). More specifically, the activity of the creative agent within the total social and historical creative process is asserted to be intellectual activity as predicted by Soar-like theories of cognition. It consists of searches in problem spaces, under various degrees and amounts of knowledge, as produced by the experiences of the agent. This does not provide a full accounting of what happens in creative activity, of why certain creative events occur on certain occasions with certain individuals, and so on. Much is buried in the social and historical contexts. The theory does say that no special processes are involved, beyond those that we understand from more mundane cognitive activities.[10]

Such a claim does not *follow* from the theory. Creativity is a phenomenon in the world, not a defined notion within the theory. Rather, such a claim obtains support (or not), as the cognitive theory of the mind is successful (or not) in explaining empirically labeled creative activities. We need to examine attempts to describe and explain creative activities, and clearly the more creative, the better.

A useful case is the research over the years by my colleague Herb Simon to understand scientific discovery in information-processing terms. This work has recently been summarized at book length (Langley et al. 1987), emphasizing that scientific discovery is problem solving as formulated in current cognitive theories. The theory that the work draws on is not a detailed cognitive architecture, such as Soar, but a more generalized formulation that is consonant with the Soar model, to wit, symbol manipulation, goal hierarchies, problem spaces, and recognition memory. The temporal grain of scientific discovery is too long to require sharp assumptions about the details of the architecture. By the same coin, this work extends the reach of a theory of the architecture, such as Soar.

The methodology employed in this research is both interesting and important. It explains historically significant events of scientific discovery—Boyle's law or Kepler's third law. These satisfy the criteria of being highly creative events. It is not possible to experiment with these events directly; they are history. Therefore, the goal is to *reproduce* these discoveries by a program. The actual data that the discoverer used is presented to a discovery program, and the program should make the actual discovery. It should produce Boyle's law, for instance. The context of what the discoverer knew is set as closely as possible according to the historical evidence. The record is only partial, especially the record of immediate knowledge and skill. But, in a positive confluence, creative scientific discoveries are exactly those on which historians of science lavish special attention, so that often much can be said. This approach is quite analogous to that of the paleoarchaeologists, who endeavor to chip flints by the methods available to early man, or to Thor Hyderdahl, with his sailing of the *Ra* from Ecuador to the Polynesian islands. Care must be taken, both in setting the stage and in interpreting the results. But the yield is new data of a particularly intriguing and relevant sort.

Figure 9.11 summarizes the yield of this research effort. The cases are taken from Langley et al. (1987), plus one more recent effort, Kekada (Kulkarni and Simon 1988), which reproduces the synthesis of urea. There have been several different programs, each of which addresses a different type of scientific discovery problem. The varieties of the Bacon program perform data-driven induction from quantitative data, Glauber and Stahl discover qualitative laws, and so on. Some of the programs provide alternatives or more complete versions of the same discovery. The exact number of cases depends on how to count, but essentially a score of examples has now been worked through. It is important to realize that these programs (Bacon, etc.) actually discover the laws. The stipulation is the context of discovery, and the program then engages in a search in the relevant problem spaces.

This research raises many questions in addition to providing support for the general proposition that creativity is continuous with problem solving on mundane tasks. Such programs require very modest search: they discover the laws quickly. Scientific discovery, as we well know, takes long efforts. Thus, there is dissonance between theory and common understanding. There are several possibilities to be explored in explaining this. Perhaps the greats, like the rest of us, never find the time actually to *do* science, so when they finally get a few hours, interesting things happen. Perhaps there is lots of scientific detailed work to be done, such as setting up experiments and tabulating data, activities not accounted for by these programs. Perhaps the problem spaces they work in are really much bigger and the problem much more difficult, but that explanation contains a disturbing reversal. Perhaps, finally, the creative activities are really located elsewhere, and the actual discovery from the data of, say, Boyle's law, is just a minor bit of routine activity. Then the programs are working on the wrong aspect. However, one should not embrace this last explanation too quickly. The events dealt with by the programs have certainly been considered central by scientific philosophers and historians and by the scientists themselves—as attested by Archimedes's cry of *Eureka!* as he leapt from a bath that could not have lasted more than a few hours.

Suppose all the above were true? Should the humanities care? The research certainly has an impact on history of science and philosophy of science. But that is to be expected, because the research speaks to them directly with the details of its findings. If, however, the research were taken to be a conclusive demonstration about the nature of creativity, it would affect all future discourse on the topic. But the research has

Bacon 1   Boyle's law, Galileo's law of uniform acceleration, Ohm's law,
           Kepler's third law

Bacon 2   (Variant of Bacon.1 with different heuristics)

Bacon 3   Ideal gas law, Kepler's third law, Coulomb's law, Ohm's law

Bacon 4   Archimedes' law of displacement, Snell's law of refraction, Black's
           law of specific heat, law of gravitation, Ohm's law, law of conserva-
           tion of momentum, chemical law of combination

Bacon 5   Snell's law of refraction, conservation of momentum, Black's specific
           heat, Joule's law

Glauber   Acids and alkalis (bases)

Stahl   Phlogiston theory, Black on Magnesium alba, Lavoisier's caloric
           theory and the discovery of oxygen

Dalton   Hydrogen and oxygen to water, plausible extension to particle phys-
           ics reactions, Mendelian genetics

Kekada   Orinthine cycle (synthesis of urea)

Fig. 9.11.   Scientific discoveries reproduced by programs of Langley et al. (1987)
and Kulkarni and Simon (1988)

focused only on scientific creativity. Many other activities are included
under the rubric of creativity—novel and impressive performances in
the fine arts, the performing arts, literature, and poetry—to list only
those in the heartland of the humanities. There is much evidence about
the separability of these various areas, each involving unique technologies to be manipulated and skills to do the manipulations. Thus, it is
possible to treat this evidence from creative scientific discovery as fragmentary. However, it would seem to raise strong enough signals to encourage seeking analogous investigations in related areas where creativity plays a similarly important role.

Speculation 4. On Knowing and Not Articulating

The issue is that humans know things they cannot articulate. This is
often said with an overtone of amazement or disbelief. One scientist cum
philosopher, Michael Polyani, even turned this observation into the central theme of his philosophic oeuvre; he called it *tacit knowledge* (Polyani
1958). A favorite example was riding a bicycle, where it seemed clear for
purposes of philosophy (i.e., without gathering empirical data) that bicycle riders could not articulate how they rode a bicycle, nor would telling
nonbicyclists how to ride, that is, what physical principles to use, enable
them to ride bicycles. The central significance of tacit knowledge has
been widely acknowledged throughout the humanities (Grene 1966),
though not always tied to Polyani.

What does the theory say? It yields a straightforward answer to why human cognition shows the phenomena of tacit knowledge. Actually, it provides two separate answers: one for extended behavior and one for immediate behavior. The extended case comes from the nature of long-term memory, which is a recognition memory, in the sense we described above. In such a memory, knowledge is accessed by means of the retrieval cues that occur in short-term working memory. Thus, knowledge is accessible only if the right cues exist. But the cues are right only if they pull out the right knowledge, and the system cannot know what the right knowledge is. That is what it is trying to find out. Thus, the system in effect must guess at the retrieval cues (although the guessing can be intelligent). This situation holds for any associative or content-addressed memory, not just the specific recognition memory system posited for Soar (fig. 9.1).

In such a memory, it is no wonder that what the system knows for some purposes is not generally available to it for another. Couple this with the fact, in Soar, that procedures are also stored this way, that is, available by recognition when the behavior is to be produced. It follows that people in general cannot articulate the knowledge of how they behave. When they do, they only construct an articulated view on the basis of the internal and external observation of their own performance.

The immediate-behavior case arises from the structure of the decision cycle (fig. 9.1). The decision cycle is composite, consisting of a sequence of production firings that accumulate the available knowledge prior to a decision actually being made. Simple reasoning occurs within a cycle as productions trigger succeeding productions. However, the decision cycle is the shortest time scale at which deliberate action can be taken. It is not possible for a person to articulate what goes on within the decision cycle. They can report various products that end up in working memory, but there is no way they can monitor the detailed processing within the cycle whereby these products originated. Soar provides an explicit picture of the lower limits of articulation. This is not, in general, what Polyani was referring to by tacit knowledge, but both types of limitations easily merge together, if there is no theoretical reason for separating them.

Suppose all the above were true? Should the humanities care? The main effect might be just debunking—to make obvious the limits on articulation, so that it would cease to play a role in larger, more profound discussions. The consequences of knowing without articulation remain, however. It remains an important ingredient in discussing artistic and literary skills and how they relate to the thoughts that artists and writers have of their own art and craft. From this standpoint, having a theory of the mechanisms that lead to the separation of knowing from articulating would seem to be extremely worthwhile.

Speculation 5. On Repression

The issue is emotion and cognition. One striking feature of modern cognitive theories is their failure to incorporate emotional behavior with the cognitive mechanisms. Soar is no exception. There have been a few efforts (Colby 1975; Mueller 1987; Oatley and Johnson-Laird 1987; Simon 1967), which mostly converge on the role of emotions in the interruption of behavior. However, they do not change the overall picture.

This situation reflects the problematic relation of emotion to reason in our society as a whole. The emotion side of the scientific literature shows the same tension. For instance, although some theories actually compute a trajectory of a person's affective state during an interaction, they have no cognitive or task dimension (Heise 1977). Yet, it seems almost undeniable that emotion and affect exist within, around, among, and throughout the mechanisms of the cognitive architecture. One potential approach is to identify cognitive mechanisms that might enter into emotional behaviors in an interesting way, as preparations for understanding how cognition and emotion might fit together into a single system.

What might the theory suggest? The snapshot on developmental mechanisms in Soar provides an interesting example. Recall (fig. 9.7) that the major system problem for Soar in the balance beam task was how to relearn in the face of prior learning that is wrong. This problem has a specific character in Soar, because chunking is the permanent acquisition of productions. Soar's solution was to create new problem spaces, without the bad learning. They did not necessarily contain all the good learning, but these new spaces were linked with the original ones, so that Soar would revert into the originals. By operating momentarily in the old space, with additional considerations from the new one to filter out the wrong behavior, it could operate successfully. Chunking in the old space gradually transfers filtered behaviors into the new space. In this respect at least, Soar would not have to return to the old space on subsequent occasions. This entire mechanism is built within Soar, using chunking, and does not involve any architectural modifications.

The purpose in reviewing this mechanism is to note what has been produced. Problem spaces that contain undesirable effects are being gradually insulated from access by the new problem spaces built in front of them. Gradually, it will become more and more difficult to access these insulated spaces. However, if on some occasion, perhaps much later, a way of working with the new space occurs which has not previously been attempted, the old space will be reentered. It could be like opening the door to a long-locked room. The mind is populated by such old spaces, since new ones get overlaid with additional new ones ad infinitum, depending on the learning history of the system.

This looks like a mechanism for repression, as Freud has taught us to understand it, namely, as central in the emotional life of the individual. The Soar mechanism was not deliberately designed for repression; this is a side effect. It was designed to let new learning become effective and not get mixed up with old learning that had been rejected. It is a cognitive mechanism for cognitive purposes. When we consider what a fully emotional mind might be like, we can imagine that the phenomenon we (as good neo-Freudians) think of as repression would involve this mechanism. This does not say that Freudian repression (more generally, affectively grounded repression) is nothing but this mechanism. We know too little about emotion within the cognitive realm to guess at that. Rather, it opens the possibility that emotional repression will inhabit and use such a mechanism, perhaps rather like the hermit crab, a mechanism defined for entirely cognitive reasons, and become an integral part of the emotional apparatus.

Suppose all the above were true? Should the humanities care? I would think so. The attempt to understand the realms of behavior of major significance to the humanities—represented here by emotion and affect—will be enriched by the use of theories of cognition. These will be a source of ideas about the character of emotion and how it is manifest. In short, such a theory of mind might end up becoming a central theoretical resource for the humanities.

CONCLUSIONS

We have had five speculations to provide some indication of what might follow if there were to emerge from the coming of the computer a theory of mind. They represent a potential yield from Soar, but Soar, in turn, represents the possibility of a unified theory of cognition, and such a theory, in its turn, represents the general and continued development of cognitive science.

These speculations are fragile, but I hope they are useful. A greater concern, perhaps, is their being something of a congeries, rather than a coherence. This arises from the method we chose, namely, to move from Soar toward the humanities. It was not within my ken to pick a central issue in the humanities and build the case for what a theory of mind might say. Scattershot seemed the only way to have a chance at contact.

The point of all the speculations is to illustrate that a theory of mind has a wealth of detail that allows sustained argument and investigation about why humans are the way they are. There are mechanisms of particular shapes and kinds behind the capacities and limits of our abilities to articulate, be logical, have insight, or repress. In this web of mechanisms lies many of the clues to our humanity—what it is like and what it can be like. The details of these speculations are not critical for this point, though to some extent their plausibility is. But most important is that they arise from the operations of a theory, not from reflections on a metaphor.

Finally, does it make any difference to the humanities which one of these two ways of viewing the matter of mind, metaphor or theory, turns out to be sustained? The two views are not symmetric. Sustain the metaphorical view and a nonevent has happened. The computer as metaphor enriches a little our total view of ourselves, allowing us to see facets that we might not otherwise have glimpsed. But we have been enriched by metaphors before, and on the whole, they provide just a few more threads in the fabric of life, nothing more. The computer as generator of a theory of mind is another thing entirely. It is an event. Not because of the computer but because finally we would have obtained a theory of mind. For a theory of mind, in the same sense as a theory of genetics or of plate tectonics, will entrain an indefinite sequence of shocks through all our dealings with mind—which is to say, through all our dealings with ourselves. And the humanities might just be caught in the maelstrom. Or so it would seem.

NOTES

1. Actually, of course, Soar is realized as a set of programs in various programming languages (Lisp and C) that run on a wide range of standard computers.

2. This and other times are asserted of human cognition; they are not the time for running Soar on a computer work station.

3. There is good reason that it should not: the upper reaches of capability are not yet well charted empirically.

4. Actually, the current Soar has a more general attribute-value representation (Laird, Newell, and Rosenbloom 1987), but we posit that humans represent external situations by forming models in this more basic representation.

5. Production systems are often referred to as *rule-based systems*. In many systems, they function as rules with a rule interpreter. In Soar, productions function as an associative recognition memory and not as rules, as that term is used in philosophical discussions of rule following.

6. There need not be a unique battleground; consider sociobiology.

7. This graph is a variant of the store-versus-compute trade-off familiar in computer science. This particular version is adapted from Berliner and Ebeling 1988.

8. The analogous inquiry for Hitech-like systems is not useful yet, because few exist and because they arise from a research community that values exploration for its own sake.

9. The slow neural technology (which runs at ms speeds) might be conjectured to be relevant. However, animals (including man) mostly must respond to other organisms, as predator, prey, and rival. Since all are constructed in the same technology, its absolute speed is probably not strongly relevant.

10. It does not, by the way, claim completeness of current cognitive theory, only that what is missing is as relevant to mundane as to creative cognition.

REFERENCES

Anderson, J. R. *The Architecture of Cognition.* Cambridge: Harvard University Press, 1983.

Berliner, H., and C. Ebeling. "Pattern Knowledge and Search: The SUPREM Architecture," *Artificial Intelligence* 38 (1988): 161–198.

Brownston, L., R. Farrell, E. Kant, and N. Martin. *Programming Expert Systems in OPS5.* Reading, Mass.: Addison-Wesley, 1985.

Chase, W. G., and H. A. Simon. "Perception in Chess," *Cognitive Psychology* 4 (1973): 55–81.

Clark, H. H., and W. G. Chase. "On the Process of Comparing Sentences against Pictures," *Cognitive Psychology* 3 (1972): 472–517.

Clark, H., and E. Clark. *The Psychology of Language: An Introduction to Psycholinguistics.* New York: Harcourt Brace Jovanovich, 1977.

Colby, K. M. *Artificial Paranoia.* Elmsford, N.Y.: Pergamon, 1975.

Dennett, D. C. *The Intentional Stance.* Cambridge: Bradford Books/MIT Press, 1988.

Fitts, P. M., and C. M. Seeger. "S-R Compatibility: Spatial Characteristics of Stimulus and Response Codes," *Journal of Experimental Psychology* 46 (1953): 199–210.

Fodor, J. A. *The Modularity of Mind.* Cambridge: Bradford Books/MIT Press, 1983.

Gardner, H. *The Mind's New Science: A History of the Cognitive Revolution.* New York: Basic Books, 1985.

Grene, M. *The Knower and the Known.* London: Faber and Faber, 1966.

Heise, D. R. "Social Action as the Control of Affect," *Behavioral Science* 22 (1977): 163–177.

John, B. E., and A. Newell. "Predicting the Time to Recall Computer Command Abbreviations," in *Proceedings of CHI'87 Human Factors in Computing Systems,* April 1987. New York: Association for Computing Machinery.

Johnson-Laird, P. *Mental Models.* Cambridge: Harvard University Press, 1983.

Kulkarni, D., and H. A. Simon. "The Processes of Scientific Discovery: The Strategy of Experimentation," *Cognitive Science* 12 (1988): 139–175.

Laird, J. E., A. Newell, and P. S. Rosenbloom. "Soar: An Architecture for General Intelligence," *Artificial Intelligence* 33 (1987): 1–64.

Langley, P., H. A. Simon, G. L. Bradshaw, and J. M. Zytkow. *Scientific Discovery: Computational Explorations of the Creative Processes.* Cambridge: MIT Press, 1987.

Latour, B., and S. Woolgar. *Laboratory Life: The Social Construction of Scientific Facts.* Beverly Hills: Sage, 1979.

Mueller, E. T. "Daydreaming and Computation: A Computer Model of Everyday Creativity, Learning, and Emotions in the Human Stream of Thought." Ph.D.

dissertation, Computer Science Department, University of California, Los Angeles, 1987.

Newell, A. *Unified Theories of Cognition.* Cambridge: Harvard University Press (in press). (The William James Lectures, Harvard University, Spring 1987).

Newell, A., and H. A. Simon. *Human Problem Solving.* Englewood Cliffs, N.J.: Prentice-Hall, 1972.

Newell, A., J. C. Shaw, and H. A. Simon. "The Processes of Creative Thinking," in H. E. Gruber, G. Terrell, and J. Wertheimer, eds., *Contemporary Approaches to Creative Thinking.* New York: Atherton, 1962.

Oatley, K., and P. N. Johnson-Laird. "Towards a Cognitive Theory of Emotions," *Cognition and Emotion* 1 (1987): 29–50.

Polyani, M. *Personal Knowledge: Toward a Post-Critical Philosophy.* Chicago: University of Chicago Press, 1958.

Siegler, R. S. "Three Aspects of Cognitive Development," *Cognitive Psychology* 8 (1976): 481–520.

Simon, H. A. "Motivational and Emotional Controls of Cognition," *Psychological Review* 74 (1967): 29–39.

Simon, H. A., and K. Gilmartin. "A Simulation of Memory for Chess Positions," *Cognitive Psychology* 5 (1973): 29–46.

Steier, D. E., J. E. Laird, A. Newell, P. S. Rosenbloom, R. A. Flynn, A. Golding, T. A. Polk, O. G. Shivers, A. Unruh, and G. R. Yost. "Varieties of Learning in Soar: 1987," in *Proceedings of the Fourth International Workshop on Machine Learning,* June 1987. Los Altos, Calif.: Morgan Kaufman.

Sternberg, R. J., ed. *Mechanisms of Cognitive Development.* New York: Freeman, 1984.

Toews, J. E. "Intellectual History after the Linguistic Turn: The Autonomy of Meaning and the Irreducibility of Experience," *The American Historical Review* 92 (1987): 879–907.

TEN

Thinking Machines:
Can There Be? Are We?

Terry Winograd

INTRODUCTION

Futurologists have proclaimed the birth of a new species, *Machina sapiens,* that will share (perhaps usurp) our place as the intelligent sovereigns of our earthly domain. These "thinking machines" will take over our burdensome mental chores, just as their mechanical predecessors were intended to eliminate physical drudgery. Eventually, they will apply their "ultra-intelligence" to solving all of our problems. Any thoughts of resisting this inevitable evolution is just a form of "speciesism," born from a romantic and irrational attachment to the peculiarities of the human organism.

Critics have argued with equal fervor that "thinking machine" is an oxymoron, a contradiction in terms. Computers, with their foundations of cold logic, can never be creative or insightful or possess real judgment. No matter how competent they appear, they do not have the genuine intentionality that is at the heart of human understanding. The vain pretensions of those who seek to understand mind as computation can be dismissed as yet another demonstration of the arrogance of modern science.

Although my own understanding developed through active participation in artificial intelligence research, I have now come to recognize a larger grain of truth in the criticisms than in the enthusiastic predictions. But the story is more complex. The issues need not (perhaps cannot) be debated as fundamental questions concerning the place of humanity in the universe. Indeed, artificial intelligence has not achieved creativity, insight, and judgment. But its shortcomings are far more mundane: we have not yet been able to construct a machine with even a modicum of common sense or one that can converse on everyday topics in ordinary language.

The source of the difficulties will not be found in the details of silicon microcircuits or of Boolean logic. The basic philosophy that has guided the research is shallow and inadequate and has not received sufficient scrutiny. It is drawn from the traditions of rationalism and logical empiricism but has taken a novel turn away from its predecessors. This new "patchwork rationalism" will be our subject of examination.

First, we will review the guiding principles of artificial intelligence and see how they are embodied in current research. Then we will look at the fruits of that research. I will argue that "artificial intelligence" as now conceived is limited to a very particular kind of intelligence: one that can usefully be likened to bureaucracy in its rigidity, obtuseness, and inability to adapt to changing circumstances. The weakness comes not from insufficient development of the technology but from the inadequacy of the basic tenets.

But, as with bureaucracy, weaknesses go hand in hand with unique strengths. Through a reinterpretation and reformulation of the techniques that have been developed, we can anticipate and design appropriate and valuable uses. In conclusion, I will briefly introduce an orientation I call "hermeneutic constructivism" and illustrate how it can lead down this alternative path of design.

THE MECHANIZATION OF RATIONALITY

In the quest for mechanical explanations of (or substitutes for) human reason, researchers in artificial intelligence are heirs to a long tradition. In his "Discourse on the Method of Properly Guiding the Reason in the Search of Truth in the Sciences" (1637), Descartes initiated the quest for a systematic method of rationality. Although Descartes himself did not believe that reason could be achieved through mechanical devices, his understanding laid the groundwork for the symbol-processing machines of the modern age.

In 1651, Hobbes described reason as symbolic calculation:

> When a man reasoneth, he does nothing else but conceive a sum total, from addition of parcels; or conceive a remainder . . . . These operations are not incident to numbers only, but to all manner of things that can be added together, and taken one out of another . . . the logicians teach the same in consequences of words; adding together two names to make an affirmation, and two affirmations to make a syllogism; and many syllogisms to make a demonstration.[1]

Leibniz (as described by Russell)

> cherished through his life the hope of discovering a kind of generalized mathematics, which he called *Characteristica Universalis*, by means of which

thinking could be replaced by calculation. "If we had it," he says, "we should be able to reason in metaphysics and morals in much the same way as in geometry and analysis. If controversies were to arise, there would be no more need of disputation between two philosophers than between two accountants. For it would suffice to take their pencils in their hands, to sit down to their slates, and to say to each other . . . 'Let us calculate.' "[2]

Behind this program of mechanical reason was a faith in a rational and ultimately understandable universe. The model of "Let us calculate" is that of Euclidean geometry, in which a small set of clear and self-evident postulates provides a basis for generating the right answers (given sufficient diligence) to the most complex and vexing problems. Reasonable men could be relied on to agree on the postulates and the methods, and therefore dispute could only arise from mistaken calculation.

The empiricists turned to physical experience and experiment as the true basis of knowledge. But in rejecting the a priori status of the propositions on which reasoning was based, they did not abandon the vision of rigorous (potentially mechanizable) logical procedures. For our purposes, it will suffice to adopt a broader characterization, in which much of both rationalism and empiricism fall within a common "rationalistic tradition."[3] This label subsumes the varied (and at times hotly opposed) inheritors of Descartes's legacy—those who seek to achieve rational reason through a precise method of symbolic calculation.

The electronic computer gave new embodiment to mechanical rationality, making it possible to derive the consequences of precisely specified rules, even when huge amounts of calculation are required. The first decades of computing emphasized the application of numerical techniques. Researchers in operations research and decision theory addressed policy questions by developing complex mathematical models of social and political systems and calculating the results of proposed alternatives.[4] Although these techniques work well in specialized cases (such as scheduling delivery vehicles or controlling the operation in a refinery), they proved inadequate for the broader problems to which they were applied. The "mathematization" of experience required simplifications that made the computer results—accurate as they might be with respect to the models—meaningless in the world.

Although there are still attempts to quantify matters of social import (for example, in applying mathematical risk analysis to decisions about nuclear power), there is an overall disillusionment with the potential for adequately reducing human concerns to a precise set of numbers and equations.[5] The developers of artificial intelligence have rejected traditional mathematical modeling in favor of an emphasis on symbolic, rather than numerical, formalisms. Leibniz's "Let us calculate" is taken in

Hobbes's broader sense to include not just numbers but also "affirmations" and "syllogisms."

THE PROMISE OF ARTIFICIAL INTELLIGENCE

Attempts to duplicate formal nonnumerical reasoning on a machine date back to the earliest computers, but the endeavor began in earnest with the artificial intelligence (AI) projects of the mid-1950s.[6] The goals were ambitious: to fully duplicate the human capacities of thought and language on a digital computer. Early claims that a complete theory of intelligence would be achieved within a few decades have long since been abandoned, but the reach has not diminished. For example, a recent book by Minsky (one of the founders of AI) offers computational models for phenomena as diverse as conflict, pain and pleasure, the self, the soul, consciousness, confusion, genius, infant emotion, foreign accents, and freedom of will.[7]

In building models of mind, there are two distinct but complementary goals. On the one hand is the quest to explain human mental processes as thoroughly and unambiguously as physics explains the functioning of ordinary mechanical devices. On the other hand is the drive to create intelligent tools—machines that apply intelligence to serve some purpose, regardless of how closely they mimic the details of human intelligence. At times, these two enterprises have gone hand in hand; at other times, they have led down separate paths.

Researchers such as Newell and Simon (two other founding fathers of artificial intelligence) have sought precise and scientifically testable theories of more modest scope than Minsky suggests. In reducing the study of mind to the formulation of rule-governed operations on symbol systems, they focus on detailed aspects of cognitive functioning, using empirical measures such as memory capacity and reaction time. They hypothesize specific "mental architectures" and compare their detailed performances with human experimental results.[8] It is difficult to measure the success of this enterprise. The tasks that have been examined (such as puzzle solving and the ability to remember abbreviations for computer commands) do not even begin to approach a representative sample of human cognitive abilities, for reasons we will examine below.

On the other side lies the goal of practical system building. In the late 1970s, the field of artificial intelligence was drastically affected by the continuing precipitous drop in computing costs. Techniques that previously demanded highly specialized and costly equipment came within the reach of commercial users. A new term, "knowledge engineering," was coined to indicate a shift to the pragmatic interests of the engineer, rather than the scientist's search for theoretical knowledge.

FACTS:

Tank #23 contains sulfuric acid.

The plaintiff was injured by a portable power saw.

RULES:

If the sulfate ion test is positive, the spill material is sulfuric acid.

If the plaintiff was negligent in the use of the product, the theory of contributory negligence applies.

Fig. 10.1.   Rules for an expert system (from D. Waterman, *A Guide to Expert Systems*, 16)

"Expert systems," as the new programs were called, incorporate "knowledge bases" made up of simple facts and "if . . . then" rules, as illustrated in figure 10.1.

These systems do not attempt to explain human intelligence in detail but are justified in terms of their practical applications, for which extravagant claims have been made.

> Humans need expert systems, but the problem is they don't often believe it. . . . At least one high-performance medical diagnosis program sits unused because the physicians it was designed to assist didn't perceive that they needed such assistance; they were wrong, but that doesn't matter. . . . There's a manifest destiny in information processing, in knowledge systems, a continent we shall all spread out upon sooner or later.[9]

The high hopes and ambitious aspirations of knowledge engineering are well documented, and the claims are often taken at face value, even in serious intellectual discussions. In fact, although a few widely known systems illustrate specific potentials, the successes are still isolated pinnacles in a landscape of research prototypes, feasibility studies, and preliminary versions. It is difficult to get a clear picture of what has been accomplished and to make a realistic assessment of what is yet to come. We need to begin by examining the difficulties with the fundamental methods these programs employ.

THE FOUNDATIONS OF ARTIFICIAL INTELLIGENCE

Artificial intelligence draws its appeal from the same ideas of mechanized reasoning that attracted Descartes, Leibniz, and Hobbes, but it differs from the more classical forms of rationalism in a critical way. Descartes wanted his method to stand on a bedrock of clear and self-evident truths. Logical empiricism sought truth through observation and the refinement of formal theories that predicted experimental results. Artificial intelligence has abandoned the quest for certainty and truth. The new patchwork rationalism is built on mounds of "micro-truths" gleaned through commonsense introspection, ad hoc programming, and so-called knowledge acquisition techniques for interviewing experts. The grounding on this shifting sand is pragmatic in the crude sense: "If it seems to be working, it's right."

The resulting patchwork defies logic. Minsky observes,

> For generations, scientists and philosophers have tried to explain ordinary reasoning in terms of logical principles—with virtually no success. I suspect this enterprise failed because it was looking in the wrong direction: common sense works so well not because it is an approximation of logic; logic is only a small part of our great accumulation of different, useful ways to chain things together.[10]

In the days before computing, "ways to chain things together" would have remained a vague metaphor. But the computer can perform arbitrary symbol manipulations that we interpret as having logical import. It is easy to build a program to which we enter "Most birds can fly" and "Tweety is a bird" and that then produces "Tweety can fly" according to a regular (although logically questionable) rule. The artificial intelligence methodology does not demand a logically correct answer but one that works sufficiently often to be "heuristically adequate."

In a way, this approach is very attractive. Everyday human thought does not follow the rigid strictures of formal deduction. Perhaps we can devise some more flexible (and even fallible) system that operates according to mechanical principles but more accurately mirrors the mind.

But this appeal is subtly deceptive. Minsky places the blame for lack of success in explaining ordinary reasoning on the rigidity of logic and does not raise the more fundamental questions about the nature of all symbolic representations and of formal (though possibly "nonlogical") systems of rules for manipulating them. There are basic limits to what can be done with symbol manipulation, regardless of how many "different, useful ways to chain things together" one invents. The reduction of mind to the interactive sum of decontextualized fragments is ultimately impossible and misleading. But before elaborating on the problems, let us first review some assumptions on which this work proceeds:

1) Intelligence is exhibited by "physical symbol systems."
2) These systems carry out symbol manipulations that correspond to some kind of "problem solving."
3) Intelligence is embodied as a large collection of fragments of "knowledge."

The Physical Symbol System Hypothesis

The fundamental principle is the identification of intelligence with the functioning of a rule-governed symbol-manipulating device. It has been most explicitly stated by Newell and Simon:

> A physical symbol system has the necessary and sufficient means for general intelligent action. . . . By 'general intelligent action' we wish to indicate the same scope of intelligence we see in human action: that in any real situation behavior appropriate to the ends of the system and adaptive to the demands of the environment can occur, within some limits of speed and complexity.[11]

This "physical symbol system hypothesis" presupposes materialism— the claim that all of the observed properties of intelligent beings can ultimately be explained in terms of lawful physical processes. It adds the claim that these processes can be described at a level of abstraction in which all relevant aspects of a physical state can be understood as the encoding of symbol structures and that the activities can be adequately characterized as systematic application of symbol manipulation rules.

The essential link is *representation*—the encoding of the relevant aspects of the world. Newell lays this out explicitly:

> An intelligent agent is embedded in a *task environment*; a *task statement* enters via a *perceptual* component and is encoded in an initial *representation*. Whence starts a cycle of activity in which a *recognition* occurs . . . of a method to use to attempt the problem. The method draws upon a memory of *general world knowledge*. . . . It is clear to us all what *representation* is in this picture. It is the data structures that hold the problem and will be processed into a form that makes the solution available. Additionally, it is the data structures that hold the world knowledge and will be processed to acquire parts of the solution or to obtain guidance in constructing it.[12] [emphasis in original]

Complete and systematic symbolic representation is crucial to the paradigm. The rules followed by the machine can deal only with the symbols, not their interpretation.

Problem Solving, Inference, and Search

Newell and Simon's physical symbol systems aspire not to an idealized rationality but to "behavior appropriate to the ends of the system and adaptive to the demands of the environment." This shift reflects the formulation that won Simon a Nobel Prize in economics. He supplanted decision theories based on optimization with a theory of "satisficing"— effectively using finite decision-making resources to come up with adequate, but not necessarily optimal, plans of action.

As artificial intelligence developed in the 1950s and 1960s, this methodology was formalized in the techniques of "heuristic search."

> The task that a symbol system is faced with, then, when it is presented with a problem and a problem space, is to use its limited processing resources to generate possible solutions, one after another, until it finds one that satisfies the problem-defining test.[13]

The "problem space" is a formal structure that can be thought of as enumerating the results of all possible sequences of actions that might be taken by the program. In a program for playing chess, for example, the problem space is generated by the possible sequences of moves. The number of possibilities grows exponentially with the number of moves and is beyond practical reach after a small number. However, one can limit search in this space by following heuristics that operate on the basis of local cues ("If one of your pieces could be taken on the opponent's next move, try moving it . . ."). There have been a number of variations on this basic theme, all of which are based on explicit representations of the problem space and the heuristics for operating within it.

Figure 10.1 illustrated some rules and facts from expert systems. These are not represented in the computer as sentences in English but as symbols intended to correspond to the natural language terms. As these examples indicate, the domains are naturally far richer and more complex than can be captured by such simple rules. A lawyer will have many questions about whether a plaintiff was "negligent," but for the program, it is a simple matter of whether a certain symbolic expression of the form "**Negligent(x)**" appears in the store of representations or whether there is a rule of the form "**If . . . then Negligent (x)**," whose conditions can be satisfied.

There has been a great deal of technical debate over the detailed form of rules, but two principles are taken for granted in essentially all of the work:

1) Each rule is true in a limited (situation-dependent), not absolute, sense.
2) The overall result derives from the synergistic combination of rules, in a pattern that need not (in fact, could not in general) be anticipated in writing them.

For example, there may be cases in which the "sulfate ion test is positive" even though the spill is not sulfuric acid. The overall architecture of the rule-manipulating system may lead to a conclusion being drawn that violates one of these rules (on the basis of other rules). The question is not whether each of the rules is true but whether the output

of the program as a whole is "appropriate." The knowledge engineers
hope that by devising and tuning such rules, they can capture more than
the deductive logic of the domain:

> While conventional programs deal with facts, expert systems handle
> 'lore' . . . the rules of thumb, the hunches, the intuition and capacity for
> judgment that are seldom explicitly laid down but which form the basis of
> an expert's skill, acquired over a lifetime's experience.[14]

This ad hoc nature of the logic applies equally to the cognitive models
of Newell and Simon, in which a large collection of separate "production
rules" operate on a symbolic store, or "working memory." Each production rule specifies a step to be carried out on the symbols in the store, and
the overall architecture determines which will be carried out in what
order. The symbols do not stand for chemical spills and law but for
hypothesized psychological features, such as the symbolic contents of
short-term memory. Individual rules do things like moving an element to
the front of the memory or erasing it. The cognitive modeler does not
build an overall model of the system's performance on a task but designs
the individual rules in the hope that appropriate behavior will emerge
from their interaction.

Minsky makes explicit this assumption that intelligence will emerge
from computational interactions among a plethora of small pieces.

> I'll call "Society of Mind" this scheme in which each mind is made of many
> smaller processes. These we'll call agents. Each mental agent by itself can
> only do some simple thing that needs no mind or thought at all. Yet when
> we join these agents in societies—in certain very special ways—this leads to
> true intelligence.[15]

Minsky's theory is quite different from Newell's cognitive architecture. In place of finely tuned clockworks of precise production rules, we
find an impressionistic pastiche of metaphors. Minsky illustrates his view
in a simple "micro-world" of toy blocks, populated by agents such as
BUILDER (which stacks up the blocks), **ADD** (which adds a single block
to a stack), and the like:

> For example, **BUILDER**'s agents require no sense of meaning to do their
> work; **ADD** merely has to turn on **GET** and **PUT.** Then **GET** and **PUT** do
> not need any subtle sense of what those turn-on signals "mean"—because
> they're wired up to do only what they're wired up to do.[16]

These agents seem like simple computer subroutines—program fragments that perform a single well-defined task. But a subsequent chapter describes an interaction between the **BUILDER** agent and the
WRECKER agent, which are parts of a **PLAY-WITH-BLOCKS** agent:

Inside an actual child, the agencies responsible for **BUILDING** and **WRECKING** might indeed become versatile enough to negotiate by offering support for one another's goals. "Please, **WRECKER,** wait a moment more till **BUILDER** adds just one more block: it's worth it for a louder crash!"[17]

With a simple "might indeed become versatile," we have slipped from a technically feasible but limited notion of agents as subroutines to an impressionistic description of a society of homunculi, conversing with one another in ordinary language. This sleight of hand is at the center of the theory. It takes an almost childish leap of faith to assume that the modes of explanation that work for the details of block manipulation will be adequate for understanding conflict, consciousness, genius, and freedom of will.

One cannot dismiss this as an isolated fantasy. Minsky is one of the major figures in artificial intelligence, and he is only stating in a simplistic form a view that permeates the field. In looking at the development of computer technology, one cannot help but be struck by the successes at reducing complex and varied tasks to systematic combinations of elementary operations. Why not, then, make the jump of the mind. If we are no more than protoplasm-based physical symbol systems, the reduction must be possible, and only our current lack of knowledge prevents us from explicating it in detail, all the way from **BUILDER**'s clever ploy down to the logical circuitry.

Knowledge as a Commodity

All the approaches described above depend on interactions among large numbers of individual elements: rules, productions, or agents. No one of these elements can be taken as representing a substantial understandable truth, but this does not matter since somehow the conglomeration will come out all right. But how can we have any confidence that it will? The proposed answer is a typical one of our modern society: "More is better!" "Knowledge is power, and more knowledge is more power."

A widely used expert systems text declares,

> It wasn't until the late 1970s that AI scientists began to realize something quite important: The problem-solving power of a program comes from the knowledge it possesses, not just from the formalisms and inference schemes it employs. The conceptional breakthrough was made and can be quite simply stated. *To make a program intelligent, provide it with lots of high-quality, specific knowledge about some problem areas.*[18] [emphasis in original]

This statement is typical of much writing on expert systems, both in the parochial perspective that inflates a homily into a "conceptual breakthrough" and in its use of slogans like "high-quality knowledge." Michie (the dean of artificial intelligence in Britain) predicts,

> [Expert systems] . . . can actually help to codify and improve expert human knowledge, taking what was fragmentary, inconsistent and error-infested and turning it into knowledge that is more precise, reliable and comprehensive. This new process, with its enormous potential for the future, we call "knowledge refining."[19]

Feigenbaum proclaims,

> The miracle product is knowledge, and the Japanese are planning to package and sell it the way other nations package and sell energy, food, or manufactured goods. . . . The essence of the computer revolution is that the burden of producing the future knowledge of the world will be transferred from human heads to machine artifacts.[20]

Knowledge is a kind of commodity—to be produced, refined, and packaged. The knowledge engineers are not concerned with the age-old epistemological problems of what constitutes knowledge or understanding. They are hard at work on techniques of "knowledge acquisition" and see it as just a matter of sufficient money and effort:

> We have the opportunity at this moment to do a new version of Diderot's *Encyclopedia,* a gathering up of all knowledge—not just the academic kind, but the informal, experiential, heuristic kind—to be fused, amplified, and distributed, all at orders of magnitude difference in cost, speed, volume, and *usefulness* over what we have now.[21] [emphasis in original]

Lenat has embarked on this task of "encod[ing] all the world's knowledge down to some level of detail." The plan projects an initial entry of about 400 articles from a desk encyclopedia (leading to 10,000 paragraphs worth of material), followed by hiring a large number of "knowledge enterers" to add "the last 99 percent." There is little concern that foundational problems might get in the way. Lenat asserts that "AI has for many years understood enough about representation and inference to tackle this project, but no one has sat down and done it."[22]

THE FUNDAMENTAL PROBLEMS

The optimistic claims for artificial intelligence have far outstripped the achievements, both in the theoretical enterprise of cognitive modeling and in the practical application of expert systems.

Cognitive models seek experimental fit with measured human behavior, but the enterprise is fraught with methodological difficulty, as it straddles the wide chasm between the engineering bravado of computer science and the careful empiricism of experimental psychology. When a computer program duplicates to some degree some carefully restricted aspect of human behavior, what have we learned? It is all too easy to write a program that would produce that particular behavior and all too hard to build one that covers a sufficiently general range to inspire confidence. As Pylyshyn (an enthusiastic participant in cognitive science) observes,

> Most current computational models of cognition are vastly undercon-
> strained and *ad hoc;* they are contrivances assembled to mimic arbitrary
> pieces of behavior, with insufficient concern for explicating the principles
> in virtue of which such behavior is exhibited and with little regard for a
> precise understanding.[23]

Newell and his colleagues' painstaking attention to detailed architecture of production systems is an attempt to better constrain the computational model, in the hope that experiments can then test detailed hypotheses. As with much of experimental psychology, a highly artificial experimental situation is required to get results that can be sensibly interpreted at all. Proponents argue that the methods and theoretical foundations that are being applied to microbehavior will eventually be extended and generalized to cover the full range of cognitive phenomena. As with Minsky, this leap from the microstructure to the whole human is one of faith.

In the case of expert systems, there is a more immediate concern. Applied AI is widely seen as a means of managing processes that have grown too complex or too rapid for unassisted humans. Major industrial and governmental organizations are mounting serious efforts to build expert systems for tasks such as air traffic control, nuclear power plant operation, and, most distressingly, the control of weapons systems. These projects are justified with claims of generality and flexibility for AI programs. They ignore or downplay the difficulties that will make the programs almost certain to fail in just those cases where their success is most critical.

It is a commonplace in the field to describe expert systems as "brittle"—able to operate only within a narrow range of situations. The problem here is not just one of insufficient engineering but is a direct consequence of the nature of rule-based systems. We will examine three manifestations of the problem: gaps of anticipation, blindness of representation, and restriction of the domain.

Gaps of Anticipation

In creating a program or knowledge base, one takes into account as many factors and connections as feasible. But in any realistically complex domain, this gives, at best, a spotty coverage. The person designing a system for dealing with acid spills may not consider the possibility of rain leaking into the building, or of a power failure, or that a labeled bottle does not contain what it purports to. A human expert faced with a problem in such a circumstance falls back on common sense and a general background of knowledge.

The hope of patchwork rationalism is that with a sufficiently large body of rules, the thought-through spots will successfully interpolate to the wastelands in between. Having written Rule A with one circumstance in mind and Rule B with another, the two rules in combination will succeed in yet a third. This strategy is the justification for the claim that AI systems are more flexible than conventional programs. There is a grain of truth in the comparison, but it is deceptive. The program applies the rules blindly with erratic results. In many cases, the price of flexibility (the ability to operate in combinations of contingencies not considered by the programmer) is irreparable and inscrutable failure.

In attempting to overcome this brittleness, expert systems are built with many thousands of rules, trying to cover all of the relevant situations and to provide representations for all potentially relevant aspects of context. One system for medical diagnosis, called **CADUCEUS** (originally **INTERNIST**), has 500 disease profiles, 350 disease variations, several thousand symptoms, and 6,500 rules describing relations among symptoms. After fifteen years of development, the system is still not on the market. According to one report, it gave a correct diagnosis in only 75 percent of its carefully selected test cases. Nevertheless, Myers, the medical expert who developed it, "believes that the addition of another 50 [diseases] will make the system workable and, more importantly, practical."[24]

Human experts develop their skills through observing and acting in many thousands of cases. AI researchers argue that this results in their remembering a huge repertoire of specialized "patterns" (complex symbolic rules) that allow them to discriminate situations with expert finesse and to recognize appropriate actions. But it is far from obvious whether the result of experience can be adequately formalized as a repertoire of discrete patterns.[25] To say that "all of the world's knowledge" could be explicitly articulated in *any* symbolic form (computational or not), we must assume the possibility of reducing all forms of tacit knowledge (skills, intuition, etc.) to explicit facts and rules. Heidegger and other phenomenologists have challenged this, and many of the strongest criticisms of artificial intelligence are based on the phenomenological analysis of human understanding as a "readiness-to-hand" of action in the world, rather than as the manipulation of "present-to-hand" representations.[26]

Be that as it may, it is clear that the corresponding task in building expert systems is extremely difficult, if not theoretically impossible. The knowledge engineer attempts to provide the program with rules that correspond to the expert's experience. The rules are modified through analyzing examples in which the original rules break down. But the patchwork nature of the rules makes this extremely difficult. Failure in a particular case may not be attributable to a particular rule but rather to a chance combination of rules that are in other circumstances quite useful. The breakdown may not even provide sharp criteria for knowing what to change, as with a chess program that is just failing to come up with good moves. The problem here is not simply one of scale or computational complexity. Computers are perfectly capable of operating on millions of elements. The problem is one of human understanding—the ability of a person to understand how a new situation experienced in the world is related to an existing set of representations and to possible modifications of those representations.

In trying to remove the potentially unreliable "human element," expert systems conceal it. The power plant will no longer fail because a reactor operator falls asleep but because a knowledge engineer did not think of putting in a rule specifying how to handle a particular failure when the emergency system is undergoing its periodic test and the backup system is out of order. No amount of refinement and articulation can guarantee the absence of such breakdowns. The hope that a system based on patchwork rationalism will respond "appropriately" in such cases is just that—a hope, and one that can engender dangerous illusions of safety and security.

The Blindness of Representation

The second problem lies in the symbol system hypothesis itself. To characterize a situation in symbolic form, one uses a system of basic distinctions, or terms. Rules deal with the interrelations among the terms, not with their interpretations in the world.

Consider ordinary words as an analogy. Imagine that a doctor asks a nurse, "Is the patient eating?" If they are deciding whether to perform an examination, the request might be paraphrased, "Is she eating at this moment?" If the patient is in the hospital for anorexia and the doctor is checking the efficacy of the treatment, it might be more like, "Has the patient eaten some minimal amount in the past day?" If the patient has recently undergone surgery, it might mean, "Has the patient taken any nutrition by mouth?" and so on. In responding, a person interprets the sentence as having relevance in the current situation and will typically respond appropriately without conscious choosing among meaning.

To build a successful symbol system, decontextualized meaning is necessary: terms must be stripped of open-ended ambiguities and shadings. A medical expert system might have a rule of the form, "**IF EATING (x)** . . . ," which is to be applied only if the patient is eating, along with

others of the form "**IF** . . . **THEN EATING (x)**," which determine when
that condition holds. Unless everyone who writes or reads a rule interprets the primitive term "Eating" in the same way, the rules have no
consistent interpretation and the results are unpredictable.

In response to this, one can try to refine the vocabulary. "Currently
Dining" and "Taking Solids" could replace the more generic term, or we
could add construal rules, such as, "in a context of immediate action, take
'Eating' to mean 'Currently Dining.' " Such approaches work for the cases
that programmers anticipate but of course are subject to the infinite regress of trying to decontextualize context. The new terms or rules themselves depend on interpretation that is not represented in the system.

Restriction of the Domain

A consequence of decontextualized representation is the difficulty of
creating AI programs in any but the most carefully restricted domains,
where almost all of the knowledge required to perform the task is special
to that domain (i.e., little commonsense knowledge is required). One can
find specialized tasks for which appropriate limitations can be achieved,
but these do not include the majority of work in commerce, medicine,
law, or the other professions demanding expertise.

Holt characterized the situation as follows:

> A brilliant chess move while the room is filling with smoke because the
> house is burning down does not show intelligence. If the capacity for
> brilliant chess moves without regard to life circumstances deserves a name,
> I would naturally call it "artificial intelligence."[27]

The brilliance of a move is with respect to a well-defined domain: the
rules of chess. But acting as an expert doctor, attorney, or engineer takes
the other kind of intelligence: knowing what makes sense in a situation.
The most successful artificial intelligence programs have operated in the
detached puzzlelike domains of board games and technical analysis, not
those demanding understanding of human lives, motivations, and social
interaction. Attempts to cross into these difficult territories, such as a
program said to "understand tales involving friendship and adultery,"[28]
proceed by replacing the real situation with a cartoonlike caricature, governed by simplistic rules whose inadequacy is immediately obvious (even
to the creators, who argue that they simply need further elaboration).

This reformulation of a domain to a narrower, more precise one can
lead to systems that give correct answers to irrelevant problems. This is
of concern not only when actions are based directly on the output of the
computer system (as in one controlling weapons systems) but also when,
for example, medical expert systems are used to evaluate the work of
physicians.[29] Since the system is based on a reduced representation of

the situation, it systematically (if invisibly) values some aspects of care while remaining blind to others. Doctors whose salaries, promotions, or accreditation depend on the review of their actions by such a program will find their practice being subtly shaped to its mold.

The attempt to encode "the world's knowledge" inevitably leads to this kind of simplification. Every explicit representation of knowledge bears within it a background of cultural orientation that does not appear as explicit claims but is manifest in the very terms in which the "facts" are expressed and in the judgment of what constitutes a fact. An encyclopedia is not a compendium of "refined knowledge" but a statement within a tradition and a culture. By calling an electronic encyclopedia a "knowledge base," we mystify its source and its grounding in a tradition and background.

THE BUREAUCRACY OF MIND

Many observers have noted the natural affinity between computers and bureaucracy. Lee argues that "bureaucracies are the most ubiquitous form of artificial intelligence. . . . Just as scientific management found its idealization in automation and programmable production robots, one might consider an artificially intelligent knowledge-based system as the ideal bureaucrat."[30] Lee's stated goal is "improved bureaucratic software engineering," but his analogy suggests more.

> Stated simply, *the techniques of artificial intelligence are to the mind what bureaucracy is to human social interaction.*

In today's popular discussion, bureaucracy is seen as an evil—a pathology of large organizations and repressive governments. But in his classic work on bureaucracy, Weber argued its great advantages over earlier, less formalized systems, calling it the "unambiguous yardstick for the modernization of the state." He notes that "bureaucracy has a 'rational' character, with rules, means-ends calculus, and matter-of-factness predominating"[31] and that it succeeds in "eliminating from official business love, hatred, and all purely personal, irrational, and emotional elements which escape calculation."[32]

> The decisive reason for the advance of bureaucratic organization has always been its purely *technical* superiority over any other form of organization. The fully developed bureaucratic apparatus compares with other organizations exactly as does the machine with the non-mechanical modes of production. Precision, speed, unambiguity, knowledge of the files, continuity, discretion, unity, strict subordination, reduction of friction and of material and personal costs—these are raised to the optimum point in the strictly bureaucratic administration.[33] [emphasis in original]

The benefits of bureaucracy follow from the reduction of judgment to the systematic application of explicitly articulated rules. Bureaucracy achieves a predictability and manageability that is missing in earlier forms of organization. There are striking similarities here with the arguments given for the benefits of expert systems and equally striking analogies with the shortcomings as pointed out, for example, by March and Simon:

> The reduction in personalized relationships, the increased internalization of rules, and the decreased search for alternatives combine to make the behavior of members of the organization highly predictable; i.e., they result in an increase in the *rigidity of behavior* of participants [which] increases the *amount of difficulty with clients* of the organization and complicates the achievement of client satisfaction.[34] [emphasis in original]

Given Simon's role in artificial intelligence, it is ironic that he notes these weaknesses of human-embodied rule systems but sees the behavior of rule-based physical symbol systems as "adaptive to the demands of the environment." Indeed, systems based on symbol manipulation exhibit the rigidities of bureaucracies and are most problematic in dealing with "client satisfaction"—the mismatch between the decontextualized application of rules and the human interpretation of the symbols that appear in them. Bureaucracy is most successful in a world that is stable and repetitive, where the rules can be followed without interpretive judgments. Expert systems are best in just the same situations. Their successes have been in stable and precise technical areas, where exceptions are not the rule.

Michie's claim that expert systems can encode "the rules of thumb, the hunches, the intuition and capacity for judgment" is wrong in the same way that it is wrong to seek a full account of an organization in its formal rules and procedures. Modern sociologists have gone beyond Weber's analysis, pointing to the informal organization and tacit knowledge in individual expertise. Without it, we get rigidity and occasional but irreparable failure.

The depersonalization of knowledge in expert systems also has obvious parallels with bureaucracy. When a person views his or her job as the correct application of a set of rules (whether human invoked or computer based), there is a loss of personal responsibility or commitment. The "I just follow the rules" of the bureaucratic clerk has its direct analogue in "That's what the knowledge base says." The individual is not committed to appropriate results (as judged in some larger human context) but to faithful application of the procedures.

This forgetfulness of individual commitment is perhaps the most subtle and dangerous consequence of patchwork rationality. The person

who puts rules into a knowledge base cannot be committed to the consequences of applying them in a situation he or she cannot foresee. The
person who applies them cannot be committed to their formulation or to
the mechanics by which they produce an answer. The result belongs to
no one. When we speak here of "commitment," we mean something
more general than the kind of accountability that is argued in court.
There is a deep sense in which every use of language is a reflection of
commitment, as we will see below.

ALTERNATIVES

We began with the question of thinking machines—devices that mechanically reproduce human capacities of thought and language. We have
seen how this question has been reformulated in the pursuit of artificial
intelligence, to reflect a particular design based on patchwork rationalism. We have argued that the current direction will be inadequate to
explain or construct real intelligence.

But, one might ask, does that mean that no machine could exhibit
intelligence? Is artificial intelligence inherently impossible, or is it just
fiendishly difficult? To answer sensibly, we must first ask what we mean
by "machine." There is a simple a priori proof that machines can be
intelligent if we accept that our own brains are (in Minsky's provocative
words) nothing but "meat machines." If we take "machine" to stand for
any physically constituted device subject to the causal laws of nature,
then the question reduces to one of materialism and is not to be resolved
through computer research. If, however, we take machine to mean
"physical symbol system," then there is ground for a strong skepticism.
This skepticism has become visible among practitioners of artificial intelligence as well as the critics.

Emergent Intelligence

The innovative ideas of cybernetics a few decades ago led to two contrasting research programs. One, which we have examined here, took the
course of symbol processing. The other was based on modeling neural
activity and led to the work on "perceptrons" a research line that was
discounted for many years as fruitless and is now being rehabilitated in
"connectionist" theories, based on "massively parallel distributed processing." In this work, each computing element (analogous to a neuron)
operates on simple general principles, and intelligence emerges from the
evolving patterns of interaction.[35]

Connectionism is one manifestation of what Turkle calls "emergent
AI."[36] The fundamental intuition guiding this work is that cognitive structure in organisms emerges through learning and experience, not through

explicit representation and programming. The problems of blindness and domain limitation described above need not apply to a system that has developed through situated experience.

It is not yet clear whether we will see a turn back toward the heritage of cybernetics or simply a "massively parallel" variant of current cognitive theory and symbol-processing design. Although the new connectionism may breathe new life into cognitive modeling research, it suffers an uneasy balance between symbolic and physiological description. Its spirit harks back to the cybernetic concern with real biological systems, but the detailed models typically assume a simplistic representational base much closer to traditional artificial intelligence. Connectionism, like its parent cognitive theory, must be placed in the category of brash unproved hypotheses, which have not really begun to deal with the complexities of mind and whose current explanatory power is extremely limited.

In one of the earliest critiques of artificial intelligence, Dreyfus compared it to alchemy.[37] Seekers after the glitter of intelligence are misguided in trying to cast it from the base metal of computing. There is an amusing epilogue to this analogy: in fact, the alchemists were right. Lead can be converted into gold by a particle accelerator hurling appropriate beams at lead targets. The AI visionaries may be right in the same way, and they are likely to be wrong in the same way. There is no reason but hubris to believe that we are any closer to understanding intelligence than the alchemists were to the secrets of nuclear physics. The ability to create a glistening simulacrum should not fool us into thinking the rest is "just a matter of encoding a sufficient part of the world's knowledge" or into a quest for the philosopher's stone of "massively parallel processing."

Hermeneutic Constructivism

Discussions of the problems and dangers of computers often leave the impression that on the whole we would be better off if we could return to the precomputer era. In a similar vein, one might decry the advent of written language, which created many new problems. For example, Weber attributes the emergence of bureaucracy to the spread of writing and literacy, which made it possible to create and maintain systems of rules. Indeed, the written word made bureaucracy possible, but that is far from a full account of its relevance to human society.

The computer is a physical embodiment of the symbolic calculations envisaged by Hobbes and Leibniz. As such, it is really not a thinking machine, but a *language machine*. The very notion of "symbol system" is inherently linguistic, and what we duplicate in our programs with their rules and propositions is really a form of verbal argument, not the workings of mind. It is tempting—but ultimately misleading—to project the image of rational discourse (and its reflection in conscious introspection) onto the design of embodied intelligence. In taking inner discourse as a model for the activity of Minsky's tiny agents, or of productions that determine what token to process next, artificial intelligence has operated with the faith that mind is linguistic down to the microscopic level.

But the utility of the technology need not depend on this faith. The computer, like writing, is fundamentally a communication medium, one that is unique in its ability to perform complex manipulations on the linguistic objects it stores and transmits. We can reinterpret the technology of artificial intelligence in a new background, with new consequences. In doing so, we draw on an alternative philosophical grounding, which I will call "hermeneutic constructivism."

We begin with some fundamental questions about what language is and how it works. In this, we draw on work in hermeneutics (the study of interpretation) and phenomenology, as developed by Heidegger and Gadamer, along with the concepts of language action developed from the later works of Wittgenstein through the speech act philosophy of Austin, Searle, and Habermas.[38]

Two guiding principles emerge: (1) *people create their world through language;* and (2) *language is always interpreted in a tacitly understood background.*

Austin pointed out that "performative" sentences do not convey information about the world but act to change that world. "You're hired," when uttered in appropriate conditions, creates—not describes—a situation of employment. Searle applied this insight to mundane language actions such as asking questions and agreeing to do something. Habermas extended it further, showing how sentences we would naively consider statements of fact have force by virtue of an act of commitment by the speaker.

> The essential presupposition for the success of [a language] act consists in the speaker's entering into a specific engagement, so that the hearer can rely on him. An utterance can count as a promise, assertion, request, question, or avowal, if and only if the speaker makes an offer that he is ready to make good insofar as it is accepted by the hearer. The speaker must engage himself, that is, indicate that in certain situations he will draw certain consequences for action.[39]

Descartes's descendants in the rationalistic tradition take the language of mathematics as their ideal. Terms are either primitive or can be fully defined; the grammar is unambiguous; and precise truth conditions can be established through formal techniques. But even in apparently simple and straightforward situations, human language is metaphorical, ambiguous, and undefinable. What we can take as fundamental is the engagement—the commitment to make good what cannot be fully made precise.

This grounding is especially evident for statements of the kind that Roszak characterizes as "ideas" rather than "information."[40] "All men are created equal" cannot be judged as a true or false description of the objective world. Its force resides in the commitments it carries for further characterization and further action. But it is critical to recognize that this social grounding of language applies equally to the mundane statements of everyday life. "The patient is eating" cannot be held up to any specific set of truth conditions across situations in which it may be uttered. The speaker is not reporting an objectively delineated state of affairs but indicating the "engagement" to enter sincerely into a dialogue of articulation of the relevant background.

This unavoidable dependence of interpretation on unspoken background is the fundamental insight of the hermeneutic phenomenologists, such as Gadamer. It applies not just to ordinary language but to every symbolic representation as well. We all recognize that in "reducing things to numbers," we lose the potential for interpretation in a background. But this is equally true of "reducing them to symbol structures."

Whenever a computer program is intended to guide or take action in a human domain, it inevitably imports basic values and assumptions. The basic nature of patchwork rationalism obscures the underlying constitutive "ideas" with a mosaic of fragmentary bits of "information." The social and political agenda concealed behind these patches of decontextualized and depersonalized belief is dangerous in its invisibility.

Language Machines

Symbol structures are ultimately created by people and interpreted by people. The computer, as a language machine, manipulates symbols without respect to their interpretation. To the extent that relations among the meanings can be adequately reflected in precise rules, the computational manipulations make sense. The error is in assuming that these manipulations capture, rather than augment or reify, parts of the meaning. If an expert system prints out "Give the patient penicillin" or "Fire the missiles now," room for interpretation is limited and meaning is lost. But instead, we can see the computer as a way of organizing, searching, and manipulating texts that are created by people, in a context, and ultimately intended for human interpretation.

We are already beginning to see a movement away from the early vision of computers replacing human experts. For example, the medical diagnostic system described above is being converted from "Internist" (a doctor specializing in internal medicine) to an "advisory system" called "QMR" (Quick Medical Reference).[41] The rules can be thought of as constituting an automated textbook, which can access and logically combine entries that are relevant to a particular case. The goal is to suggest and justify possibilities a doctor might not otherwise have considered. The program need not respond with an evaluation or plan for action but is successful through providing relevant material for interpretation by an expert. Similarly, in areas of real-time control (like a nuclear power plant), an advisory system can monitor conditions and provide warnings, reports, and summaries for human review. In a similar vein, an interactive computer-based encyclopedia need not cover all of human knowledge or provide general purpose deduction in order to take advantage of the obvious computer capacities of speed, volume, and sophisticated inferential indexing.

Another opportunity for design is in the regularities of the structure of language use. As a simple example, a request is normally followed in coherent conversation by an acceptance, a rejection, or a request to modify the conditions. These, in turn, are followed by other language acts in a logic of "conversation for action" oriented toward completion (a state in which neither party is awaiting further action by the other). The theory of such conversations has been developed as the basis for a computer program called The Coordinator, which is used for facilitating and organizing computer-message conversations in an organization.[42] It emphasizes the role of commitment by the speaker in each speech act and provides the basis for timely and effective action.

Howard has studied the use of computer systems by professionals evaluating loan applications for the World Bank. He argues that their use of computers while on field missions increases the "transparency" of their decision-making process, hence increasing their accountability and enhancing opportunities for meaningful negotiation. The computer serves as a medium of discourse in which different commitments and their consequences can be jointly explored.

> As a result, the dialogue between them [the bankers and their clients] suddenly becomes less about the final results—"the numbers"—and more about the assumptions behind the numbers, the criteria on which decisions are themselves based. . . . [quoting a bank professional] "Instead of just saying, 'I don't believe you, my opinion is X,' we explore it. We say, 'let's see what the consequences of that are.' And, sometimes, we end up changing our assumptions."[43]

Current expert systems methodologies are not well suited to this kind of dialogue. They separate the construction of the knowledge base from the use of its "expertise." The experts (with the help of knowledge engineers) enter the knowledge in the laboratory, and the users apply it in the field to get results. But we might instead use the computer to support the discourse that creates the reality—as a tool for the cooperative articulation of the characterizations and rules that will be applied. Rather than seeing the computer as working with objectified refined knowledge, it can serve as a way of keeping track of how the representations emerge from interpretations: who created them in what context and where to look for clarification.

CONCLUSION

The question of our title demands interpretation in a context. As developed in this essay, it might be formulated more precisely, "Are *we* machines of the kind that researchers are building as 'thinking machines'?" In asking this kind of question, we engage in a kind of projection—understanding humanity by projecting an image of ourselves onto the machine and the image of the machine back onto ourselves. In the tradition of artificial intelligence, we project an image of our language activity onto the symbolic manipulations of the machine, then project that back onto the full human mind.

But these projections are like the geometric projection of a three-dimensional world onto a two-dimensional plane. We systematically eliminate dimensions, thereby both simplifying and distorting. The particular dimensions we eliminate or preserve in this exercise are not idiosyncratic accidents. They reflect a philosophy that precedes them and that they serve to amplify and extend.

In projecting language as a rule-governed manipulation of symbols, we all too easily dismiss the concerns of human meaning that make up the humanities and indeed of any socially grounded understanding of human language and action. In projecting language back as the model for thought, we lose sight of the tacit embodied understanding that undergirds our intelligence. Through a broader understanding, we can recapture our view of these lost dimensions and in the process better understand both ourselves and our machines.

NOTES

1. Hobbes, *Leviathan,* quoted in Haugeland, *Artificial Intelligence: The Very Idea,* 24.

2. Russell, *A History of Western Philosophy,* 592.

3. See chap. 2, Winograd and Flores, *Understanding Computers and Cognition.*

4. One large-scale and quite controversial example was the MIT/Club of Rome simulation of the world social and economic future (*The Limits of Growth*).

5. See, e.g., the discussions in Davis and Hersh, *Descartes' Dream.*

6. See Gardner, *The Mind's New Science,* for an overview of the historical context.

7. These are among the section headings in Minsky, *The Society of Mind.*

8. See, e.g., Newell and Simon, *Human Problem Solving,* and Laird et al., *Universal Subgoaling and Chunking.*

9. Feigenbaum and McCorduck, *The Fifth Generation,* 86, 95, 152.

10. Minsky, *The Society of Mind,* 187. Although Minsky's view is prevalent among AI researchers, not all of his colleagues agree that thought is so open-endedly nonlogical. McCarthy (cofounder with Minsky of the MIT AI lab), for example, is exploring new forms of logic that attempt to preserve the rigor of ordinary deduction, while dealing with some of the properties of commonsense reasoning, as described in the papers in Bobrow, ed., Special Issue on Nonmonotonic Logic.

11. Newell and Simon, "Computer Science as Empirical Inquiry" (their speech accepting the ACM Turing Award, the computer science equivalent of the Nobel Prize).

12. Newell, "The Knowledge Level," 88.

13. Newell and Simon, "Computer Science as Empirical Inquiry," 121.

14. Michie and Johnston, *The Creative Computer,* 35.

15. Minsky, *The Society of Mind,* 17.

16. Ibid., 67.

17. Ibid., 33.

18. Waterman, *A Guide to Expert Systems,* 4.

19. Michie and Johnston, *The Creative Computer,* 129.

20. Feigenbaum and McCorduck, *The Fifth Generation,* 12, 40.

21. Ibid., 229.

22. Lenat, "CYC," 75.

23. Pylyshyn, *Computation and Cognition,* xv.

24. Newquist, "The Machinery of Medical Diagnosis," 70.

25. See the discussion in H. Dreyfus and S. Dreyfus, *Mind Over Machine.*

26. See, e.g., H. Dreyfus, *What Computers Can't Do,* and Winograd and Flores, *Understanding Computers and Cognition.*

27. Holt, "Remarks Made at ARPA Principal Investigators' Conference," 1.

28. See the discussion of the BORIS program in Winograd and Flores, *Understanding Computers and Cognition,* 121 ff.

29. See Athanasiou, "High-tech Politics: The Case of Artificial Intelligence," 24.

30. Lee, "Bureaucracy as Artificial Intelligence," 127.

31. Weber, *Economy and Society,* 1002.

32. Ibid., 975.

33. Ibid., 973.

34. March and Simon, *Organizations,* 38.

35. For a historical account and analysis of the current debates, see H. Dreyfus, "Making a Mind vs. Modeling the Brain." For a technical view, see Rumelhart and MacLelland, *Parallel Distributed Processing.* Maturana and Varela, in *The Tree of Knowledge,* offer a broad philosophy of cognition on this basis.

36. Turkle, "Romantic Reactions."

37. H. Dreyfus, "Alchemy and Artificial Intelligence."

38. See chap. 5 of Winograd and Flores, *Understanding Computers and Cognition,* for an overview.

39. Habermas, *Communication and the Evolution of Society,* 61.
40. Roszak, *The Cult of Information.*
41. Newquist, "The Machinery of Medical Diagnosis," 70.
42. See Flores, "Management and Communication in the Office of the Future"; Winograd and Flores, *Understanding Computers and Cognition;* and Winograd, "A Language/Action Perspective on the Design of Cooperative Work."
43. Howard, "Systems Design and Social Responsibility."

REFERENCES

Athanasiou, Tom. "High-tech Politics: The Case of Artificial Intelligence," *Socialist Review* (1987): 7–35.

Austin, J. L. *How to Do Things with Words.* Cambridge: Harvard University Press, 1962.

Bobrow, Daniel, ed. Special Issue on Nonmonotonic Logic, *Artificial Intelligence* 13:1 (January 1980).

Club of Rome, *The Limits to Growth.* New York: Universe Books, 1972.

Davis, Philip J., and Reuben Hersh. *Descartes' Dream: The World According to Mathematics.* San Diego: Harcourt Brace Jovanovich, 1986.

Dreyfus, Hubert. "Alchemy and Artificial Intelligence," Rand Corporation Paper, December 1965, 3244.

———. *What Computers Can't Do: A Critique of Artificial Reason.* New York: Harper and Row, 1972 (2d ed. with new preface, 1979).

———. "Making a Mind versus Modeling the Brain: Artificial Intelligence Back at a Branchpoint" *Daedalus* 117:1 (Winter 1988): 14–44.

Dreyfus, Hubert L., and Stuart E. Dreyfus. *Mind Over Machine: The Power of Human Intuition and Expertise in the Era of the Computer.* New York: Macmillan/The Free Press, 1985.

Feigenbaum, Edward A., and Pamela McCorduck. *The Fifth Generation: Artificial Intelligence and Japan's Computer Challenge to the World.* Reading, Mass.: Addison-Wesley, 1983.

Flores, C. Fernando. "Management and Communication in the Office of the Future," Ph.D. dissertation, University of California, Berkeley, 1982.

Gardner, Howard. *The Mind's New Science: A History of the Cognitive Revolution.* New York: Basic Books, 1985.

Habermas, Jürgen. *Communication and the Evolution of Society,* trans. Thomas McCarthy. Boston: Beacon Press, 1979.

Haugeland, John. *Mind Design.* Cambridge: Bradford/MIT Press, 1981.

———. *Artificial Intelligence: The Very Idea.* Cambridge: Bradford/MIT Press, 1985.

Holt, Anatol. "Remarks Made at ARPA Principal Investigators' Conference," Los Angeles, February 6–8, 1974 (unpubl. ms.).

Howard, Robert. "Systems Design and Social Responsibility: The Political Implications of 'Computer-Supported Cooperative Work,' " address delivered at the First Annual Conference on Computer-Supported Cooperative Work, Austin, Texas, December 1986.

Laird, John, Paul Rosenbloom, and Allen Newell. *Universal Subgoaling and Chunking: The Automatic Generation and Learning of Goal Hierarchies.* Hingham, Mass.: Kluwer, 1986.

Lee, Ronald M. "Bureaucracy as Artificial Intelligence," in L. B. Methlie and R. H. Sprague, eds., *Knowledge Representation for Decision Support Systems.* New York: Elsevier (North-Holland), 1985. 125–132.

———. "Automating Red Tape: The Performative vs. Informative Roles of Bureaucratic Documents," *Office: Technology and People* 2 (1984): 187–204.

Lenat, Douglas. "CYC: Using Common Sense Knowledge to Overcome Brittleness and Knowledge Acquisition Bottlenecks," *AI Magazine* 6:4 (1986): 65–85.

March, James G., and Herbert A. Simon. *Organizations.* New York: Wiley, 1958.

Maturana, Humberto R., and Francisco Varela. *The Tree of Knowledge.* Boston: New Science Library, 1987.

Michie, Donald, and Rory Johnston. *The Creative Computer.* New York: Viking, 1984.

Minsky, Marvin. *The Society of Mind.* New York: Simon and Schuster, 1986.

Newell, Allen. "The Knowledge Level," *Artificial Intelligence* 18 (1982): 87–127.

Newell, Allen, and Herbert Simon. "Computer Science as Empirical Inquiry: Symbols and Search," *Communications of the ACM* 19 (March 1976): 113–126. Reprinted in J. Haugeland, ed., *Mind Design,* 35–66.

———. *Human Problem Solving.* Englewood Cliffs, N.J.: Prentice-Hall, 1972.

Newquist, Harvey P., III. "The Machinery of Medical Diagnosis," *AI Expert* 2:5 (May 1987): 69–71.

Pylyshyn, Zenon. *Computation and Cognition: Toward a Foundation for Cognitive Science.* Cambridge: Bradford/MIT Press, 1984.

Roszak, Theodore. *The Cult of Information: The Folklore of Computers and the True Art of Thinking.* New York: Pantheon, 1986.

Rumelhart, David, and James MacLelland. *Parallel Distributed Processing: Explorations in the Microstructures of Cognition.* 2 vols. Cambridge: Bradford/MIT Press, 1986.

Russell, Bertrand. *A History of Western Philosophy.* New York: Simon and Schuster, 1952.

Simon, Herbert. *Models of Thought.* New Haven: Yale University Press, 1979.

Turkle, Sherry. "Romantic Reactions: Paradoxical Responses to the Computer Presence," chap. 11, this volume.

Waterman, Donald. *A Guide to Expert Systems.* Reading, Mass.: Addison-Wesley, 1986.

Weber, Max. *Economy and Society: An Outline of Interpretive Sociology.* Berkeley, Los Angeles, London: University of California Press, 1968.

Winograd, Terry. "A Language/Action Perspective on the Design of Cooperative Work," *Human-Computer Interaction* 3:1 (1987–88): 3–30.

Winograd, Terry, and Fernando Flores. *Understanding Computers and Cognition: A New Foundation for Design.* Norwood, N.J.: Ablex, 1986.

ELEVEN

Romantic Reactions: Paradoxical Responses to the Computer Presence

Sherry Turkle

EVOCATIVE OBJECTS

In the eighteenth century, Newton's physics gave rise to a clockwork and rationalist view of human nature.[1] It also eventually gave rise to the opposite: a romantic reaction to considering reason as what made humans unique declared that sensibility was more important than logic, the heart more human than the mind.

Responses in our contemporary culture to the computer presence have a similar dialectical quality. Computers and computational ideas have entered popular thinking to support images of mind as mechanism, as program, as information processor. Yet even as these images have spread through the culture, they have provoked a new romantic reaction. When people use information-processing models to explain more and more of their behavior, they often feel compelled to isolate as "their core" something they can think of as privileged and undetermined, something fundamentally "beyond information." The very qualities of computers that foster mechanistic views of human nature also lead people to emphasize the importance of feelings, spontaneity, holism, sensuality, and spirituality in defining what is uniquely human. For some people, the appropriation and disavowal of computational images of the self take the form of a pendulum swing; for others, the competing views of the self exist simultaneously: there is no victory, only ambivalence.

I have been a student of these popular "romantic reactions" to the computer for over a decade.[2] I have reported that in the presence of the computer, there is a tendency for people to define themselves as what computers are not or cannot do. But defining people too starkly as what computers cannot do in terms of *performance* leaves one in a vulnerable position, with definitions of what is unique in human nature trying to run ahead of what clever engineers might come up with next. This happened (to choose only one out of many examples) when in the early 1960s, philosopher Hubert Dreyfus insisted that a computer could not beat him at chess because chess required intuition and experience, a "knowing how" rather than a "knowing that." When a chess program was able to triumph over him (and other even more skilled players), Dreyfus had to retreat to the position that "real chess" was the kind of chess computers could not play.[3] With many such experiences of computer competency behind them, people have learned to look for a more modulated response. In my studies, I find that people begin by admitting that human minds are some kind of computer and then go on to find ways to think of people as something more as well.

Faced with "smart machines," professional philosophers respond by cataloging principles of human uniqueness. They find them in human intentionality, emotion, and biology. Faced with a computer that follows *rules*, philosophers see humans as unique because their knowledge is socially and physically situated, not rule based but embodied, concrete, and experiential.[4] These responses from a professional community are echoed in the popular culture. When confronted with a computer that in some ways seems to think like a person, people use everyday language to capture their sense of human uniqueness. They talk about feelings, flesh, intuition, spark, direct experience, or, as Joseph Weizenbaum summed it up, the things we know but cannot say, the wordless glance that a father and mother share over the bed of their sleeping child.[5]

People analogize mind to computer but then take care to undermine the analogy by attributing to people what one eighteen-year-old I interviewed called "a saving grace." In her mind, "that saving grace, the difference between people and computers, is emotion. And that's the line you can draw. That's where you say, this thing may be able to do something like thinking, but it can't love anybody." I have found this response widespread.

Since the mid-1970s, the media have touted the prowess of expert systems, the large computer programs that embody the information and rules that professionals use to make everyday decisions. With a general cultural understanding that rule-based, information-rich computers can do amazing things, many people have come to believe that there is such a thing as computer "cognition" and see information processing as a model for an important aspect of human rationality.[6] But often, at the same time, almost in defense, their sense of identity becomes increasingly focused on whatever they define as "not cognition," "beyond information." People concede to the rule-based computer some power of reason and then turn their attention to the soul and the spirit in the human machine.

Most recently, however, the story of computers and "romantic reactions" has taken a dramatic new turn. Romantic reations to the computer are being met by a movement within the technical community which rejects programs and rules to focus on "emergent" intelligence. This movement puts forward new images of machines that bring together many of the characteristics the romantic reaction used to mark the boundary between people and mechanism. These images are of computation without programming, of machines that are unpredictable and undetermined. Such are the "romantic machines" of emergent artificial intelligence (AI). Emergent AI insists that it does not teach the computer but allows the machine to learn; it does not give the computer rules to follow but expects intelligence to emerge from the interaction of agents or entities within the computer system.

The guiding metaphors here are not logical but biological, not mechanistic but social. Theorists of a "connectionist" or "neural net" school of AI believe that if neuronlike entities in the machine are left to interact, they will organize themselves to produce intelligent behavior. They treat the computer as a black box that houses the emergent processes.[7] Their way of approaching computers is more like the one we use to approach people in everyday life. We do not need to know the specific rules of our human companions' behavior; we have a general feeling for how they do things and allow ourselves the pleasure of surprise. In a "society of mind" model, Marvin Minsky and Seymour Papert describe an inner world of "dumb" interacting agents. Complexity of behavior, emotion, and thought emerges from the cacophony of their opposing views, their conflicts and their compromises.[8]

A vision of emergent intelligence was present from the earliest days of AI, but for many years it went underground, leaving the field to a more rationalistic and "rule-driven" tradition, symbolic information processing.[9] But recently, the emergent tradition has resurfaced, with a vengeance. As Paul Smolensky put it, "In the past half-decade the connectionist approach to cognitive modeling has grown from an obscure cult claiming a few true believers to a movement so vigorous that recent meetings of the Cognitive Science Society have begun to look like connectionist pep rallies."[10] My studies show that in the popular culture, people are trying to describe human uniqueness in terms of what computers cannot do, while in the professional computer culture, scientists are starting to talk about machines in images ever closer to those we use to describe people. Now, both people *and* computers are presented as fundamentally "beyond information."

Thus, the scientists of emergent AI—a classification I use to include connectionist (neural net) and society of mind models—are themselves part of the romantic reaction. Assimilating their research to a romantic reaction does not challenge the validity or importance of their mathematical methods. It is, however, an assertion about the appeal of the problem to which the mathematics is applied. While traditional AI represented thought as an essentially logical process, connectionism sees it as a natural phenomenon governed by mathematical laws in the same way that the rest of nature is. The influences that bear on this construction of the problem are not just technical but social, cultural, and psychological.

With the resurgence of emergent approaches to AI, the story of romantic reactions to the computer presence comes full circle. Images of the machine as unstructured and undetermined meet images of people as unstructured and undetermined, some of these put forth in response to computers in the first place. With this "effet de retour," the story of romantic reactions to the computer presence can no longer be told from one side as the story of people responding to their reflection in the mirror of the machine. There is movement through the looking glass.

The computer is a psychological machine, not only because it might be said to have its own very primitive psychology but also because it causes us to reflect on our own. Marginal objects play important roles in theory construction. On the line between categories, they draw attention to how we have drawn the lines and in the process call them into question.[11] Emerson said that "dreams and beasts are two keys by which we find out the secrets of our own nature. They are test objects."[12] Like dreams and beasts, the computer stands on the margins. It is mind and not yet mind; it is inanimate and yet interactive. It does not think, yet neither is it external to thought. It is poised between the thought and the thought of. As behaving systems, computers sit on the boundary between the physical and the psychological. In that position, they provoke thinking about the boundaries between matter, life, and mind.

From this perspective, which takes the computer as a test object, what I have called an "evocative object," the question is not whether we will ever build machines that think like people but whether people have always thought like machines.[13] And if this is the case, if we see ourselves as in some ways kin to the computer, are these the most important things about us? Is what we share with the computer what is most essential about being human?

Such questions have traditionally been the province of philosophers and psychologists. With the advent of personal computers in the 1970s, these questions moved out into the culture at large, carried by people's relationships with an object they could touch, use, and own. Computers became "objects to think with," carrier objects for thinking about the self, and this for two reasons.[14] First, as I have noted, computers are at the margins. The machines do things—like interact and respond to queries—that provoke reflection on what it means to interact and respond. And if one of the things that makes you feel alive is "I think therefore I am," the computer's "almost" thinking is provocative. Second, although computers engage in complex behaviors, they present no simple window onto their inner structure. They are opaque. People use computers to reflect on the human. In this process of using machines to think about mind, what the machines can actually do is important, but how people think about them is more so. Thus, the story is being played out on the boundary, not between minds and machines but between ideas about minds and ideas about machines.

TRANSPARENCY TO OPACITY/PHYSICS TO PSYCHOLOGY

When scientists speak about their childhood experiences, many refer to the intensity of their relationships with objects. For example, an MIT faculty member I shall call "Sandy" told of the many happy hours he had spent with a beloved broken radio.

> I had no idea what any of the parts did: capacitors and resistors and parts I didn't know the names of, tubes that plugged in and things like that. What I did assimilate was that it was made of lots of pieces, and that the pieces were connected in special patterns, and that one can discover truth or something like that by looking through the patterns that connect this device. Obviously, some kind of influences flowed between these connections, and they sort of communicated. And you could see that the radio had lots of littler, simpler devices that communicated with each other so that the whole thing could work.
>
> A lot of the parts came in little glass tubes. I could see through the glass. And some of them had different patterns than the others. So I could figure out that the parts came in different classes. And the different patterns could help you figure out the arrangements that they needed to communicate with each other. And it was a great thrill to have thought of that. I can remember that there was this tremendous charge I got from that, and I thought I would spend the rest of my life looking for charges just like that one.

Although Sandy never fixed the broken radio, several things happened to him in the course of working on it. He came to see himself as a special sort of person, the kind of person who is good with "things" and with "figuring things out." He came to understand the importance of interconnections and of breaking things down to simpler systems within a more complex device. And when he had such insights, Sandy felt an exhilaration to which he became addicted. Sandy's charges came not from external success but from his inner conviction that he had understood something important. In other words, when we watch Sandy with his radio, we watch Sandy the child developing the intellectual personality of Sandy the scientist.

Scientists' recollections of their youth are highly subjective data. But there is another source of data for exploring the developmental role of objects as carriers of ideas: direct observation of children. I have observed many children who remind me of how Sandy describes himself at five.[15] Like Sandy, they puzzle about how things work; like him, they take things apart and theorize about their structure. The objects at the center of their play and theorizing include refrigerators (another of Sandy's childhood passions, the object to which he "graduated" after radios), air-conditioning machines, heaters, Legos, erector sets, model trains, motors, and bicycles. Notable for their absence are modern radios. The favored objects (let us call them "traditional objects") have a great deal in common with one another and with the four-tube radio that offered itself up to Sandy's fascinated observation.

The most significant thing they have in common is "transparency." An object is transparent if it lets the way it works be seen through its physical structure. The insides of a modern radio do not provide a window onto the patterns and interconnections of parts that so impressed Sandy. Sandy's portable four-tube radio was transparent. Its solid-state contemporary cousin is opaque.

With the words "solid-state," I have invoked the most dramatic example of the shift to opacity in the object world. Unlike Sandy's radio, integrated circuits have no easily visible "parts" from the point of view of the curious eye and the probing hand that are the only equipment children bring to such things. They hide their structure while performing miracles of complexity of function.

At five, Sandy could look inside his radio and make enough sense of what he saw to develop a fruitful theory about how it worked. But when you take off the back of an electronic toy or computer, all that the most persistently curious child finds is a chip or two, some batteries, and some wire. Sandy was able to use the radio to think with by thinking about its physical structure. He could make it his own not only because he could see it but because he could work it in his head, drawing on a coherent system of thought that was part of his child knowledge. This was knowledge of physical movement. Sandy spoke of some unknown "stuff" moving through the connections between the different parts of the radio. He says he thought of the stuff as influences, and as he got older, he learned to think of the influences as current.

Computers (taken as physical objects) present a scintillating surface, and the "behavior" they exhibit can be exciting and complex, but there is no simple, mechanical way to understand how they work. They are opaque. If their "behavior" tempts one to anthropomorphize, there is no way to "open the hood," to "pull off the cover," and reassure oneself that mechanism stands behind. When children try to think about the physical working of the computer, they find themselves with little to say. ("It's the batteries," they tell me, frustrated at finding themselves at a dead end.) When this happens, children turn to a way of understanding in which they have more to say—a psychological way of understanding. In doing so, they draw on another kind of child knowledge than that which Sandy used, knowledge not of the body and its motion but of the mind and its thought and emotion. Sandy was able to use the radio to approach the ways of thinking of physical science through his knowledge of how people move (the influences and their connections). Contact with computational objects leads children to approach psychological ways of thinking through their intuitive knowledge about how people think.

In sum, children use computers as "objects to think with" by identifying with them as psychological machines. One nine-year-old, Tessa, made this point very succinctly in a comment about the chip she had seen when her computer was being serviced. "It's very small, but that does not matter. It doesn't matter how little it is, it only matters how much it can remember." The physical object is dismissed. The psychological object becomes the center of attention and elaboration. The development of this kind of discourse begins with much younger children. There, the computer enters into how they sort out the metaphysically charged questions to which childhood must give a response.

When, in the 1920s, Swiss psychologist Jean Piaget first studied what children thought was alive and not alive, he found that children home in on the concept of life by making finer and finer distinctions about the kind of physical activity that is evidence of life. For the very young child, said Piaget, everything active may be alive: the sun, the moon, a car, the clouds. Later, only things that seem to move on their own without anybody giving them a push or a pull can be seen as alive. And finally, the concept of "motion from within" is refined to include a notion of subtle life activity: growth, metabolism, and breathing become the new criteria.[16]

Children build their theories of what is alive and what is not alive as they build all other theories. They use the things around them: toys, people, technology, the natural environment. Children today are confronted with highly interactive computer objects that talk, teach, play, and win. Children are not always sure whether these should be called alive or not alive. But it is clear, even to the youngest children, that physical movement is not the key to the puzzle. The child perceives the relevant criteria not as physical or mechanical but as psychological. For example, in the case of a computer game that plays tic-tac-toe, is it aware, is it conscious, does it have feelings, even, does it cheat?[17]

Children use psychology to talk about the aliveness of inanimate things other than computers. One five-year-old told me that the sun is alive "because it has smiles." Another said that a cloud is alive "because it gets sad. It cries when it rains." But if an eight-year-old argues that clouds or the sun are alive, the reasons given are almost always related to their motion—their way of moving across the sky or the fact that they seem to do so of their own accord. In contrast, as children become older and as they become more sophisticated about computers, their arguments about the computer's aliveness or lack of aliveness become focused on increasingly refined psychological distinctions. The machines are "sort of alive" because they think but do not feel, because they learn but do not decide what to learn, because they cheat but do not know they are cheating.

Piaget told a relatively simple story that accounted for increasing sophistication about the question of aliveness through the development of notions of physical causality. My observations of children discussing the aliveness of computers agree with those of many investigators who stress the greater complexity of children's animistic judgments. For example, in *Conceptual Change in Childhood,* Susan Carey demonstrates that alongside the development Piaget traces, something else is going on: the development of biological knowledge.[18] Children's encounters with computers underscore the importance of a third area of relevant knowledge: psychological knowledge and the ability to make psychological distinctions. Carey discusses how children develop an intuitive psychology that is prebiological, a way of interpreting biological aspects of life as aspects of human behavior. (As when a child answers the question, "Why do animals eat?" by saying that "they *want* to" rather than they must "eat to live.") When I refer to children's responses about the nature of the computer's aliveness as psychological, I am talking about something else—aspects of psychology that will not be replaced by a biological discourse but will grow into mature psychological distinctions, most significantly, the distinction between thought and feeling.

The computer evokes an increasingly sophisticated psychological discourse just as Carey points out that involvement with and discussion about animals evokes a more developed biological discourse. Non-computational machines—for example, cars and telephones—entered into children's thinking but in essence did not disturb the "traditional" pattern. Cognitive psychologists Rochel Gelman and Elizabeth Spelke say why. There is a great difference between "traditional machines" and computers. "A machine may undergo complex transformations of states that are internal and unseen. But it lacks the capacity for mental transformations and processes." In their work, "for purposes of exposition," they "disregard or set aside modern man-made machines that mimic in one way or more the characteristics of man."[19] Their intuition that the computer would be disruptive to their expository categories is correct. The marginal computer does upset the child's constructed boundaries between thing and person.

A long tradition of Western science has drawn a line between the worlds of psychology and physics and has tried, at least programmatically, to take the laws of motion of matter as the fundamental handle for grasping the things it found in the physical world. Sandy's investigation of the radio and Piaget's reports of how children used motion to sort out the question of what is alive in the world of traditional objects showed them conforming to this way of thinking. Tessa's summary comment of what "matters" when you try to understand a chip ("that it remembers") does not conform. Nor do scenes of children discussing whether a computer is alive by cataloging its qualities of consciousness, its degree of intentionality, whether or not it "cheats."[20]

In the present context, what is most important is that the new psychologized language for talking about the machine world influences how children think about people. The discussion of the computer's cheating leads them into a discussion of intentions: people have them, computers do not. Discussion about the computer's origins leads them to distinctions between free will and programming: people think their own ideas, computer ideas are put in by their makers. Some children move from this distinction to another between rote thinking, which computers are said to do, and creative thinking, which they do not.

Among such distinctions, perhaps the most important is how children isolate the cognitive from the rest of psychology. While young children tend to throw together such undifferentiated observations as that a computer toy is happy, smart, or gets angry, by the ages of nine and ten, children comfortably manipulate such ideas as "the computer thinks like a person—does the math things you know—but it doesn't have feelings," or "the computer can't dream, only people can," or "the computer only does things that can come out in typing."

The position toward which children tend as they develop their thinking about people in relation to computers is to split psychology into the cognitive and the affective: the psychology of thought and of feeling. It is no longer that something has a psychology or it does not. While younger children often say that a computer or computer toy is alive "because it has feelings," older children tend to grant that the machine is intelligence and is thus "sort of alive" but then distinguish it from people because of its lack of feelings. Confronted by a personlike machine, a machine that plays on the boundary, people want to make the boundary firmer.

ROMANTIC SELVES

Traditionally, children came to define what was special about people in contrast to what they saw as their nearest neighbors, the animals: their pet dogs, cats, and horses. Pets have desires, but what stands out dramatically about people is how intelligent they are, their gifts of speech and reason. Computers upset this distinction. The machine presents itself to the child as a thing that is not quite a thing, a mind that is not quite a mind. As such, it changes the way children think about who are their nearest neighbors. The Aristotelian definition of man as a "rational animal" (powerful even for children when it defined people in contrast to their nearest neighbors, the animals) gives way to a different distinction.

Today's children appropriate computers through identification with them as psychological entities and come to see them as their new nearest neighbors. And they are neighbors that seem to share in or (from the child's point of view) even excel in our rationality. Children stress the machines' prowess at games, spelling, and math. People are still defined in contrast to their neighbors. But now, people are special because they feel. Many children grant that the computer is able to have a "kind of life," or a "sort of life," but what makes people unique is the kind of life that computers do not have, an emotional life. If people were once rational animals, now they are emotional machines. This is their romantic reaction.

As children tell it, we are distinguished from machine intelligence by love and affection, by spiritual urges and sensual ones, and by the warmth and familiarity of domesticity. In the words of twelve-year-old David, "When there are computers who are just as smart as people, the computers will do a lot of the jobs, but there will still be things for the people to do. They will run the restaurants, taste the food, and they will be the ones who will love each other, have families and love each other. I guess they'll still be the ones who go to church." Or we are distinguished from the machines by a "spark," a mysterious element of human genius.

Thirteen-year-old Alex plays daily with a chess computer named Boris which allows its human user to set its level of play. Although Alex always loses if he asks the computer to play its best game, Alex claims that "it doesn't feel like I'm *really* losing." Why? Because as Alex sees it, chess with Boris is like chess with a "cheater." Boris has "all the most famous, all the best chess games right there to look at. I mean, they are inside of him." Alex knows he can study up on his game, but Boris will always have an unfair advantage. "It's like in between every move Boris could read all the chess books in the world." Here, Alex defines what is special about being a person not in terms of strengths but in terms of a certain frailty.

For this child, honest chess is chess played within the boundaries of human limitations. His heroes are the great chess masters whose skill depends not only on "memorizing games" but on "having a spark," a uniquely human creativity.

In my studies of adults in the computer culture, I have found that many follow essentially the same path as do children when they talk about human beings in relation to the new psychological machines. This path leads to allowing the possibility of unlimited rationality to computers while maintaining a sharp line between computers and people by taking the essence of human nature to be what computers cannot do. The child's version: the human is the emotional. The adult's version, already foreshadowed in Alex's formulation of the human "spark": the human is the unprogrammable.

Few adults find it sufficient to say, as did David, that machines are reason and people are sensuality, spirituality, and emotion. Most split the human capacity for reason. Then, the dichotomy that David used to separate computers and people becomes a way to separate aspects of human psychology. One student speaks of his "technology self" and his "feelings self," another of her "machine part" and her "animal part."

Or, people talk about those parts of the psyche that can be simulated versus those parts that are not subject to simulation, frequently coupled with the argument that simulated thinking is real thinking, but simulated feeling is not real feeling. Simulated love is never love. Again, this is a romantic response, with the computer making a new contribution to our formulas for describing the divided self. We have had reason and passion, ego and id. Now, on one side is placed what is simulable; on the other, that which cannot be simulated, that which is "beyond information."

THE ROMANTIC MACHINES OF EMERGENT AI

This, of course, is where new directions in artificial intelligence become central to our story. Because emergent AI presents an image of the computer as *fundamentally beyond information.*

For years, AI was widely identified with the intellectual philosophy and methodology of information processing. Information-processing AI has roots in mathematician George Boole's intellectual world, in logic.[21] It relies on the manipulation of propositions to obtain new propositions and the combination of concepts to obtain new concepts. But artificial intelligence is not a unitary enterprise. It is a stuff out of which many theories can be fashioned. And beyond information processing, there is emergent AI.

Emergent AI is indissociable from parallel computation. In a traditional, serial computer, millions of units of information sit in memory doing nothing as they wait for the central processor to act on them, one at a time. Impatient with this limitation, the goal of emergent AI is "pure" computation. The whole system is dynamic, with no distinction between processors and the information they process. In some versions of emergent AI, the processors are neuronlike entities connected in networks; in others, they are anthropomorphized societies of subminds. In all cases, they are in simultaneous interaction. The goal, no less mythic in its proportions than the creation of a strand of DNA, is the generation of a fragment of mind. From the perspective of emergent AI, a rule is not something you give a computer but a pattern you infer when you observe the machine's behavior, much as you would observe a person's.

The two AIs have fueled very different fantasies of how to build mind out of machine. If information-processing AI is captured by the image of the knowledge engineer, hungry for rules, debriefing the human expert to embody that expert's methods in algorithms and hardware, emergent AI is captured in the image of the computer scientist, "his young features rebelling, slipping into a grin not unlike that of a father watching his child's first performance on the violin," running his computer system overnight so that the agents within the machine will create intelligence.[22]

The popular discourse about emergent intelligence tends to stress that the AI scientists who work in this paradigm set up experiments in the computer and let them run, not knowing in advance what the interactions of agents within the system will produce. They stress the drama and the suspense.

> To train NETalk to read aloud, Sejnowski had given his machine a thousand-word transcription of a child's conversation to practice on. The machine was reading the text over and over, experimenting with different ways of matching the written text to the sound of spoken word. If it got a syllable right, NETalk would remember that. If it was wrong, NETalk would adjust the connections between its artificial neurons, trying new combinations to make a better fit. . . . NETalk rambles on, talking nonsense. Its voice is still incoherent, but now the rhythm is somewhat familiar: short and long bursts of vowels packed inside consonants. It's not English, but it sounds something like it, a crude version of the nonsense poem "The Jabberwocky." Sejnowski stops the tape. NETalk was a good student. Learning more and more with each pass through the training text, the voice evolved from a wailing banshee to a mechanical Lewis Carroll.[23]

Such descriptions of neural net "experiments" reflect the AI scientists' excitement in doing what feels like "real" laboratory science rather than running simulations. But at the same time that they are excited by the idea of AI as an experimental science, they are drawn to the mystery and unpredictability of what is going on inside of the machine. It makes their material seem more lifelike.

We are far from the language of data and rules that was used to describe the large expert systems of the 1970s. The agents and actors of emergent AI programs are most easily described through anthropomorphization. Take, for example, a very simple case of emergent intelligence, the perceptron, a pattern-recognition machine designed in the late 1950s. In the perceptron, inner agents, each of whom has a very narrow decision rule and access to a very small amount of data, essentially "vote." The perceptron weights their voices according to each agent's past record of success. It is able to take advantage of signals saying whether it has guessed right or wrong to create a voting system where agents who have guessed right get more weight. Perceptrons are not programmed but learn from their own "experiences." In an information-processing system, behavior follows from fixed rules. The perceptron has none. What is important is not what an agent knows but who it knows, its place in a network, its interactions and connections. While information processing begins with formal symbols, perceptrons operate on a subsymbolic and subformal level.

In the brain, damage seldom leads to complete breakdown. It usually leads to a degradation of performance proportional to its extent. Perceptrons show the graceful degradation of performance that characterizes the brain. With disabled "voter-agents," the system still works, although not as well as before. This connection with the brain is decisive for the theorists of the most successful of the trends in emergent AI: connectionism or neural nets.

In the early 1960s, the atmosphere in AI laboratories was heady. Researchers were thinking about the ultimate nature of intelligence. The goal ahead was almost mythic: mind creating mind. Perceptrons and perceptronlike systems had their successes and their adherents as did information-processing approaches with their attempts to specify the rules behind intelligence, or in Boole's language, the "laws of thought."

But for almost a quarter of a century, the pendulum swung away from one computational aesthetic and toward another, toward rules and away from emergence. In its influence on psychology, AI became almost synonymous with information processing. Allen Newell and Herbert Simon posited that the human brain and the digital computer shared a level of common functional description. "At this level, both the human brain and the appropriately programmed digital computer could be seen as two different instantiations of a single species of device—a device that generated intelligent behavior by manipulating symbols by means of formal rules."[24] Newell and Simon developed rule-based systems in their purest form, systems that simulated the behavior of people working on a variety of logical problems. The method and its promise were spelled out in the Newell and Simon physical symbol system hypothesis:

> A physical symbol system has the necessary and sufficient means for general intelligent action. By necessary we meant that any system that exhibits general intelligence will prove upon analysis to be a physical symbol system. By sufficient we meant that any physical symbol system of sufficient size can be organized further to exhibit general intelligence.[25]

Thus, simulations of what came to be called "toy problems" promised more: that mind could be built out of rules. But the ideas of information processing were most successful in an area where they fell far short of building mind. This was in the domain of expert systems. With the worldly success of expert systems in the 1970s, the emphasis was taken off what had been most mythic about the AI of the 1950s and early 1960s and placed on what computer scientists had learned how to do with craftsman's confidence—gather rules from experts and code them in computer programs.

However, I have noted that in the late 1970s and early 1980s, the pendulum swung again. There was new, powerful, parallel hardware and new ideas about how to program it. The metaphors behind programming languages shifted. They were no longer about lists and variables but about actors and objects. You could think about traditional programming by analogies to the step-by-step instruction of a recipe in a cookbook. To think about the new object-oriented programming, the analogies had to be more dynamic: actors on a stage. With these changes came a rebirth of interest in the concept of neural nets, reborn with a new capturing mnemonic, connectionism.

More than anyone else, Douglas Hofstadter captured the aesthetic of the new movement when he spoke about computation "waking up from the Boolean dream."[26] For connectionists, that dream had been more like a nightmare. Like the romantics, connectionists sought to liberate themselves from a constraining rationalism of program and rules. They take pride in the idea that the artificial minds they are trying to build have an aspect that, if not mystical, is at the very least presented as mysterious. From the point of view of the connectionists, a certain amount of mystery fits the facts of the case.

We cannot teach an information-processing computer the rules for most aspects of human intelligence that people take for granted because we simply do not know them. There is no algorithm for recognizing a face in a crowd. The connectionists approach this state of affairs with a strategy made possible by the new availability of massively parallel computing: build a computer that at least in some way looks like a brain and make it learn by itself. Unlike symbolic information processing, which looked to programs and specified locations for information storage, the connectionists do not see information as being stored "anywhere" in particular. Rather, it is stored everywhere. Information is better thought of as "evoked" than "found."[27] The computer is treated as a black box that houses emergent processes.

There is an irony here. The computer presence was an important influence toward ending the behaviorist hegemony in American psychology in the late 1970s. Behaviorism forbade the discussion of inner states or entities. One could not talk about memory, only the behavior of "remembering." But the fact that computers had memory and inner states provided legitimation for discussing people as having them as well. Behaviorism presented mind as a black box. Information processing opened the box and filled it with rules, trying to ally itself as closely as possible with commonsense understandings. But this was a vulnerability from the point of view of nonprofessionals who were then exposed to these understandings. They seemed *too* commonsense. People had to be more than information and rules. Now connectionism closes the box again. What is inside these more opaque systems can once again be thought of as mysterious and indeterminate.

Philosopher John Searle exploited the vulnerability of information-processing models when he pursued a thought experiment that took as its starting point the question of what might be going on in a computer that could "speak Chinese." Searle, who assures us that he does not know the Chinese language, asks us to imagine that he is locked in a room with stacks and stacks of paper, say, index cards. He is given a story written in Chinese and then is passed slips of paper on which are written questions about the story, also in Chinese. Of course, he does not know he has a story, and he does not know that the slips of paper contain questions about the story. What he does know is that "clever programmers" have given him a set of rules for what to do with the little pieces of paper he is passed. The rules tell him how to match them up with other little pieces of paper that have Chinese characters on them, which he passes out of the room. The rules say such things as "The squiggle-squiggle sign is to be followed by the squoggle-squoggle sign."[28] He becomes extraordinarily skillful at following these rules, at manipulating the cards in his collection. We are to suppose that his instructions are sufficiently complete to enable him to "output" Chinese characters that are in fact the correct answers to the questions about the story.

All of this is set up for the sake of argument in order to ask one rhetorical question in plain English: Does the fact that he sends out the correct answers prove that he understands Chinese? For Searle, it is clear that the answer is no.

... I can pass the Turing test for understanding Chinese. But all the same
I still don't understand a word of Chinese and neither does any other
digital computer because all the computer has is what I have: a formal
program that attaches no meaning, interpretation, or content to any of the
symbols.[29]

In the end, for Searle, the system is only a "paper shuffler." He described
the innards of the machine in terms so deeply alien to the ways most
people experience the inner workings of their minds that they felt a
shock of "nonrecognition." For many people, it fueled a sense that Searle
had captured what always seemed wrong with AI. The disparity between
the description of the paper shuffler and one's sense of self supported
the view that such a system could not possibly understand the meaning
of Chinese in the same sense that a person does.

Connectionism is less vulnerable to the Searlean argument. Its models
postulate emergence of thought from "fuzzy" process, so opening up the
box does not reveal a crisply defined mechanism that a critic can isolate
and make to seem psychologically implausible. Connectionists only admit
just enough of a view onto the inside of their system to create a general
feeling for its shape. And for many people, that shape feels right—in the
way that Searle made rule-driven systems feel wrong. That shape is resonant with brainlike processes: associations and networks. Perhaps for
these grown-up AI scientists, neural nets have something of the feel that
the four-tube radio had for Sandy the child. The theoretical objects "feel
right," and the theory does not require that they be pinned down to a high
degree of specificity. And similar to Sandy, these scientists' "charges," their
sense of excitement and achievement, depends not only on instrumental
success but on the sense of being in touch with fundamental truths. In this,
the connectionists, like Sandy, are romantics-in-practice.

Winograd worked as a young scientist in a very different intellectual
culture, the culture of symbolic AI. This is the culture of which Dreyfus
could say, "any domain must be formalizable." And the way to do AI is to
"find the context-free elements and principles and to base a formal,
symbolic representation on this theoretical analysis."[30] In other words,
the goal is a limpid science, modeled on the physical sciences, or as
Winograd put it, "We are concerned with developing a formalism, or
'representation,' with which to describe . . . knowledge. We seek the
'atoms' and 'particles' of which it is built, and the 'forces' that act on it."[31]
From the point of view of this intellectual aesthetic of transparency, the
connectionist black box is alien and unacceptable. In other terms, the
classic confronts the romantic.

Indeed, referring to the connectionist's opaque systems, Winograd
has said that people are drawn to connectionism because it has a high
percentage of "wishful thinking."[32] Perhaps one could go further. For

connectionism, wishful thinking is a point of method. They assert that progress does not depend on the ability to specify process. In other words, for connectionists, computers can have the same "opacity" as the brain. Like the brain, they are boxes that can remain closed; this does not interfere with their functioning as models of mind.

SOCIETIES OF MIND

Winograd has made a similar point about the wishful thinking in another branch of emergent AI that has come to be known as the "society theory" of mind.[33] Marvin Minsky and Seymour Papert have built a computational model that sees the mind as a society of interacting agents that are highly anthropomorphized, discussed in the terms one usually reserves for a whole person. But their agents do not have the complexity of people. Instead, the society theory is based (as is the idea of perceptrons) on these agents being "dumb." Each agent has a severely limited point of view. Like the voting agents in a perceptron model, this narrowness of vision leads them to different opinions. Intelligence emerges from their interactions and negotiations. In its construction of a highly anthropomorphized inner world, society theory uses a language about mind that is resonant with the object-relations tradition in psychoanalytic thinking.[34]

In classical psychoanalytic theory, a few powerful inner structures (e.g., the superego) act on memories, thoughts, and wishes. Object relations theory posits a dynamic system in which the distinction between processed and processor breaks down.[35] The parallel with computation is clear: in both cases, there is movement away from a situation in which a few inner structures act on more passive stuff. Psychoanalyst W. R. D. Fairbairn replaced the Freudian dichotomy of ego and id, structure and drive energy with independent agencies within the mind who think, wish, and generate meaning in interaction with one another.

The Minsky-Papert computational model evokes the world of Fairbairn. In the case of both psychoanalysis and society theory, a static model (on the one hand, based on drive and on the other, based on information) is replaced by an active one. A model that seems mechanistic and overly specified as something that could encompass the human psyche is replaced by a model with a certain mystery, a model of almost chaotic interactions. The most elaborated presentation of the society model is Minsky's *The Society of Mind*.[36] There, instead of what Winograd describes as the "finely tuned clockwork" of information-processing AI, we get an "impressionistic pastiche of metaphors." In a microworld of toy blocks, Minsky describes how agents that at first blush seem like simple computational subroutines work together to perform well-defined tasks like building towers and tearing them down. But then comes the wishful thinking, what Winograd here calls the "sleight of hand."[37] Minsky speculates how, within an actual child, the agents responsible for BUILDING and WRECKING might become versatile enough to offer support for one another's goals. In Minsky's imaginative text, they utter sentences like, "Please WRECKER, wait a moment more till BUILDER adds just one more block: it's worth it for a louder crash."[38] Winograd points out that Minsky has moved from describing the agents as subroutines to speaking of them as entities with consciousness and intention. And his reaction is sharp:

> With a simple "might indeed become versatile," we have slipped from a technically feasible but limited notion of agents as subroutines, to an impressionistic description of a society of homunculi, conversing with one another in ordinary language. This sleight of hand is at the center of the theory. It takes an almost childish leap of faith to assume the modes of explanation that work for the details of block manipulation will be adequate for understanding conflict consciousness, genius, and freedom of will.
>
> One cannot dismiss this as an isolated fantasy. Minsky is one of the major figures in artificial intelligence and he is only stating in a simplistic form a view that permeates the field.[39]

Winograd attributes the sleight of hand to Minsky's faith that since we are no more than "protoplasm-based physical symbol systems, the reduction must be possible and only our current lack of knowledge prevents us from explicating it in detail, all the way from BUILDER's clever play down to the logical circuitry." In other words, Winograd attributes the sleight of hand to Minsky's belief in the physical symbol system hypothesis. I interpret it somewhat differently. Minsky's leap of faith, his confidence in the power of the agents, is based on his belief—one that I see at the core of the romantic reaction in artificial intelligence—that the interaction of agents causes something to emerge *beyond* what is possible through the manipulation of symbols alone.

Winograd's critique reflects his model of what Minsky's audience wants to hear, of the culture Minsky is writing to. Winograd believes that they want to hear a vindication of physical symbols, that they want to hear that symbols and rules will ultimately tell the story. The way I see it, Minsky's audience, like the audience for connectionism, wants to hear precisely the opposite. In the 1970s, the culture of AI enthusiasts was committed to a rule-based model, but now things have changed. Both professionals and the lay public are drawn to society theory and to connectionism not because they promise specificity but because they like their *lack* of specificity. W. Daniel Hillis, designer of the "Connection Machine," a massively parallel computer, puts the point well:

> It would be very convenient if intelligence were an emergent behavior of randomly connected neurons in the same sense that snowflakes and whirl-pools are emergent behaviors of water molecules. It might then be possible to build a thinking machine by simply hooking together a sufficiently large network of artificial neurons. The notion of emergence would suggest that such a network, once it reached some critical mass, would spontaneously begin to think.
>
> *This is a seductive idea because it allows for the possibility of constructing intelligence without first understanding it.* Understanding intelligence is difficult and probably a long way off, so the possibility that it might spontaneously emerge from the interactions of a large collection of simple parts has considerable appeal to the would-be builder of thinking machines.
>
> *. . . Ironically, the apparent inscrutibility of the idea of intelligence as an emergent behavior accounts for much of its continuing popularity.*[40]

The strength of object theories in both psychoanalysis and artificial intelligence is a conceptual framework that offers rich possibilities for models of interactive process; the weakness, which is of course what Winograd is pointing to, is that the framework may be *too* rich. The postulated objects may be too powerful when they explain the mind by postulating many minds within it.[41] Object theory confronts both fields with the problem of infinite regress, but Minsky is writing to a professional audience that has sensitized itself to its heady possibilities. Computer scientists are used to relying on recursion, a controlled form of circular reasoning; it would not be going too far to say that some have turned it into a transcendent value. For Douglas Hofstadter, computation and the power of self-reference weave together art, music, and mathematics into an eternal golden braid that brings coherency and a shared aesthetic to the sciences and the arts. His vision is, to say the least, romantic. In *Gödel, Escher, Bach,* he speaks of it as a kind of religion.[42] Hofstadter's brilliant and accessible writing has done a great deal to legitimate the circularity implicit in accounting for the entities that are then to account for thought in the wider culture.

In the 1970s, Minsky said, "The mind is a meat machine." The phrase became famous. During my research program in the late 1970s and early 1980s, I interviewed hundreds of people in both the technical and lay cultures about their beliefs about computers, about how smart the machines were then and how smart they might someday be. In these conversations, Minsky's words were often cited as an example of "what was wrong" with AI. They provoked irritation, even disgust. I believe they seemed unacceptable not so much because of their substance but because of then-prevalent images of what kind of machine the mind's meat machine might be. These images were mechanistic. But now, a source of connectionism's appeal is precisely that it proposes an artificial meat machine, a computational machine made of biologically resonant components. And with a changed image of the machine, the idea that the mind is one becomes far less problematic.

Even those who were most critical of rule-driven AI are somewhat disarmed by emergent models that turn away from rules and toward biology. Dreyfus, for example, had criticized symbolic information-processing AI in terms of a broader critique of a purely syntactic, representational view of the relation of mind to reality. Pointing to the work of Martin Heidegger and the later Ludwig Wittgenstein, he made the point that "Both these thinkers had called into question the very tradition on which symbolic information processing was based. Both were holists, both were struck by the importance of everyday practices, and both held that one could not have a theory of the everyday world."[43] Now, he sees neural networks in a position to prove them right and him as well:

> If multilayered networks succeed in fulfilling their promise, researchers will have to give up the conviction of Descartes, Husserl, and early Wittgenstein that the only way to produce intelligent behavior is to mirror the world with a formal theory in mind. . . . Neural networks may show that Heidegger, later Wittgenstein and Rosenblatt [an early neural net theorist] were right in thinking that we behave intelligently in the world without having a theory of that world.[44]

While cautious, Dreyfus is receptive to the technical possibilities and philosophical importance of connectionist research in a way that he never was toward traditional AI. Similarly, cultural critics such as Leo Marx, long skeptical about the impact of technology on liberal and humanistic values, have found the "contextual, gestaltist, or holistic theory of knowledge implicit in the connectionist research program" to be "particularly conducive to acquiring complex cultural understanding, a vital form of liberal knowledge."[45] Although the sympathetic response here is less to connectionism than to its metaphors, his warm feelings, like those of Dreyfus, show how connectionism has new possibilities for intellectual imperialism. Connectionism has received good press as a more "humanistic" form of AI endeavor, with the stress on its respect for the complexity and mystery of mind.

THINKING OF YOURSELF AS AN ANTI-LOVELACE MACHINE

In a memoir she wrote in 1842, Lady Ada Lovelace, a friend and patroness of Charles Babbage, inventor of the "analytical engine," was the first person to go on record with a variant of the often-quoted phrase, "The computer only does what you tell it to do, nothing more, nothing less."[46] Most people are used to thinking of computers with the "Lovelace" model. It captures the aesthetic of information processing.[47] But it does not speak to emergent AI. For emergent AI, the point is precisely to make computers do *more* than they were programmed to do, indeed, in a certain sense, not to have to program them at all. It has become common-place to quote Lovelace to object to the possibility of AI. "People are not computers. They don't follow rules. They learn. They grow." But to the degree that emergent AI is characterized by "anti-Lovelace" representa-tions of the computer, it breaks down resistance to seeing continuity between computers and people by describing computers that learn and grow. And it describes computers whose workings are mysterious.

In emergent AI, the effort is to have surprising global complexity emerge from local simplicity. Even in the small neural net programs that can run on standard personal computers, watching such phenomena emerge can have the "feel" of watching life. Indeed, one of the first computer demonstrations that played on this idea was a program called the "GAME OF LIFE." Patterns grow, change, and evolve before the eye of the beholder. It is not surprising that AI scientists use such systems to study evolutionary phenomena. This kind of evolving, "unfolding" ma-chine does not seem to "offend" in the same way as did its programmed cousin. One MIT hacker I interviewed told me that if you make the system complicated enough, for example, the simultaneous operation of a society of millions of interacting programs, you might be able to create in a machine "that sense of surprising oneself . . . that makes most peo-ple feel that they have free will, perhaps even . . . a soul." Another told me that "with the idea of mind as society, Minsky is trying to create a computer complex enough, indeed beautiful enough, that a soul might want to live in it." If you romanticize the machine in this way, you have a new chance to see the machine as like the human and the human as like the machine.

If you see computers as Lovelace machines, people are the opposite of computers, or if they are to be analogized with computers, the human psychology that emerges is resolutely mechanistic. But connectionists in-sist that computation should not be reduced to specifications, and al-though the adherents of society models are more committed to one day being able to specify what is within the black box, that day is far off and the theory need not wait. Emergence offers an appealing retort to the Love-lace objection. For Hillis, "emergence offers a way to believe in physical causality while simultaneously maintaining the impossibility of a reduc-tionist explanation of thought. For those who fear mechanistic explana-tions of the human mind, our ignorance of how local interactions produce emergent behavior offers a reassuring fog in which to hide the soul."[48]

Connectionist machines, romantic machines whose emergent properties can "hide the soul," have a cultural resonance in our time of widespread disaffection with instrumental reason. For Papert, speculating on
the identity of the "Prince Charming" who awoke the sleeping connectionism, a shift of cultural values has created a more welcoming milieu
for connectionist ideas. The new resonance depends on a "generalized
turn away from the hard-edged rationalism of the time connectionism
last went into eclipse and a resurgent attraction to more holistic ways of
thinking."[49]

For years I have documented how people construct romantic images
of mind when confronted with the image of the computer as an
information-processing machine. Today there is a more complex picture
as people also confront increasingly romantic images of the machine.

When sociobiology presents an image of the human as a "bundle of
genes," people rebel. They listen to the theory, and they say that is "not
me." When AI presents an image of the human as a "bundle of programs," there is the same "not me" response, the same reaction that was
exploited by Searle with powerful rhetorical effect. When programs became refined as "heuristic" (defined by rules of thumb rather than
rules), the response softens, but the idea of people as a "bundle of
heuristics" does not go far enough for people to accept such systems as a
reflection of who they are. But the idea that "I" am a bundle of neuronlike agents that communicate with one another and whose intelligence emerges from their interactions sounds enough like how we have
always thought about the brain to start to feel comfortable, like "me."

The mathematical theory of connectionism might not be any more
accessible to lay thinking than technical papers on information processing; indeed, their advanced mathematics usually makes them less so. But
when object- and agent-oriented theories are popularized and move out
into the general culture, they have special appeal, the direct appeal of
actors on a stage. At one time or another, we all have the sense of not
feeling "at one" with ourselves: inner voices offer conflicting advice,
reassurance, and chastisements. These experiences are easily and satisfy-
ingly translated into a drama of inner objects. The objects and agents of
emergent AI are engaging because they are concrete; it is easy to "play"
with them. They are resonant with popular understandings of Freud
that represent ego, superego, and id as competing inner actors. Like
Freud's trio, the agents provide a way to interpret our common experiences of inner conflict. The rational bias of our culture presents consis-
tency and coherency as natural, but, of course, feelings of fragmentation
abound. Indeed, it has been argued that they characterize contemporary
psychological life.[50] And so, theories that speak to the experience of a
divided self have particular power.

Thus, emergent AI is a seductive theory for many reasons. It presents itself as escaping the narrow determinism of information processing. Its images are biologically resonant. The language of "neural nets" is inexact but metaphorically effective, presenting mind processes as the kinds of things that could be going on in a brain. Its constituent agents offer a theory for the felt experience of multiple inner voices. Like "fuzzy logic" or "chaos," two other ideas that have captured the popular and professional imagination, emergent AI speaks to our technological society's disappointments with the cold, sharp edges of formal logic. It is resonant with a general turn to "softer" epistemologies that emphasize concrete methodologies over algorithmic ones in the sciences as well as the arts.[51] It is resonant with a criticism of traditional Western philosophy, which, for Heidegger, is defined from the start by its focusing on facts in the world while "passing over" the world as such.[52]

And finally, to come full circle, the constituent agents of emergent AI offer almost tangible "objects to think with." In a paradoxical but comforting way, they get one back to a version of Sandy's experience with the four-tube radio. They try to explain the world to us in terms of familiar interactive systems, in terms of "parts" that do this or that to one another, and in terms of physics. The connection strengths that are posited between the neuronlike entities can be translated into the simple physics of moving things closer together and farther apart.

Freudian ideas about slips of the tongue became well known and gained acceptance for reasons that had little to do with assessments of their scientific validity. Slips are almost tangible ideas. They are manipulable. Slips are appealing as objects to think with. You can analyze your own slips and those of your friends. As we look for slips and start to manipulate them, both seriously and playfully, psychoanalytic ideas, at the very least the idea that there is an unconscious, start to feel more natural. The theory of slips allowed psychoanalytic ideas to weave themselves into the fabric of everyday life. They made the theory more concrete and appropriable. Similarly, people like to think about the ideas behind mind as connection and mind as society. To take the simplest case (which is the only case that matters when you look for the "whys" behind a theory's cultural popularity), you can imagine and play with Minsky's ideas of agents by taking on their personae. As in the case of psychoanalytic models, you can imagine yourself in the role of the psychic entities, and acting out these roles feels enough like an acting out of the theory to give a sense of understanding it. One may forget the details of each theory, but they offer experiences of theoretical play that break down resistance to seeing mind as irrational or seeing mind as machine. Romantic machines pave the way for the idea of mind as machine to become an acceptable part of everyday thinking.

In their reaction to new science and technology, the romantics split passion from reason, the sensuous from the analytic. T. S. Eliot, reflecting on the loss of the ability to integrate "states of mind and states of feeling," called it the "dissociation of sensibility."[53] Information processing led to the position that if computers closely resemble people in their thinking, they differ from them in their lack of feeling. It, too, set the stage for a dissociation of sensibility. The information-processing paradigm and the consequent reaction to it deepened the gulf between affect and cognition. Within the academic world, this movement was both reflected and reinforced in the emergence of a new, computationally inspired, branch of psychology: cognitive science.

The Freudian experience has long ago taught us that resistance to a theory is part of its cultural impact. Resistance to psychoanalysis with its emphasis on the unconscious led to an emphasis on the rational aspect of human nature, to an emphasis on people as logical beings. Resistance to a computational model of people as programmed information systems led to a new articulation of the position that what is essential in people is what cannot be captured in language, rules, and formalism. This resistance, in a form that I have called "romantic," put positive emphasis on the importance of aspects of human nature that are not simulable—on love, human connection, and sensuality—and on the importance of the embodiment of human knowledge within individuals and social groups. But it tended to reinforce a too-radical split between affect and cognition, between the psychology of thought and the psychology of feeling. When thought and feeling are torn from their complex relationship with each other, the cognitive can become reduced to mere logical process and the affective to the visceral. What was most powerful about Freud's psychological vision was its aspiration to look at thought and feeling as always existing together, at the same time and in interaction with each other. In psychoanalytic work, the effort is to explore the passion in the mathematician's theorem and the reason behind the most primitive fantasy. The unconscious has its own, highly structured language that can be deciphered and analyzed. Logic has an affective side, and affect has a logic. The too-easy acceptance of the idea that computers closely resemble people in their thinking and differ only in their lack of feeling supports a dichotomized and oversimplified view of human psychology.

We might hope that the theorists of emergent machine intelligence will further our appreciation and understanding of the human integration of thought and feeling. We must fear that they are not. Indeed, while we feared before that the human would be reduced to the analytic through neglect of feelings, the inclusion of feelings in AI models raises its own problems. The point is dramatized by the way Minsky appropriates Oedipus. In *The Society of Mind*, Minsky looks at the Oedipus complex through its computational prism: "If a developing identity is based upon that of another person, it must become confusing to be attached to two dissimilar adult 'models.' "[54] Thus, "Oedipus" intervenes, a mechanism designed to facilitate the construction of a simple-enough agent by removing "one [of the models] from the scene."[55]

With this scenario, Minsky has entered a domain of human experience where pure information processing did not often care to wander. The tenor of his theory—romantic, loose, emergent—makes him confident that he can build agents that represent complex human attributes. But when he does so, he turns the Oedipal moment (traditionally thought of in terms of jealousy, sexuality, and murderous emotion) into a problem closer to cognitive dissonance. A discussion of primitive feelings is turned into a discussion of a kind of thinking. Information processing left affect dissociated; emergent AI may begin to integrate it only to leave it reduced.

We must acknowledge a profound change in our cultural images of the machine. The question remains: What will its effect be on our images of people?

Through the mid-1980s, many who criticized the computer as the embodiment of rationality feared that it would lead people to a view of themselves as cold mechanism. In fact, we have seen that resistance to images of computation as information processing led to a resurgence of romantic ideas about people: what made them special was all that the analytical engine was not. Now we face an increasingly complex situation.

For the foreseeable future, emergent machine intelligence will exist in only the most limited form. But already, there is widespread confidence in its intellectual and economic importance and familiarity with elements of its language, its way of talking about the problem of mind. This language provides a way to talk about machines which makes them seem more like people. It serves as a mediator between the computer culture and the culture of mind in a way that the language of information processing never could. The language of neurons, connections, associations, agents, and actors makes it easier to talk about oneself as "that kind" of a machine. The similarities in the language of computational "society" models and object-relations psychoanalysis makes the new models seem resonant with the concerns of a professional culture widely perceived as least hidebound by narrow logicism. And finally, I have noted that with the move away from rules and toward biology, philosophical critics seem disarmed in their traditional objections. In its simplest form, arguing that people do not think "linearly" is no longer an argument for why parallel machines are not "really" thinking.

Through such intellectual detours, romantic machines may have the effect that critics feared from rational ones. Resistance to the rational machines fostered a romantic view of people. The romantic machines offer a way for people to accept the idea of the human as a meat machine. But this acceptance comes at a high cost. John Searle has argued that thought is a product of our specific biology, the product of a human brain.[56] When Searle talks about human biology, he means neurons and the chemistry of the synapse, as when he speculates that "as far as we know, the functional aspect of the neuron is the nondigital variation in [its] rate of firing."[57] But our specific biology means more than having a brain just as it means more than being made of meat. Our specific biology places us in the human life cycle: we are born, nurtured by parents, grow, develop sexually, become parents in our turn. And we die. This cycle brings us the knowledge that comes from understanding the certainty of loss, that those we love will die and so will we. In these ways, we are alien to a being that is not born of a mother, that does not feel the vulnerability of childhood, that does not know sexuality or anticipate death. We may be machines, but these experienced aspects of our biology (the consequences of there being meat in our meat machines) compel a search for transcendence. People look for it in religion, history, art, the relationships through which we hope to live on.

Emergent AI does not offer us minds that are born of mothers, grow up in families, or know the fear of death. When AI offered a rational and rule-driven machine, it led to a romantic reaction. Current romanticizations of the machine may lead to a rationalistic one: a too-easy acceptance of the idea that what is essential about human beings can be captured in what makes us kin to mechanism.

NOTES

1. This article grew out of many long hours of conversation with Seymour Papert. I am indebted to him as a dialogue partner and critical reader.

2. My work on romantic reactions in the computer culture among children and adults is ethnographic and clinical. See Sherry Turkle, *The Second Self: Computers and The Human Spirit* (New York: Simon and Schuster, 1984), esp. chap. 1, "Child Philosophers: Are Smart Machines Alive," 29–63; chap. 8, "Thinking of Yourself as a Machine," 271–305; and "On Method: A Sociology of Sciences of Mind," 315–323.

3. Turkle, *The Second Self,* 239–240.

4. See John Searle, "Minds, Brains, and Programs," *The Behavioral and Brain Sciences* 3 (1980): 417–424, for an emphasis on biology; Hubert L. Dreyfus, *What Computers Can't Do: The Limits of Artificial Intelligence,* 2d ed. (New York: Harper and Row, 1979), for an emphasis on "embodiment" and situated knowledge ("knowing how vs. knowing that"); and Joseph Weizenbaum, *Computer Power and Human Reason: From Judgment to Calculation* (San Francisco: W. H. Freeman,

1976), for an emphasis on the ineffable, on knowledge that cannot be formally expressed.

5. Weizenbaum, *Computer Power and Human Reason,* 201.

6. Turkle, *The Second Self,* chap. 8.

7. See David E. Rumelhart, James L. McClelland, and the PDP Research Group, *Parallel Distributed Processing: Explorations in the Microstructure of Cognition,* vol. 1 (Cambridge: Bradford Books/MIT Press, 1986).

8. Marvin Minsky, *The Society of Mind* (New York: Simon and Schuster, 1987), and Seymour Papert, *Mindstorms: Children, Computers, and Powerful Ideas* (New York: Basic Books, 1981), 167–170.

9. For a more detailed discussion of the dichotomy between emergent and information-processing AI, see Seymour Papert, "One AI or Many?" and Sherry Turkle, "Artificial Intelligence and Psychoanalysis: A New Alliance," in *Daedalus* 117, 1 (Winter 1988): 1–14, 241–268.

10. Cited in Hubert L. Dreyfus and Stuart E. Dreyfus, "Making a Mind versus Modeling the Brain: Intelligence Back at a Branchpoint," *Daedalus* 117, 1 (Winter 1988): 35.

11. My discussion of the evocative properties of "betwixt and between" objects owes much to the work of Victor Turner on liminal objects and Mary Douglas on category maintenance. See, for example, Victor Turner, *The Ritual Process* (Chicago: Aldine, 1966), and Mary Douglas, *Purity and Danger* (London: Routledge and Kegan Paul, 1966).

12. W. H. Auden and Louis Kronenberger, eds., *The Viking Book of Aphorisms* (New York: Penguin, 1981), 24.

13. Turkle, *The Second Self,* 24.

14. My use of the idea of "objects to think with" owes much to Claude Levi-Strauss's notion of "bricolage," the use of concrete materials to think through scientific problems. See Claude Levi-Strauss, *The Savage Mind* (Chicago: University of Chicago Press, 1968).

15. In the field studies for *The Second Self,* I worked with over 200 children and adolescents, ages 4 to 16. My first formulation of how children use "objects to think with" came out of that research experience. Since 1984, my research with children has turned more directly to differences of personal style in relationships with objects, both computational and traditional; my new studies include clinical, projective, and observational materials on a closely studied group of 20 fifth-graders.

16. Jean Piaget, *The Child's Construction of the World* (Totowa, N.J.: Littlefield, Adams, 1960).

17. For example, in a sample of 88 children, ages 4 through 14, 68% used physical criteria and 11% psychological criteria to discuss the "aliveness" of non-computational or "traditional" objects, but when they turned to computational objects, the proportions were reversed. Then, 17% used physical criteria, and 67% used psychological criteria. See Turkle, *The Second Self,* "Children's Psychological Discourse: Methods and Data Summary," 324–332.

18. Susan Carey, *Conceptual Change in Childhood* (Cambridge: MIT Press, 1985).

19. Rochel Gelman and Elizabeth Spelke, "The Development of Thoughts About Animate and Inanimate Objects: Implications for Research on Social Cognition," in John H. Flavell and Lee Ross, eds., *Social Cognitive Development: Frontiers and Possible Choices* (Cambridge: Cambridge University Press, 1981).

20. See Turkle, *The Second Self,* chap. 1, for detailed descriptions of children in "psychological" discussions about computational objects.

21. George Boole, *The Laws of Thought,* vol. 2 of *Collected Works* (La Salle, Ill.: Open Court Publishing Company, 1952).

22. William F. Allman, *Apprentices of Wonder: Inside the Neural Network Revolution* (New York: Bantam, 1989), 1.

23. Ibid., 2.

24. Dreyfus and Dreyfus, "Making Mind vs. Modeling the Brain," 16.

25. Allen Newell and Herbert Simon, "Computer Science as Empirical Inquiry: Symbols and Search," reprinted in John Haugeland, ed., *Mind Design* (Cambridge: MIT Press, 1981), 41.

26. Douglas R. Hofstadter, *Metamagical Themes: Questing for the Essence of Mind and Pattern* (New York: Basic Books, 1985).

27. David E. Rumelhart and Donald A. Norman, "A Comparison of Models," in Geoffrey Hinton and James Anderson, eds., *Parallel Models of Associative Memory* (Hillsdale, N.J.: Lawrence Erlbaum Associates, 1981), 3. In Rumelhart, McClelland, and the PDP Research Group, *Parallel Distributed Processing,* the PDP model of learning is contrasted with that of traditional AI:

> In most models, knowledge is stored as a static copy of a pattern. . . . In PDP models, though, this is not the case. In these models, the patterns themselves are not stored. Rather, what is stored is the *connection strengths* between units that allow these patterns to be recreated. . . . Learning must be a matter of finding the right connection strengths so that the right patterns of activation will be produced under the right circumstances. This is an extremely important property of this class of models, for it opens up the possibility that an information processing mechanism could learn, as a result of tuning its connections, to capture the interdependencies between activations that it is exposed to in the course of processing. (31–32)

28. John Searle, "The Myth of the Computer," *The New York Review of Books,* April 29, 1982, 5.

29. Ibid.

30. Dreyfus and Dreyfus, "Making a Mind vs. Modeling the Brain," 25.

31. Cited in Ibid., 25.

32. *Science 86* (May 1986): 27.

33. Terry Winograd, "Thinking Machines: Can There Be? Are We?" See chap. 10, this vol.

34. See Turkle, "Artificial Intelligence and Psychoanalysis."

35. For a presentation of psychoanalytic theory in terms of the dichotomy between a drive and an object model, see Jay R. Greenberg and Stephen A. Mitchell, *Object Relations in Psychoanalytic Theory* (Cambridge: Harvard University Press, 1983).

36. Minsky, *The Society of Mind.*

37. Winograd, "Thinking Machines," chap. 10, this vol.

38. Ibid.

39. Ibid.

40. W. Daniel Hillis, "Intelligence as an Emergent Behavior," *Daedalus* 117, 1 (Winter 1988): 175–176. Italics mine.

41. Psychoanalytic writers have taken object-relations theorists to task on this point. See, e.g., Roy Schafer, *A New Language for Psychoanalysis* (New Haven: Yale University Press, 1976), and Thomas H. Ogden, "The Concept of Internal Object Relations," *The International Journal of Psychoanalysis* 64 (1983).

42. Douglas Hofstadter, *Gödel, Escher, Bach: An Eternal Golden Braid* (New York: Basic Books, 1978).

43. Dreyfus and Dreyfus, "Making a Mind vs. Modeling the Brain," 26.

44. Ibid., 35.

45. Leo Marx, "Is Liberal Knowledge Worth Having?" Address to the Conference of the Association of Graduate Liberal Studies Programs, DePaul University, Chicago, October 7, 1988, unpub. ms., 10–11.

46. Lovelace put it like this: "The analytical Engine has no pretensions whatever to originate anything. It can do whatever we know how to order it to perform."

47. Although this statement is true in spirit, large and complex programs are not predictable in any simple sense.

48. Hillis, "Intelligence as an Emergent Behavior," 176.

49. Papert, "One AI or Many?" 14.

50. Christopher Lasch, *The Culture of Narcissism* (New York: Norton, 1979).

51. For a discussion of the turn to the concrete and away from algorithm, see Sherry Turkle and Seymour Papert, "Epistemological Pluralism: Styles and Voices Within the Computer Culture," in *Signs: Journal of Women in Culture and Society* 16, 1 (Sept. 1990).

52. Cited in Dreyfus and Dreyfus, "Making a Mind vs. Modeling the Brain," 24–25.

53. T. S. Eliot, "The Metaphysical Poets," in *Selected Essays 1917–1932* (New York: Harcourt Brace and Co., 1932), 241–250.

54. Minsky, *The Society of Mind,* 182.

55. Ibid.

56. Searle, "Minds, Brains, and Programs."

57. John Searle, "Minds and Brains Without Programs," in Colin Blakemore and Susan Greenfield, eds., *Mindwaves: Thoughts on Intelligence, Identity and Consciousness* (New York: Basil Blackwell, 1987), 219.

TWELVE

Biology, Machines, and Humanity

Stuart Hampshire

In addressing the subjects of biology and humanity as well as machines and humanity, I feel the necessity of mentioning human bodies, which often get left out although they are among the rather conspicuous facts about human beings, that they possess them. The philosophy in which I was largely brought up, Anglo-American empiricist philosophy, sometimes seems a prolonged conspiracy to overlook the fact that human beings have bodies and that we live in them and, most important of all, that we exist because of them. We often know what our bodies are doing and what is going on inside them from sources other than the five senses that we use to observe objects other than our own bodies. These sources of knowledge about bodily movement and action are more intimate, because internal, sources. If we did not know without observation that we were moving our eyes and our hands, we would not know by observation about external things. I said all this some years ago in *Thought and Action*[1] but not sufficiently aggressively, I now think.

The overwhelming and obvious lack of any significant similarity between machines of any kind, as far as we know, and human beings, is due to the fact that machines do not have bodies. I believe they have frames or mainframes. This limits their minds. The more the intellect's calculative abilities and the memories of machines are developed and increased, the less, in certain respects, they become like human beings. That is why they are sometimes spoken of, not unreasonably, as inhuman. When I hear that they are regularly defeating the human grand masters at chess (and we have been waiting for some years for this to happen), I shall know that they have become even less human. You may remember a very brilliant novel by Nabokov about chess masters that brought up the human aspects of successful chess playing. An increase in machines' intellectual powers and their powers of coherent memory might correctly be described, in summary fashion, as an increase in their powers of mind. There is nothing incorrect about that. But these words might be misleading if they were taken to imply that their minds as a whole had been developed and their total powers of mind increased.

The fact is that just two commonly distinguished powers of mind, distinguished for practical and social purposes, would have been abstracted from the huge amalgam that constitutes the mind and then been further developed and increased. As was stressed, both by Terry Winograd and Sherry Turkle, all sorts of humanly interesting mental powers and dispositions would remain at zero. I am thinking of the dispositions and powers associated with sexuality, with all that sexuality entails in family relationships and emotional attachments, the enjoyment of sports and of games of skill that are played outside and are less abstract than chess, of sculpture, of dancing, of mimicry (as opposed to reproduction), of dramatic performance, of inappropriate and sudden laughter, of groans and scowls out of season and not on cue, of tones of voice in speech and in singing. Obviously, I could continue this list indefinitely. I have not mentioned the pleasures of thirst, cultivated thirst and controlled intoxication, of conviviality and of old-fashioned greed, which was once mentioned charmingly by one of Sherry Turkle's twelve-year-old subjects. One could go on. Yet the competition between man and machines remains.

The important thing about machines is that they have remarkably copious and definite memories—efficient, clear, and unconfused—which we do not. Together, this makes up a fairly small part of what we should properly include under the title of mind and not necessarily the most interesting or productive part. If we take a long historical view of culture, and of a person's individuality, it is a matter of the expression in an eye or the way a person walks or stands or speaks; it is half physical. No one who has seen it will forget the way that a certain dancer's neck, a Russian dancer, Ulanova, fitted on to her head when she danced. It was quite unforgettable. The style and expression (I do not mean feeling) were unique. Think of the tainted history of the word *reason*, pictured as master to slave, as in Plato, or upside down, as in Hume, where it is subject to another total and hopeless abstraction called feeling, reason being the slave. The history of the word *reason* is tainted because Aristotle began by associating powers of reason with the doctrine of the Scala Universi, the great Chain of Being, which puts reason at the top, near to God the Father, or God the Holy Ghost in the sky, our animal nature lower down the scale of being, and the "trancelike life of plants" just above the sticks and stones. This picture of the great Chain of Being is just a pleasing and rather self-glorifying fiction, which models God's creation, as has been several times remarked, on a properly stratified social order, and the social order is indeed a human creation. This picture is a denial of complexity of living things and of the many different powers of development that can be traced in nature, all in the interest of some form of social tidiness.

If there is no clear view of God at the top of the ladder, or perhaps a little above it, it is not clear what is higher and lower in the order of human powers and dispositions. Nor is it clear why we should think in terms of scales at all. There is no valid reason, it seems to me, to place the noncomputational, or nonstorage, or nonlogical, aspects of the mind lower than so-called pure reason, apart from the dreams of the disembodied survival of the soul, which the myth of pure reason preserves. If we forget this recurring, haunting dream of an ideal Manichaeanism, we can insist on the equal priority in the human mind of imagination, of physical play, of poetry, painting, and the performing arts, in the definition of humanity. We can think of individuality in handwriting and script. We ought not, it seems to me, to have this academic competition of higher or lower. Maybe, for some ulterior moral argument, one picks out distinctive human powers and dispositions where we could probably look better, compared with other animal species, or we may think of the surprisingly variable and unstructured nature of human sexuality, which leads to various family structures. Second, since we learn an enormous variety of natural languages, variety within the species is important and distinctive, as is the peculiarly confused store of our memories.

Let me also address memories, because they came up in Roger Hahn's essay and elsewhere. Ours are confused in comparison with the machine's. In an interesting and productive way, human beings, compared with other animals, are obsessed with their past, as Bernard Williams has remarked. Not merely their own past but their family's past, the tribe's and nation's past. These various pasts are lodged in their minds both as individuals and as tribes or nations, as a mixture of history and myth, truth and falsity. Memories are blurred (at any rate, mine is), smudged with the vast complicated network of unplanned, unique, and largely unconscious associations in the process of condensation of memory.

Assuming an individual's memories are an inextricable and innovative muddle, an interfusion of elements, forming and reforming as experience goes on in a person's life. When the muddle becomes sufficiently rich and many layered, like a compost heap, and when reason has been kept in its place, we call the muddled memory "imagination." However, when machines have impaired memories, they become "defective," and we are stuck with them, and they do not breed as compost does.

Hahn proposed a certain revision of standard histories of science in relation to the scientific revolution. He drew a contrast between the role of mechanical devices, particularly in the sixteenth and seventeenth centuries, which are plentifully illustrated in the books of the time (they illustrated new concepts of physical understanding), and, equally important, a new confidence in human abilities. If you understand it, you can make it, and often you can convert that proposition and say you can make it if you can understand it. This principle is referred to as the *verum factum* principle. It introduced a notion of causality connected with experimental action, with doing something in contrast to mere observation: the recording in the eye, of what the eye sees or receives. Now the Platonic and hence Peripatetic tradition had put the recording eye, not the ingenious manipulator, on top of the scale of value, and Plato, as is often remarked, had always used metaphors of vision to explain what the acquisition of knowledge is. The ingenious manipulator was a craftsman, lower on the social scale. As Keller points out, the terms that we use, such as competition, are derived from new social realities. There is an interesting difference that Hahn brought out, because the eye is, according to Hegel, the most ideal of the human senses, which means it is the least bodily part of the body, the least, as it were, closely material, the most expressive, the nearest to the mind through being nearest to the brain. We have this interesting view of true empiricism as being the doctrine that we can reconstruct natural creatures, and to reconstruct is to understand. It is not to have a map of a possible reconstruction but an actual reconstruction that is most enlightening about the nature of understanding.

NOTE

1. Stuart Hampshire, *Thought and Action* (New York: Viking Press, 1960).

PART THREE

Coda

Coda

James J. Sheehan

Never before have the conceptual boundaries of humanity been less secure. Perhaps, as Anthony Flew has recently argued, we are now at a point where a persuasive definition of what it means to be human is impossible. There is no guarantee, Flew maintains, "that in every case which we may in the future meet, we shall be able—once given all the relevant facts—to return an unhesitatingly correct answer to the question: 'Is this a human being or not?'" It may be, as Walter Burkert has suggested, that the definition of human nature has collapsed into its own history: "What has been assumed to constitute 'human nature' turns out to be just the tradition of mankind as developed in a unique historical process up to the present day." This would make humanity the best illustration of Nietzsche's dictum that "only that which has no history is definable."[1]

From the very beginning, people have tried to define humanity by clarifying the differences between humans and those creatures and things with which we share this planet. Again and again in the Western tradition, we humans have assured ourselves that we are unique, separated from everything else by special gifts and qualities. Made in God's image, possessors of a soul, spiritual as well as corporeal, humans stood apart from and above the rest of the earth. But however firmly they may have believed in these anthropocentric barriers, people have always been fascinated by the thought of crossing them. Since ancient times, poets have written about humans who take on animal form and animals that seem to act like humans. There is a special place in the literature of horror for creatures dwelling in an intermediate zone between the species—werewolves, vampires, and beasts in human shape. People have also wondered about the creation of human life from nonliving things, the task Pygmalion accomplished with art and, centuries later, Dr. Frankenstein achieved with science. In recent times, machines that assume the guise of humans have taken their place alongside biological monsters in the world of fantasy.[2]

As long as the frontiers protecting humanity's uniqueness were guaranteed by divine authority, images of human exile and nonhuman infiltration could remain in the realm of metaphor or imagination. But when humans lost their heavenly patron, the boundaries of humanity became much more problematic. The mechanistic cosmologies that developed in the seventeenth and eighteenth centuries offered explanations of the entire material world, including human beings. In the nineteenth century, Darwin and his followers demonstrated that human evolution was part of—and subject to the same laws as—the rest of nature. Looking back on this process in 1925, Alfred North Whitehead wrote, "Man, who at times dreamt of himself as a little lower than the angels, has submitted to become the servant and minister of nature. . . . It still remains to be seen whether the same actor can play both parts." Neither part became easier to play in the succeeding decades as the scientific assault on human uniqueness steadily intensified. "The turf separating animal and machine is shrinking," Melvin Konner recently wrote, "and it is only human to wonder whether there will always be a place for us, and us alone, to stand."[3]

As we have seen in this volume, both sociobiology and artificial intelligence directly challenge the concept of human uniqueness. While neither questions that there are important differences between humans and animals and humans and machines, each insists that humans can best be understood if we acknowledge our essential kinship with these other entities. "*Homo sapiens,*" according to Edward Wilson, "is a conventional animal species." In a parallel statement, Allen Newell argues that "our minds are a technology—like other technologies in being a set of mechanisms for the routine solution of a class of problems." To the sociobiologist, animals can be shown to possess many of those qualities traditionally held to be distinctively human—language, emotions, social structure. Wilson believes that "civilization is not intrinsically limited to humanoids. Only by accident was it linked to the anatomy of bareskinned, bipedal mammals and the peculiar qualities of human nature."[4] Similarly, some advocates of artificial intelligence believe that it will be possible to create machines at least equal and very likely superior to human intelligence. Of course, not everyone is sure that this will be altogether a good thing:

> Once artificial intelligences start getting smart, they are going to get smart very fast. What's taken humans and their society tens of thousands of years is going to be a matter of hours with artificial intelligences. If that happens at Stanford, say, the Stanford AI lab may have immense power all of a

sudden. It's not that the United States might take over the world, it's that Stanford's AI Lab might.[5]

Thus, Edward Fredkin, of MIT.

Fredkin's somewhat facetious remark underscores the fact that sociobiology and artificial intelligence have institutional locations, internal politics, and distinctive disciplinary cultures. The profound conflicts that these enterprises have generated—conflicts within the disciplines themselves, as well as between their advocates and critics—are simultaneously scientific and personal, empirical and philosophical, methodological and ideological. Such conflicts may be especially characteristic of scientific disciplines during their formative period, when internal struggles for intellectual leadership often coincide with external struggles for recognition and legitimacy. Nor should we overlook the fact that there is a great deal at stake in these struggles: research support and faculty billets, scholarly prestige and public influence.[6]

At the core of sociobiology and AI are powerfully complex and rewarding programs for empirical research. These programs are connected with and sustained by some of the most important theoretical and technological discoveries made in the past fifty years: sociobiology, as we have seen, draws on genetics, population biology, and animal behavior; AI, on computer science and cognitive psychology. Given the two disciplines' accomplishments and connections, it is not surprising that some of their practitioners have developed ambitions well beyond the empirical limits of their research programs. Wilson, for example, imagines sociobiology as a "new synthesis," which will provide "the most direct bridge from the natural sciences to the study of human nature and thence to the social sciences." At times, Wilson has written as if he were prepared to colonize not only psychology and sociology but also such normative disciplines as moral philosophy: "Scientists and humanists should consider together the suggestion that the time has come for ethics to be removed temporarily from the hands of the philosophers and biologized." In his essay for this volume, Allen Newell seems to approach a similar position from a different direction. A unified, mechanistic science is becoming increasingly possible, he believes, because of "the amazing emergence of biology to match in power and elegance the older physical sciences" and the parallel ability of artificial intelligence to create a theory of mind.[7]

In making these claims, scientists like Wilson and Newell seem to be operating within two powerful modern traditions. The first, which goes back at least to the eighteenth century, includes thinkers like La Mettrie, Feuerbach, Marx, Nietzsche, and Freud, all of whom sought to reveal humanity's true natural essence by stripping away the final residues of spiritual illusion. The fervor with which some modern researchers insist on the biological basis of behavior or the technological character of thought reminds us that they are still locked in a long, twilight struggle against the soul. No less important than this struggle, however, has been the desire to replace spiritual illusions with scientifically based values. This, too, is a tradition that reaches back to the Enlightenment, when thinkers began to turn to our apparently certain knowledge about nature for models to replace our manifestly imperfect understanding of humanity. Since the eighteenth century, science has increasingly become the most significant source of our "sustaining myths," which are now, in Stephen Toulmin's phrase, "not so much anthropomorphic as mechanomorphic." Viewed historically, sociobiology and AI appear to be the most recent in a long series of attempts to create a synthesis of science and value that would at once explain the natural world and guide human affairs.[8]

Even many of those who applaud sociobiology and AI as research programs question their partisans' ambitions to provide a new scientific synthesis. Stephen Jay Gould, for instance, does not doubt the usefulness of sociobiological studies of nonhuman animals, but he is skeptical that sociobiology can say anything very "interesting" about human behavior. Instead, the "worst excesses" of sociobiology appear when it is applied to humans, in part because "we have so little data about a slow-breeding species that cannot be overtly manipulated for experimental purposes," in part because "the nongenetic process of cultural evolution often mimics the results of Darwinian (genetic) adaptation." But despite these inherent methodological difficulties, "our inordinate interest in *Homo sapiens*" tempts us to accept sociobiology's crude speculations without demanding the same scientific rigor we would expect in the study of other species.[9]

Critics of AI are equally disturbed by the inflated ambitions of some of the discipline's spokesmen. Seymour Papert, himself a distinguished researcher in the field, warns his colleagues about jumping from an analysis of one sort of mental activity to an analysis of the "mind" as a whole. This is, he believes, "a category error" because it supposes "that the existence of a common mechanism provides both an explanation and a unification of all systems, however complex, in which this mechanism might play a central role." C. S. Peirce made a similar point in more general terms when he noted, "There is no greater nor more frequent mistake in practical logic than to suppose that things that resemble one another strongly in some respects are any more likely for that to be alike in others." The fact that both humans and machines can learn to play chess may suggest a number of interesting things about the human brain and mechanical intelligence, but it does not suggest that the two are necessarily alike in any other ways.[10]

In an astute and largely sympathetic examination of computers and culture, David Bolter points out that it is wrong to equate AI models of mind with physicists' models of nature.

> The problem here is that the artificial intelligence specialist has nothing but a model. Having abandoned the idea that electronic circuits can be made to mirror the organization of human neurons, he has no natural phenomena left to study. . . . [W]hat can the computer programmer find in the brain or the mind of which his binary coded instructions are a model?

There can be no science of mind comparable to physics, Bolter maintains. There can only be "metaphors that capture more or less aptly our mental experiences." Despite their claims to model or mimic the mind, computer scientists have done no more than create a richly suggestive and culturally resonant metaphor that can help us to think about what it means to think.[11]

Richard Lewontin argues that sociobiology also rests on a metaphorical foundation. To talk about animal behavior in human terms characteristically involves what he calls "a process of backward etymology" through which "human social institutions are laid on animals, metaphorically, and then the human behavior is rederived from the animals as if it were a special case of a general phenomenon that had been independently discovered in other species." This backward etymology can lead in some very odd directions. For example, after reading Anne Fausto-Sterling's analysis of David Barash's description of "rape" among ducks, it is difficult not to agree with her conclusion that "sociobiologists do strange things with language." But while the case of the rapist duck may be an extreme instance of sociobiologists' linguistic eccentricity, it does call to our attention an endemic difficulty in the discipline: sociobiologists can only describe the kind of animal behavior in which they are interested by using the language of human social action. And because this language is fundamentally anthropocentric, it inevitably imposes human categories on nonhuman actions. This is why Gould is correct to insist that "we cannot write, study, or even conceive of other creatures, except in overt or implied comparison with ourselves." Just as specialists in AI cannot find a "mind" with which to test their model, so sociobiologists cannot create an alternative vocabulary with which to test their assertion that human and animal behaviors are alike.[12]

W. V. Quine once observed that metaphorical thinking is especially apparent along "the philosophical fringes of science," where "old idioms are bound to fail . . . and only metaphor can begin to limn the new order." The history of science suggests that these metaphors can develop in two directions. Sometimes, they can be absorbed by the research programs they helped to stimulate; they are then replaced by empirically based models expressed in what Quine calls a "literalistic idiom." This is what happened to the metaphor of the body as a "heat engine." But some scientific metaphors develop a life of their own, next to or separate from a disciplinary research program. Sustained by political, social, and cultural forces, the most important of these become what Stephen Pepper named "root metaphors," images of such scope and authority that they provide the basis for universally applicable explanations of the world. In both its nineteenth- and twentieth-century formulations, Darwinism became such a root metaphor. The same thing seems to be happening to the computer, the machine that has replaced clock and engine as our most potent technological metaphor.[13]

Sociobiology and artificial intelligence are still on "the philosophical fringes of science," where they make two very different claims to our attention. As research programs, they produce important information and hypotheses about the natural world. As metaphors, they draw on and help to shape our answers to the persistent question of what it means to be human.

NOTES

1. Anthony Flew, *A Rational Animal and Other Philosophical Essays on the Nature of Man* (Oxford: Clarendon Press, 1978), 23; Walter Burkert, *Structure and History in Greek Mythology and Ritual* (Berkeley and Los Angeles: University of California Press, 1979), xiii; Friedrich Nietzsche, *On the Genealogy of Morals* (New York: Vintage Books, 1967), 80.

2. J. David Bolter, *Turing's Man: Western Culture in the Computer Age* (Chapel Hill: University of North Carolina Press, 1984), explores these various metaphors.

3. Alfred North Whitehead, *Science and the Modern World* (Mentor ed., New York, 1958); Melvin Konner, "On Human Nature: Love Among the Robots," *The Sciences* 27, 2 (1987): 13.

4. E. O. Wilson, *On Human Nature* (New York: Bantam Books, 1979), 24, 48.

5. Pamela McCorduck, *Machines Who Think: A Personal Inquiry into the History and Prospects of Artificial Intelligence* (San Francisco: W. H. Freeman, 1979), 351.

6. For an introduction to the disciplinary histories of sociobiology and artificial intelligence, see Arthur Caplan, ed., *The Sociobiology Debate: Readings on Ethical and Scientific Issues* (New York: Harper and Row, 1978), and Howard Gardner, *The Mind's New Science: A History of the Cognitive Revolution* (New York: Basic Books, 1987).

7. Wilson, in his introduction to Caplan, *The Sociology Debate*, xiii; Mary Midgley, *Beast and Man: The Roots of Human Nature* (Ithaca: Cornell University Press, 1978), 169.

8. This point is developed in Howard Kaye, *The Social Meaning of Modern Biology: From Social Darwinism to Sociobiology* (New Haven: Yale University Press, 1986). See also Toulmin's *The Return to Cosmology: Postmodern Science and the*

Theology of Nature (Berkeley, Los Angeles, London: University of California Press, 1982).

9. *The New York Review of Books*, Sept. 25, 1986.

10. Seymour Papert, "One AI or Many?" in Stephen Graubard, ed., *The Artificial Intelligence Debate: False Starts, Real Foundations* (Cambridge: MIT Press, 1988), 2. Peirce, quoted in Michael Crowe, *The Extraterrestrial Life Debate, 1750–1900* (New York: Cambridge University Press, 1986), 552.

11. Bolter, *Turing's Man*, 207.

12. R. C. Lewontin, Steven Rose, and Leon Kamin, *Not in Our Genes: Biology, Ideology, and Human Nature* (New York: Pantheon Books, 1984), 249; Anne Fausto-Sterling, *Myths of Gender: Biological Theories about Women and Men* (New York: Basic Books, 1985), 160; Gould, in *The New York Review of Books,* June 25, 1987. For more on these issues, see Evelyn Fox Keller's essay in Part I.

13. W. V. Quine, "A Postscript on Metaphor," in Sheldon Sacks, ed., *On Metaphor* (Chicago and London: University of Chicago Press, 1978), 159; Stephen Pepper, *World Hypotheses* (Berkeley and Los Angeles: University of California Press, 1942).

Contributors

ARNOLD I. DAVIDSON is Associate Professor of Philosophy and a member of the Committee on the Conceptual Foundations of Science and the Committee on General Studies in the Humanities at the University of Chicago. He is also the Executive Editor of *Critical Inquiry*. He has published articles on the history of psychiatry and medicine, moral and political philosophy, and contemporary continental philosophy. He is currently working on the history of horror as it relates to the epistemology of norms and deviations.

JOHN DUPRÉ is Associate Professor of Philosophy at Stanford University. His interest is the philosophy of science, especially the philosophy of evolutionary theory. He is editor of *The Latest on the Best: Essays on Evolution and Optimality* (Cambridge: MIT Press, 1987).

ROGER HAHN is Professor of History at the University of California, Berkeley. His interest is the history of science and technology, particularly in the eighteenth century. His books include *Laplace as a Newtonian Scientist* (Los Angeles: Clark Library, 1967) and *The Anatomy of a Scientific Institution: The Paris Academy of Sciences, 1666–1803* (Berkeley and Los Angeles: University of California Press, 1971; pb. ed. 1986).

STUART HAMPSHIRE is Professor Emeritus of Philosophy at Stanford University. He has written extensively on moral philosophy, philosophy of mind, and the philosophy of the European Enlightenment. He is a Fellow of both the British Academy and the American Academy of Arts and Sciences.

EVELYN FOX KELLER is, since 1988, Professor of Women's Studies and Rhetoric, University of California, Berkeley. Formerly Professor of Mathematics and Humanities at Northeastern University and Visiting Professor in the Program in Science, Technology, and Society at the Massachusetts Institute of Technology, she is the author of *A Feeling for the Organism: The Life and Work of Barbara McClintock* (San Francisco: W. A. Freeman, 1983) and *Reflections on Gender and Science* (New Haven: Yale University Press, 1985).

MELVIN KONNER, an anthropologist and M.D., is Samuel Dobbs Professor of Anthropology, Associate Professor of Psychiatry, and Affiliate Scientist at the Yerkes Regional Primate Research Center, Emory University. He is the author of *Becoming a Doctor* (New York: Viking, 1987) and *The Tangled Wing: Biological Constraints on the Human Spirit* (New York: Holt, Rinehart, and Winston, 1983).

ALLEN NEWELL is University Professor of Computer Science at Carnegie Mellon University. A leading theorist of cognitive science, his books include *Human Problem Solving* (Englewood Cliffs, N.J.: Prentice-Hall, 1972) and *Computer Structures* (New York: McGraw-Hill, 1986). In 1986, he delivered the William James Lectures at Harvard University.

HARRIET RITVO is Associate Professor in the Department of Humanities, Massachusetts Institute of Technology. Her primary interest is the cultural history of Victorian England. She is the author of *The Animal Estate: The English and Other Creatures in the Victorian Age* (Cambridge: Harvard University Press, 1987).

JAMES J. SHEEHAN is Dickason Professor of Humanities and Professor of History, Stanford University. A specialist in modern European history, he is the author of *German Liberalism in the Nineteenth Century* (Chicago and London: University of Chicago Press, 1978) and *German History, 1770–1866* (Oxford: Oxford University Press, 1989).

MORTON SOSNA is a Fellow of the Humanities Center and Lecturer in American Studies, Stanford University. He is the author of *In Search of the Silent South: Southern Liberals and the Race Issue* (New York: Columbia University Press, 1977) and co-editor of *Reconstructing Individualism: Autonomy, Individuality and the Self in Western Thought* (Stanford: Stanford University Press, 1986).

SHERRY TURKLE is Associate Professor of Sociology in the Program in Science, Technology, and Society, Massachusetts Institute of Technology.

Her current interest is in the relationship between artificial intelligence and psychoanalysis. She is the author of *Psychoanalytic Politics* (New York: Basic Books, 1978) and *The Second Self: Computers and the Human Spirit* (New York: Simon and Schuster, 1984).

BERNARD WILLIAMS, formerly Provost of King's College, Cambridge, England, is now Monroe Deutsch Professor of Philosophy at the University of California, Berkeley. His many philosophical writings include *Ethics and the Limits of Philosophy* (Cambridge: Harvard University Press, 1985); *Morality* (New York: Harper and Row, 1972); *Descartes: The Project of Pure Enquiry* (Oxford: Penguin, 1978).

TERRY WINOGRAD, Associate Professor of Computer Science, Stanford University, wrote an early artificial intelligence program, *Understanding Natural Language* (New York: Academic Press, 1972), and has done extensive research and writing on computer models of human language: *Language as a Cognitive Process* (New York: Addison-Wesley, 1983). He has collaborated with Fernando Flores in a critique of work in artificial intelligence and in developing a theory of language that serves as a basis for the design of computer systems: *Understanding Computers and Cognition* (New York: Addison-Wesley, 1987). He is also a founding member and current national president of Computer Professionals for Social Responsibility.

INDEX